FOCUS ON MACBETH

SHAKESPEARE

CRITICAL STUDIES
In 36 Volumes

FOCUS ON MACBETH

JOHN RUSSELL BROWN

Routledge
Taylor & Francis Group
LONDON AND NEW YORK

First published in 1982

Reprinted in 2005 by
Routledge

2 Park Square, Milton Park, Abingdon, Oxfordshire, OX14 4RN
270 Madison Avenue, New York NY 10016

Routledge is an imprint of the Taylor & Francis Group

First issued in paperback 2010

British Library Cataloguing in Publication Data
A CIP catalogue record for this book
is available from the British Library

Focus on Macbeth
ISBN 13: 978-0-415-33086-2 (set)
ISBN13: 978-0-415-35276-5 (hbk)
ISBN 13: 978-0-415-61217-3 (pbk)
Miniset: Critical Studies
Series: Routledge Library Editions – Shakespeare

Focus on
Macbeth

Edited by
John Russell Brown

ROUTLEDGE & KEGAN PAUL
London, Boston and Henley

First published in 1982
by Routledge & Kegan Paul Ltd
39 Store Street, London WC1E 7DD,
9 Park Street, Boston, Mass. 02108, USA and
Broadway House, Newtown Road,
Henley-on-Thames, Oxon RG9 1EN

Set in IBM Baskerville by
Donald Typesetting, Bristol
and printed in Great Britain by
The Thetford Press Ltd, Thetford, Norfolk

Library of Congress Cataloging in Publication Data

Main entry under title:

Focus on Macbeth.

Includes index.
Contents: Images of death/R.A. Foakes –
The Kingdom, the power, and the glory in
Macbeth/Brian Morris - A new gorgon/
D.J. Palmer – [etc.]
1. Shakespeare, William, 1564-1616. Macbeth
– Addresses, essays, lectures. I. Brown, John Russell.
PR2823.F65   822.3'3   81-17855

ISBN 0-7100-9015-3   AACR2

Contents

Contents

Contributors

John Russell Brown is Professor of English at the University of Sussex and Associate Director of the National Theatre, London; his most recent books are *Theatre Language, Free Shakespeare* and *Discovering Shakespeare*.

Derek Russell Davis was until recently Professor of Mental Health at the University of Bristol; he has contributed many studies to the *British Medical Journal*, the *British Journal of Medical Psychology*, etc.

Gareth Lloyd Evans is Reader in Dramatic Literature at the University of Birmingham and drama critic for the *Guardian* and other journals; he has published a five-volume guide to Shakespeare's plays and a study of *J.B. Priestley, Dramatist*.

R.A. Foakes is Professor of English at the University of Kent; he has edited plays for the New Arden Shakespeare and his most recent book is *Shakespeare: from Satire to Celebration*; he is editing Coleridge's Shakespearean criticism.

Michael Goldman is Professor of English at Princeton University; he is author of *Shakespeare and the Energies of Drama*.

Robin Grove teaches in the Department of English, the University of Melbourne; his contribution to this volume is related to his account of recent studies of *King Lear* that he published in the *Critical Review*.

Contributors

Sir Peter Hall is Director of the National Theatre, London; of the major tragedies of Shakespeare, he has directed both *Hamlet* and *Macbeth* twice, and *Othello* once.

Michael Hawkins is Reader in History at the University of Sussex and is at present completing a study of Wardship in Elizabethan and Jacobean England.

Brian Morris was until recently Professor of English at the University of Sheffield; in 1980 he became Principal of St David's University College, Lampeter. He is a General Editor of the Mermaid Plays and the New Arden Shakespeare.

D.J. Palmer is Professor of English at the University of Manchester; he is a General Editor of *Stratford-upon-Avon Studies* and a frequent contributor to *Critical Quarterly* and *Shakespeare Survey*.

Marvin Rosenberg is Professor of Drama at the University of California, Berkeley; he has published full-scale stage-histories of *Othello, King Lear* and *Macbeth*, and is completing one of *Hamlet*.

Peter Stallybrass is Lecturer in English at the University of Sussex.

Introduction

In recent years three productions of *Macbeth* have filled
London theatres, although critical reception has varied from
outright condemnation to eager, eloquent praise. The play
exercises a strange influence over readers and playgoers, as
if it is a mystery that holds attention as well as the dramatic
power of speech and action. The words of the text offer
no easy clue to meaning or significance. In dramatic structure
it is so different from other tragedies by Shakespeare – most
obviously in the presentation of Macbeth and Lady Macbeth,
in the scenes for the witches and in its compression – that
any assessment must suggest exceptional purposes in its
writing or entry into hitherto unexplored regions of human
experience. At times the language is dark and forbidding,
but it can also grip the very nerves of actors and silent
readers.

Many kinds of study are needed if we are to understand
The Tragedy of Macbeth as well as possible, and so the present
book has been commissioned. As editor I have not attempted
to develop a single interpretation or approach, but rather to
provide a wide range of studies that respect the individuality
of the text and examine it from different viewpoints.

I was fortunate to be involved as assistant director in the
rehearsals for the National Theatre's production by Peter
Hall, in which Albert Finney and Dorothy Tutin took the
leading parts. This gave me a close and practical knowledge of
the text and its theatrical possibilities, and also suggested a
number of the questions that I posed to the contributors to
this volume.

At the head of the book are three studies of *Macbeth*'s

1

themes and structure. Various ideas are followed through the play, such as ambition, heroic valour, power and guilt, and these are related to changes in characterization and narrative, and to the same themes as they occur in other tragedies and, especially, the history plays. R.A. Foakes is concerned with the nature of Macbeth's inner life and motivation, while Brian Morris relates ideas expressed in the play to the central tenets of Christian belief and worship. D.J. Palmer's contribution starts from an examination of recurrent visual effects, rather than crucial words and narrative development. The shape of the play is a continuous interest of all three authors.

Two separate parts then study the play in performance. The first examines actual productions: Marvin Rosenberg shows the means whereby actors and actresses triumphed in the two central roles during the eighteenth and nineteenth centuries, and Gareth Lloyd Evans looks at the varied fortunes of the play at the hands of the Shakespeare Memorial Company and then the Royal Shakespeare Company at Stratford-upon-Avon in the years since the Second World War. A special feature of this latter contribution is an assessment of Laurence Olivier's memorable and innovatory interpretation of Macbeth. The following part is concerned with some of the clues to performance that are to be discerned in the *minutiae* of the text. Robin Grove seeks out tonal, rhythmic, echoing and re-echoing effects which can operate on a playgoer's senses unconsciously. Michael Goldman examines the mental and physical actions that an actor needs to create if he is to sustain the role of Macbeth, making his words truly at one with his performance.

Part 4 contains specialist studies. In rehearsals at the National, I became very aware of the unusual nature of political relationships in the play: what are 'thanes'? How are these kings chosen and what maintains them in power, and what are their powers and responsibilities? Why do Duncan's sons flee from court on the murder of their father, the king? What are the rival claims of king, country, family and loyalty? These and related issues I have asked a specialist historian, Michael Hawkins, to consider in the light of political thought and reality of the time when the play was written. In a similar way I asked Peter Stallybrass to examine the role of witchcraft, bringing contemporary belief and practices to illuminate the text of the play and proceeding to look at how this has affected both structure and significance. Derek Russell Davis then brings twentieth-century terminology to consider the protagonists as people involved in a case of murder and its consequences; systems theory is the particular psychopathological means he has used, being especially relevant to the dramatic presentation of man and wife involved together in a crime against a person with whom they have further and different relationships.

The last section of this book contains Peter Hall's assessment of the play's power in the theatre and its hold over his own imagination. In an interview he answers questions about his two productions and what the text suggests to him. The book concludes with an Afterword in which I draw upon the eleven contributions to this volume in assessing our present knowledge of this great play.

All quotations from Shakespeare's plays and all references to them are from Peter Alexander's edition, London, 1958.

John Russell Brown

Part 1

Themes and structure

1

Images of death: ambition in *Macbeth*

R. A. Foakes

Macbeth is Shakespeare's last and most original play on the theme of the ambitious prince finally overthrown. Its roots lie deep in the medieval and Renaissance preoccupation with tragedy as the fall of great men or women, brought low by fortune's wheel and so exemplifying the mutability of human life, or overreaching themselves and illustrating the retribution visited upon the proud and sinful. It was natural for Shakespeare to explore the possibilities for tragedy of

> sad stories of the death of kings:
> How some have been depos'd, some slain in war,
> Some haunted by the ghosts they have depos'd,
> Some poison'd by their wives, some sleeping kill'd,
> All murder'd.
>
> (*Richard II*, III.ii.156–60)

In writing his early plays he had the impact of Marlowe to absorb, who had broken the moralising pattern of such stories as mirrors for magistrates by showing Tamburlaine striding on to ever further conquests, and endowed with a mind aspiring to beauty and poetry as well as to power and an earthly crown. The *Henry VI* plays are full of aspiring princes, and culminate in the rise of Gloucester, whose ruthless ambition is qualified by his wit and energy; these plays, and *Richard III*, nevertheless remain within the conventional pattern. A much more complex study of an ambitious prince is realised in Bolingbroke, who, without seeming to recognise the extent of his ambitions, overthrows and effectively murders Richard II, and achieves the throne, only to be punished by ill health,

7

by constant rebellions, and by the vagaries of Prince Hal. A further variant is developed in Brutus, whose confidence in his own rectitude, the name of 'honour' for which his line has always been noted, blinds him to the true nature of the murder of Caesar. Then, in *Hamlet*, Shakespeare was to develop still subtler variations, in Claudius, a 'good' and effective monarch who, we discover, has gained the throne by murder, and in Hamlet himself, driven by events to act as if he were indeed, as he says to Ophelia, 'very proud, revengeful, ambitious' (*Hamlet* III.i.124), but delaying and avoiding action in an attempt to escape from the implications of what he feels he must do, kill Claudius.

Superficially, *Macbeth* seems to return to a more conventional mode, and on one level it is much more straightforwardly a play about an ambitious prince who overreaches himself in murdering the King, and who brings about his own downfall in the end. But it goes beyond Shakespeare's earlier treatments of the theme, notably in two ways. One is the new dimension given by the witches, and the sense of evil which is generated largely through their presence in the play; for this enables Shakespeare to show a more profound spiritual change in Macbeth than in any of his earlier protagonists. Bolingbroke and Claudius feel their guilt, but Macbeth is shown as creating his own hell. In this the play has links with Marlowe's *Doctor Faustus*, but whereas Faustus achieves nothing in return for selling his soul, and in the end, terrified at the prospect of punishment, is whisked off by devils into a traditional stage hell-mouth, Shakespeare expresses dramatically through his presentation of Macbeth that subtler idea of hell verbalised in Mephistopheles' description of it as 'being depriv'd of everlasting bliss' (Scene III, l.82). Faustus himself seems to begin to understand this in his curses at the end:

> curse Lucifer
> That hath depriv'd thee of the joys of heaven;
> (Scene XIX, ll.181–2)

but in Marlowe's play hell as deprivation remains merely a concept. It remained for Shakespeare to realise on stage what this means in terms of character.

A second way in which Shakespeare breaks new ground in *Macbeth* is in his deeper study of the nature of ambition, which is the special concern of this essay. Ambition is usually

8

understood in its straightforward sense as an eagerness to gain promotion and power, to rise in the world, and, as Duncan's general in the field, Macbeth might be expected to fit Bacon's conception in 'Of Ambition': 'Good Commanders in the Warres, must be taken, be they never so *Ambitious* . . . . And to take a Soldier without *Ambition*, is to pull off his Spurres.' Charles Lamb saw further than this in a striking comment provoked by the actor G.F.Cooke's playing of Richard III as a 'very wicked man' who kills for pleasure:[1]

> The truth is, the Characters of Shakespeare are so much the objects of meditation rather than of interest or curiosity as to their actions, that while we are reading any of his great criminal characters – Macbeth, Richard, even Iago, – we think not so much of the crimes which they commit, as of the ambition, the aspiring spirit, the intellectual activity, which prompts them to overleap those moral fences.

Lamb was led to notice something especially significant in *Macbeth* – that the emphasis when we *read* the play is less on what he does than on the activity of mind connected with his deeds. Lamb strikingly linked, perhaps equated, ambition, aspiration and intellectual activity, in a way which now may seem a little eccentric. For on the one hand, the meaning of ambition is more restricted than this on the one occasion when Macbeth speaks the word, at that point towards the end of Act I when he comes nearest to abandoning the murder of Duncan. At this moment of revulsion against the killing of the King,

> We will proceed no further in this business,
>
> (I.vii.31)

Macbeth reduces all that has been exciting him in the contemplation of the death of Duncan to 'only vaulting ambition', the mere desire to be King. This would seem to justify the claim that[2]

> Macbeth has not a predisposition to murder; he has merely an inordinate ambition that makes murder itself seem to be a lesser evil than failure to achieve the crown.

On the other hand, Lamb's comment reduces to a subordinate

role the moral issues which to many have seemed of primary importance. The play has been seen as effectively a morality, with an action that can be summarised thus:[3]

> Its hero is worked upon by forces of evil, yields to temptation in spite of all that his conscience can do to stop him, goes deeper into evil-doing as he is further tempted, sees the approach of retribution, falls into despair, and is brought by retribution to his death.

This way of regarding *Macbeth* as an exemplary play displaying the degeneration of a great criminal who has 'no morally valid reason for killing Duncan',[4] has satisfied many, although it does not account for a sense that somehow, in spite of everything, Macbeth retains an heroic stature at the end, when 'in the very act of proclaiming that life "is a tale told by an idiot, *signifying nothing*" personal life announces its virtue, and superbly *signifies itself.*'[5] Lascelles Abercrombie's extraordinary use here of the word 'virtue' may be related to Wilson Knight's view that Macbeth 'has won through by excessive crime to an harmonious and honest relation with his surroundings . . . . He now knows himself to be a tyrant confessed, and wins back . . . integrity of soul.'[6]

The word 'ambition' is used only three times in the play, and always in simple relation to the idea of worldly power, of gaining the throne, as when Lady Macbeth says her husband is 'not without ambition' (I.v.16), or Ross explains the supposed guilt of Malcolm and Donalbain for the death of Duncan in terms of 'thriftless ambition' (II.iv.28). The compulsion that drives Macbeth is more complex than this, and requires further analysis. A better understanding of why Macbeth does what he does may in turn help to explain the curious contradictions that tend to emerge in the common moralistic accounts of the play, which are torn between condemning him as a criminal and rescuing a grandeur, integrity, even virtue for him at the end. A sense of this difficulty has in part prompted a recent account of Macbeth as lacking 'the requisite moral sense and agony of conscience that any proper tragic hero must have';[7] this is a response to critics who see Macbeth as essentially good, when he has 'neither moral sense nor awareness of its existence'.[8] Such an account of Macbeth may seem a strange, even perverse, reading, but it stems from a genuine problem, and involves an important recognition, that Macbeth's 'imagination is not under his control; he is its creature.'[9] For another common assumption about Macbeth is that because he has great poetry to speak he must be an 'intellectual giant',[10] when a very important question the text raises is how far Macbeth understands his own words.

Moralistic accounts of Macbeth as falling into temptation, committing a terrible crime and ending in despair, pass too readily by the question that haunts the first two acts, why does Macbeth kill Duncan? It seems plain that he has thought of such a possibility before meeting the witches, or at least that his starting at their greetings of him (I.iii.51) registers his awareness at this moment that what they say gives conscious expression to a half-formed image; and this is confirmed by the first scene in which Lady Macbeth appears, for the death of Duncan is already an idea familiar to her, even to the murder weapon, the 'keen knife' that is to do the deed (I.v.49). If the thought of murdering Duncan is already there, so to speak, in the minds of Macbeth and Lady Macbeth, then the notion of Macbeth as tempted needs further scrutiny. The Weird Sisters announce that Macbeth will be king, and since their other prophecy, that he will be Thane of Cawdor, is immediately fulfilled, what they say might rather prompt him to sit tight than to plot to murder the King. Whatever it is that tempts Macbeth to do the deed is in himself and in his wife. And yet, hard on receiving notice of his new 'honour', the title of Thane of Cawdor, Macbeth reveals that he is already thinking of murder.

The context for all this is the opening of the play, with its emphasis on the butchery of war. According to Holinshed Macdonwald killed himself in his castle, and Macbeth, finding the dead body, and 'remitting no piece of his cruel nature',[11] cut the head off and sent it as a present to Duncan. In the play the bleeding Captain describes a much stranger image of death. Macbeth, brandishing his sword, 'which smok'd with bloody execution', as if burning with rage, or steaming with hot blood, 'carv'd' a passage through men to confront the living Macdonwald:

> Which ne'er shook hands, nor bade farewell to him,
> Till he unseam'd him from the nave to th' chops,
> And fix'd his head upon our battlements.

(I.ii.21–3)

11

The suggestion of ripping Macdonwald's flesh like cloth from the navel to the jaws completes an image of startling ferocity, quite overshadowing the attribute of courage in 'brave Macbeth . . . . Like Valour's minion'. It is as if Macbeth delights in such brutal killing, and loves

> to bathe in reeking wounds
> Or memorize another Golgotha,
>
> (I.ii.40-1)

Is the force of this to suggest that in the heat of battle Macbeth and Banquo destroy all indiscriminately who come in their way, turning the battlefield into another place of a skull, or dead bones? Are they being likened to the soldiers who crucified Christ?

The bleeding captain's narrative of the battle is supported by the report of Ross, who, on the immediate sentencing of Cawdor to death, is sent to greet Macbeth from the King:

> He finds thee in the stout Norweyan ranks
> Nothing afeard of what thyself didst make,
> Strange images of death.
>
> (I.iii.95-7)

Here, in these opening scenes, if anywhere, Macbeth comes near to being represented as a 'butcher' (V.viii.69), so habituated to the horror of the battlefield that he is untroubled by the 'strange images of death' he makes and sees all round him.

Yet it is at this point he learns he is Thane of Cawdor: the Weird Sisters have told two truths – he is Thane of Glamis 'by Sinel's death' (I.iii.71), and Thane of Cawdor because the previous holder of the title has just been executed. Shakespeare omits to tell his audience that Sinel was, according to Holinshed, Macbeth's father, and so leaves us to suppose that Sinel too may have met a violent end. Within a short space Macbeth has his first soliloquy[12] in the form of a long aside on 'the imperial theme' (I.iii.129) which has already been troubling his imagination, and he now sees an image of death he cannot face so easily:

> why do I yield to that suggestion
> Whose horrid image doth unfix my hair

And make my seated heart knock at my ribs
Against the use of nature? Present fears
Are less than horrible imaginings:
My thought, whose murder yet is but fantastical,
Shakes so my single state of man
That function is smother'd in surmise,
And nothing is but what is not

(I.iii.134–42)

The 'horrid image' of murder is stranger than any of the earlier images of death, and it both terrifies him and excites him. It is part of the 'swelling act Of the imperial theme', with the promise of the crown as reward, and at the same time it fills him with present fears and horrible imaginings. He attributes the suggestion or image to 'supernatural soliciting', as if the Weird Sisters have incited or importuned him, and are responsible for the disturbance of his mind; but they have merely announced that he will be King, and as Macbeth knows, 'chance may crown me Without my stir' (I.iii.143–4). He has realised a new kind of challenge, one which so shakes his 'single state of man', suggesting something like an earthquake afflicting his individual little kingdom or 'state', that ordinary activity is stifled, and only 'what is not', those 'horrible imaginings', seems real. The speech records Macbeth's horror at, and fascination with, a new vision of death – not the brutal and casual slaughter of the battlefield, but the calculated murder of a king.

In Holinshed's account,[13] the Weird Sisters first appear after the conclusion of peace between the Scots and the Danes, when Macbeth and Banquo meet them. Shakespeare introduces them in the opening scene, so that they contribute to the creation of atmosphere right away, and establish a sense of distance from the world of the audience. The first few scenes build up the suggestion of a barbaric and violent world, one in which Macbeth is habituated to images of death. The new image that first confronts him in I.iii, 'My thought, whose murder yet is but fantastical', fascinates him as a new challenge. In Holinshed,[14] Macbeth only thinks of using force against Duncan after Malcolm has been nominated as 'successor in the kingdome', but in the play Macbeth has already imagined the death of the King before the advancement of Malcolm is mentioned in I.iv, echoing in his word 'fantastical' Banquo's question to the Weird Sisters, 'Are ye

13

fantastical, or that indeed / Which outwardly ye show?' (I.iii. 53-4). The boundary between the fantastical, the imaginary or illusory, and actuality is indeterminate, as Macbeth proceeds to create a new image of death.

For Macbeth the gap between the familiar images of death on the battlefield or by execution and the new image is terrifying, and his speeches, especially the soliloquies, in the scenes leading up to the killing of Duncan, record his difficulties in bridging that gap. His sense of the enormity of the act is made all the more impressive in relation to the Weird Sisters, whose stark malevolence is brought home in their vindictiveness towards the 'master o' th' *Tiger*' (I.iii.7); it is also presented in sharp contrast to Lady Macbeth's coolness, for her unfamiliarity with images of death perhaps makes it easy for her to contemplate the murder of Duncan without anxiety. Coleridge thought of her as having a 'visionary and day-dreaming turn of mind', 'accustomed only to the Shadows of the Imagination, vivid enough to throw the every day realities into shadows, but not yet compared with their own correspondent realities';[15] it seems to me rather that Shakespeare presents her as lacking a fullness of imagination, as able only to envisage the deed as a triumph of the will. In her terrible soliloquy in I.v she turns herself by an act of will into another Weird Sister, shedding her sex ('unsex me here', I.v.38) and suppressing pity and remorse, so that when Macbeth enters at the end of it she greets him with an echo of the Weird Sisters' greeting in I.iii:

> Great Glamis! Worthy Cawdor!
> Greater than both, by the all-hail hereafter!
>
> (I.v.52-3)

She has indeed been 'transported' beyond the present, and feels 'The future in the instant', as if she were a wizard; so she has no thought of *him* as a man, of his battle-scars, of what he has endured,[16] and overleaps the past and present in the glow of anticipated success. At the same time, she has no experience of death itself, and her confused image of the murder obscures it as if she is unable to see the deed:

> Come, thick night,
> And pall thee in the dunnest smoke of hell,
> That my keen knife see not the wound it makes,

Nor heaven peep through the blanket of the dark
To cry, "Hold, hold."

(I.v.50–4)

'Thick night' is so to obscure 'thee' (Duncan? or the knife?) that the wound will not be seen; and the distancing of the deed from herself under a pall of smoke is accentuated by the transference of vision from herself to the knife, which is not to 'see' what it does. Metaphorically the knife becomes a free agent acting on its own; her words evade the deed, as if she cannot bear to see the weapon, or the wound it makes, or the actual shape of the man to be murdered.

Macbeth, by contrast, sees the weapon and the deed clearly enough. Familiar as he is with images of death, the unpremeditated slaughter of the battlefield, this new image, requiring the planning of a murder, makes him 'afeard', and brings a new strain to bear on the courage and imagination of 'brave Macbeth'. He has to contemplate what he is about:

He's here in double trust:
First, as I am his kinsman and his subject –
Strong both against the deed; then, as his host,
Who should against his murderer shut the door,
Not bear the knife myself.

(I.vii.12–16)

It is more than a 'double trust' – Duncan is his kinsman, his King, his guest in his own home, and, Shakespeare suggests, a surrogate father-figure, and a holy man. Here again Holinshed's account is transformed, in which Duncan and Macbeth are roughly the same age, while Duncan, 'soft and gentle of nature',[17] is merely a rather weak and incompetent monarch. Shakespeare changes their relationship so as to maximise the horror and challenge in the killing of the King. It is no ordinary murder, but rather the equivalent in its own kind of, say, breaking through the sound barrier for the first time. Macbeth fully recognises the 'deep damnation' of such a deed, and sees what it will give birth to, the 'naked babe' of pity, stirring universal sorrow for the victim, and hatred for the murderer.

His soliloquy at the beginning of I.vii ends with his one reference to ambition, as the only 'spur' to prick on his intention, and at this point he has talked himself into abandoning the project. Lady Macbeth enters to rouse him by

15

calling him 'coward', invoking a concept of manliness, and reducing the issue to gaining the crown:

> Wouldst thou have that
> Which thou esteem'st the ornament of life,
> And live a coward in thine own esteem,
> Letting 'I dare not' wait upon 'I would'?

$$(I.vii.41-4)$$

As earlier, she avoids confronting the murder itself, or translates it into a more familiar, if revolting, image of what she *might* have done, in dashing out the brains of her own child. For her it is a matter of Macbeth screwing 'his courage to the sticking place', and she seems to miss a dimension present in Macbeth's,

> I dare do all that may become a man;
> Who dares do more is none.

$$(I.vii.46-7)$$

What does it 'become' a man to do? In one sense this suggests actions that grace a man, as in the penitent death of Cawdor,

> Nothing in his life
> Became him like the leaving it.

$$(I.iv.7-8)$$

At the same time Macbeth's words raise a question about the limits of human action; at what point should daring stop? Daring is what Macbeth is known for, as 'valour's minion' (I.ii.19), and Lady Macbeth effectually prompts him in terms that remind him of this; she displaces his brooding on the enormity of the deed and its consequence with the renewed sense of challenge, and he goes off resolved to

> bend up
> Each corporal agent to this terrible feat.

$$(I.vii.79-80)$$

She is oblivious to the terror of the feat, but succeeds in making it again for him part of the fascination of a daring beyond anything he has faced before.

This is brought home in his soliloquy in the next scene, in

that 'fatal vision' (II.i.36) of the dagger, fatal as deadly, as foreboding his own as well as Duncan's death, and as inescapable, fateful. The dagger of the air is terrifying, but embodies too Macbeth's desire to achieve the deed. The dagger of the mind is, in its way, as real as the one Macbeth draws, though conjured out of words. At first it is a duplicate of the one he holds, but as it ushers him towards Duncan the illusory dagger changes:

> I see thee still,
> And on thy blade and dudgeon gouts of blood,
> Which was not so before.
>
> (II.i.45–7)

At first symbolising his terror and desire to do the deed, it then becomes an emblem of the deed achieved, and as the vision fades, Macbeth's soliloquy ends with a series of images willing his identification with the powers of darkness, even as they register the 'present horror' of the moment. The lines suggest a link with the Weird Sisters, in their reference to witchcraft and to Hecate, and mark Macbeth's awareness that he is aligning himself with evil; but his full sense of the terrible nature of the murder he is about to do also makes the overcoming of his own scruples, of the horror he feels, of all the large part of himself that rebels against it, so much the greater challenge. The central lines of his soliloquy register this:

> Thou marshall'st me the way that I was going,
> And such an instrument I was to use.
> Mine eyes are made the fools o' th' other senses,
> Or else worth all the rest.
>
> (II.i.42–5)

These lines reaffirm the double nature of that image of the death of Duncan which Macbeth sees here in the visionary dagger; his eyes are worth all the other senses in so far as they show through this illusion what is compelling him from within. When in the next scene Macbeth returns from the murder with two bloody daggers, one in each hand, the vision of his soliloquy here is made actual on the stage, and characteristically, this moment of triumph is also the moment when his sense of terror and guilt are maximised:

17

I am afraid to think what I have done;
Look on't again I dare not.

(II.ii.51-2)

This scene powerfully registers Macbeth's feelings immediately after the murder, when he is appalled by what he has done. The revulsion of the moment, marvellously expressed in the image of the blood on his hands staining the seas and 'Making the green one red' (II.ii.63), confirms the magnitude as well as the horror of the deed. But this quickly passes, for we learn in the next scene that Macbeth has returned to the scene of the crime to confront another image of death when he kills the grooms, accounting for it in terms of anger and love for Duncan. Whatever other explanations may be adduced for Lady Macbeth fainting at this point, the news of the killing of the grooms is enough to account for it. Here Macbeth's explanation shows how far he has gone beyond her in taking the initiative on his own; killing the grooms in addition to the King was not in her thoughts, and this marks the point at which she begins to lose him. He was at first horrified at his own deed in killing Duncan, but can return to look on the dead King and kill the grooms without a qualm:

Here lay Duncan,
His silver skin lac'd with his golden blood;
And his gash'd stabs look'd like a breach in nature
For ruin's wasteful entrance: there, the murderers,
Steep'd in the colours of their trade, their daggers
Unmannerly breech'd with gore. Who could refrain,
That had a heart to love, and in that heart
Courage to make's love known?

(II.iii.110-7)

Killing the grooms is nothing for him after killing Duncan, but paradoxically it shocks Lady Macbeth as a consequence she had not foreseen when she said, 'The sleeping and the dead Are but as pictures' (II.ii.53-4). For Macbeth the murder of Duncan was the equivalent in mountaineering terms of scaling Everest, and after this he has no trouble with lower hills; but Lady Macbeth never feels the magnitude or the horror of killing the King,[18] whose murder is for her merely the means of fulfilling her ambition that her husband shall wear the crown, 'the golden round' (I.v.25), and she supposes that the death of Duncan finishes the business:

> A little water clears us of this deed;
> How easy is it then!
>
> (II.ii.67-8)

The further killing of the grooms begins also to bring home to her what Macbeth has felt all through, not how easy, but how difficult it is both to kill a king, and then to be 'clear' of the deed, and 'trammel up the consequence' (I.vii.3).

Although Macbeth felt the weight of the consequences of the murder,

>   that we but teach
> Bloody instructions, which being taught return
> To plague th'inventor,
>
> (I.vii.8-10)

he did not foresee what they would be. The worst is that having scaled Everest, he finds soon that he must overcome an obstacle almost as great, another kingly figure who fills him with dread:

>   Our fears in Banquo
> Stick deep; and in his royalty of nature
> Reigns that which would be fear'd.
>
> (III.i.48-50)

The 'bloody instructions' he gives the murderers return to plague him in the banquet scene, when the ghost of Banquo sits in his place.

When Simon Forman saw the play at the Globe in the spring of 1611 he recorded the way in which the first entry of the ghost was played:[19]

> The next night, being at supper with his noble men whom he had bid to a feast to the which also Banquo should have come, he began to speak of Noble Banquo, and to wish that he were there. And as he thus did, standing up to drink a Carouse to him, the ghost of Banquo came and sat down in his chair behind him. And he turning about to sit down again saw the ghost of Banquo, which fronted him so, that he fell into a great passion of fear and fury.

Lady Macbeth, who does not see the ghost, relates this apparition to the 'air-drawn dagger' Macbeth saw in II.i, and many leading actors, from John Philip Kemble in 1786 and Edwin Booth in 1828 down to Ian McKellen in 1976, have treated the ghost as another figment of Macbeth's 'heat-oppressed brain'.[20] A good actor can indeed create a sense that he alone sees some appalling vision which terrifies him, and perhaps this is more acceptable to modern audiences less ready to believe in ghosts; but it seems that in Shakespeare's time an actor played the ghost, and Macbeth and the audience actually witnessed here another image of death. The ghost with his 'gory locks' echoes visually the First Murderer who came with blood upon his face (III.iv.13) to report the death of Banquo, and the blood smeared upon the faces of the grooms accused by Macbeth of killing Duncan (II.ii.50, 56; II iii.114). Macbeth recognises the Ghost simultaneously as real, 'Avaunt, and quit my sight!' (III.iv.93), and unreal,

> Hence, horrible shadow!
> Unreal mock'ry, hence!
>
> (III.iv.106-7)

It is appropriate that the audience should have this sense too, and see embodied on stage the cause of Macbeth's fear. Macbeth can boast with reason 'What man dare, I dare' (III.iv.99), for he has achieved a most 'terrible feat' in killing Duncan and Banquo; but the consequences include something he had not bargained for at all, the 'strange infirmity' (III.iv.86) that unmans him in trembling, as his murders leave him still 'bound in To saucy doubts and fears' (III.iv.24-5). ·

The banquet scene brings him to an important recognition about his condition:

> I am in blood
> Stepp'd in so far that, should I wade no more,
> Returning were as tedious as go o'er.
>
> (III.iv.136-8)

This picks up again the image of the multitudinous seas stained with blood, but with a difference marked especially in the word 'tedious': now, wading in that flood of blood he has spilt, he begins to realise that the excitement has gone, and the only way left for him is the repetitive boredom of further bloodshed as he ensures that 'All causes shall give way' (III.iv.136). His next move is to bully the Weird Sisters, confronting them as if he could command them; 'More shall they speak' he had said at the end of the banquet scene (III.iv.134), and his imperative echoes in 'I conjure you . . . answer me' (IV.i.50–1). Perhaps the best justification for the Hecate scene is that it exposes Macbeth's desperation and the emptiness of his imperatives, which are countered by those of Hecate:

> that, distill'd by magic sleights,
> Shall raise such artificial sprites
> As, by the strength of their illusion,
> Shall draw him on to his confusion.
>
> (III.v.26–9)

The three apparitions produced by the Weird Sisters rise and descend, if the Folio directions are followed, requiring actors to play them, or perhaps a kind of voice-over or ventriloquism by one of the witches. They must be seen by everyone on stage and the audience. The first, an armed head, both suggests Macduff ('Beware the thane of Fife'), and anticipates the bringing on of the head of the dead Macbeth at the end of the play. The second, a bloody child, seems at once an image of birth and death, saying to Macbeth that none of woman born shall harm him, but connecting for the audience with the other images of the spilling of blood in the play, and anticipating Macbeth's readiness to murder even the children of Macduff. The third, a child crowned with a tree in its hand, seems to promise security to Macbeth, but symbolises too what is brought home in the final 'show' of kings, that Banquo's line will inherit the throne. These are all externally created shows, stage-managed by the Witches, culminating in another appearance of the Ghost of Banquo, bloody as in III.ii, who must be played by an actor,

> For the blood-bolter'd Banquo smiles upon me,
> And points at them for his.
>
> (IV.i.123–4)

So the visions Macbeth imagined earlier, the air-drawn dagger, and the Ghost of Banquo unseen by the others at the banquet, were more 'real' and emotionally disturbing than those apparitions or shows witnessed by all. This scene marks the change in Macbeth; the dagger and the Ghost terrified him as images of murder that appalled him, and these figures of his imagination embodied his moral fear, his conscience and sense of guilt as well as his deep desire and compulsion to achieve the ultimate in killing. Now, in seeking out the Witches, and demanding to see the worst they can show, he is no longer afraid of such images. The culmination of the scene is the return of Banquo's ghost, an image which sears Macbeth's eyeballs, but not with terror any more, merely with anger. Macbeth's ability to face these images and ask for more until he is confronted again by the murdered Banquo, shows how far he has travelled morally and mentally since the opening of the play; once unable to look on what he has done, or to think of what he was about to do without perturbation, he is now no longer troubled by sights that might appal. He has lost his sense of fear, and is no longer shocked or disturbed by blood and killing. He has found his routine, and the tedium that goes with it.

At this point, the end of IV.i, Shakespeare removes his protagonist from the stage for the equivalent of about an act of the play, or roughly 420 lines. This is in accordance with his practice in the other central tragedies, and quite apart from giving the leading actor a well-earned rest, it serves a deeper function. Macbeth has passed beyond the point of no return, and terrible deeds no longer shock or disturb him. What remains in action is the confirmation of this in the murder of Lady Macduff and her children, and the gathering of the forces that will bring about Macbeth's downfall; for Macbeth himself there is yet to come the full recognition of what has happened to him, of the wasteland he has created for himself. The destruction of the innocent mother and children can be seen as analogous to Richard III's murder of the princes in the Tower, as marking the last degradation of the criminal, but in Macbeth's case the effect is more complex, for it is also in some sense a breakthrough for him, a liberation from the 'terrible dreams' and 'torture of the mind' (III.ii.18,21) which afflicted him. In relation to this Shakespeare's finest stroke of irony is to place Lady Macbeth's sleep-walking scene before the reappearance of Macbeth. The two have moved in opposite directions mentally, and she is now in a condition not unlike that of Macbeth before the murder of Duncan; when he saw visionary daggers and imagined nothing could wash away his blood-guilt, she had no apparent sense of horror; but as he has moved from a state of emotional turmoil and moral anxiety to one of blank indifference, so her cool self-command has given way, and the disturbance of her mind is now expressed in nightmare images like that of the blood on her hand and the bell striking 'One, two; why then 'tis time to do't' (V.i.33–4).

Here the horror of the murder of Duncan is borne in on us again just prior to the return of Macbeth, who, by contrast feels nothing, so that even the news of her death has no effect on him, except to prompt his last and most profound acknowledgment of his loss of all sense of guilt or feeling for others. The difference between Macbeth in IV.i and Macbeth in V.v lies not in his condition, but in his discovery of its nature and implications, and of the price he has paid for his liberation from fear. This is most marked not in the merely selfish disappointment at losing the social rewards and pleasures of growing old, such as 'honour, love, obedience, troops of friends' (V.iii.25), but in the wider reverberations of his inability to respond to the death of his wife:

> To-morrow, and to-morrow, and to-morrow,
> Creeps in this petty pace from day to day,
> To the last syllable of recorded time,
> And all our yesterdays have lighted fools
> The way to dusty death. Out, out, brief candle!
> Life's but a walking shadow, a poor player,
> That struts and frets his hour upon the stage,
> And then is heard no more; it is a tale
> Told by an idiot, full of sound and fury,
> Signifying nothing.
>
> (V.v.19–28)

Here the collapse of time, the future ('to-morrow'), the present (marvellously signalled in the word 'creeps'), and past ('All our yesterdays'), into the boredom of mere re-petition betrays Macbeth's crushing sense of deprivation, and now what reverberates is not the loss merely of social rewards, but of any reason for remaining alive.

In this speech too the image of the 'poor player' is especially poignant. It daringly reminds us of the actor playing the King, and by extension of ourselves playing roles, strutting and fretting, and so generates sympathy for Macbeth; at the same time, it brings home to us, through the weight of the action of the play that lies behind the lines, how inadequate such a definition of life is. For life had meant more for Macbeth than this, in his ambition to be King, to rule in Scotland and found a dynasty, to be a 'man', an heroic warrior, to be honoured and loved. Another meaning for life has been established for the audience through the play's Christian frame of reference, notably the sketching in of Duncan as a 'most sainted' monarch (IV.iii.109), and the account of Edward the Confessor, both showing up the image of the 'poor player' as reductive against a proper sense of the purpose and value of using time to a good end, against fulfilment to be thought of in the terms in which Edward is described:

> sundry blessings hang about his throne
> That speak him full of grace.

(IV.iii.158-9)

The play ends, as it began, with a battle, in which Macbeth again confronts death as a warrior, killing young Siward before he is himself slain by Macduff. The last image of death is one Macbeth has not looked for, when his head is brought on, probably as in Holinshed's account, on a pole, recalling the armed head among the apparitions of IV.i, and the bloody head of Banquo's ghost. If Macbeth's head was brought on in this way at the Globe (a possibility hinted at in Macduff's lines at V.viii.25-6, 'We'll have thee . . . . Painted upon a pole'), it would have suggested the image of an executed criminal, like the heads mounted on London Bridge; this marks the devaluation of Macbeth for Malcolm and his allies from the powerful tyrant of Scotland into 'this dead butcher' (V.viii.69). It is the last irony of the play that Macbeth should himself become an image of death that no longer terrifies anyone. The audience knows more than Malcolm, however, having experienced with Macbeth all that has happened; Malcolm sees merely the death of a hated tyrant and usurper, which is certainly what Macbeth has become for his own people. But this is to conceive Macbeth's ambitions on a basic and elementary level as merely concerned with power. What we have witnessed is something much more complex. If anyone embodies this cruder sense of ambition it is Lady Macbeth, whose one thought in the early scenes is to gain the crown for her husband.

The action of the play reveals how little Macbeth understands himself when he says ambition to leap into Duncan's seat is the only spur that pricks him on to murder. The phrase occurs in one of his great soliloquies which expresses an emotional turmoil rather than a grasp of issues. Here, as in his incantatory speeches in III.ii in relation to the murder of Banquo, his words express more than he understands, and the sense is so complicated that, as I have put it elsewhere, theatre audiences cannot fully comprehend what is being said:[21]

> in the theatre the rhetoric dominates over the sense,
> which permits only tortured glimpses into the dark
> recesses of Macbeth's state of mind, and establishes a
> mood in which, with Lady Macbeth, we marvel at his
> words; and the point of it all arguably is to bring home the
> extent to which Macbeth himself understands the force
> of what he says, but not the implications.

So, in Macbeth's soliloquy in I.vii, the final images are muddy and compressed, and reverberate with significances which can be teased out through pages of commentary;

>   pity, like a naked new-born babe
> Striding the blast, or heaven's cherubin hors'd
> Upon the sightless couriers of the air,
> Shall blow the horrid deed in every eye,
> That tears shall drown the wind. I have no spur
> To prick the sides of my intent, but only
> Vaulting ambition, which o'erleaps itself,
> And falls on th'other
>
>   (I.vii.21–8)

The sudden shifts from the 'babe' to cherubs 'horsed' on the winds, to tears flooding to 'drown', to another kind of horse in the spur-pricking intent, do not allow any clear grasp of Macbeth's meaning, and dramatically establish that he does not fully understand himself; his words and images convey the anguish of his tortured mind, and a sense of bewilderment.

Macbeth does not comprehend the reasons why he is drawn, in spite of his full consciousness of the 'deep damnation of his taking-off', to murder Duncan. If the spur were merely ambition for the crown, he could overcome it; he has in any case the prophecy of the Witches that he will be King. The play explores more profoundly the compulsion that drives him in the series of 'strange images of death' it presents. A warrior, accustomed to killing on the battlefield, Macbeth, to be fully a 'man' in this limited sense, is driven to face the challenge of killings of a different kind, and his inner drive, embodied in the air-drawn dagger that marshals him towards Duncan, overcomes for him his revulsion at the deed. It is reinforced by Lady Macbeth:

> Art thou afeard
> To be the same in thine own act and valour
> As thou art in desire?
>
> (I.vii.39–41)

Her desire is for the crown, but his is larger, the urge to fulfil himself, as we now say, and in pursuing this Macbeth appals by what he does, and excites admiration for his ability to meet such a challenge, for the sheer daring of it. In order to bring this across to an audience, Macbeth has to be established as a rugged fighter, whose world is that of slaughter, as opposed to the saintly, gentle Duncan, whose world is that of the court. Macbeth is young as imagined in the play, as Duncan's lines show:

> I have begun to plant thee, and will labour
> To make thee full of growing;
>
> (I.iv.28–9)

but Macbeth has begun as a killer, and his growth and fulfilment lie in confronting further and more terrible images of death. The play reveals, of course, the price Macbeth pays in achieving his desire, and exposes too the inadequacies of self-fulfilment as a goal; and yet there remains a sympathy for the tough and indomitable figure who ends in a hell of his own creating. The 'great intellect' of the play is Shakespeare's, realising dramatically through the magnificent compressed poetry given to Macbeth the inner impulses that he does not fully understand, but which drive him to overcome his scruples and fulfil himself in terms of what he is good at, killing. So finally *Macbeth* is a play that escapes from ordinary moral boundaries and judgments; it is less about a criminal who must be morally condemned than about a great warrior who breaks through the fear-barrier only to find on the other side not the release and fulfilment he looks for, but a desert of spiritual desolation.

In this way Shakespeare adds a new dimension to the theme of the ambitious prince finally brought low. He had earlier shown an awareness of the mixture of emotions and motives that could be involved in ambition, as, for instance, in his treatment of Caesar and Brutus in *Julius Caesar*. He understood the contradictory viewpoints which might make ambition appear sinful, foul, pitiful or thriftless, on the one hand, and 'divine' (*Hamlet*, IV.iv.49) on the other, as Macbeth himself begins from 'the big wars That makes ambition virtue' (*Othello*, III.iii.353–4). In *Macbeth* he went further. To start with he brilliantly dramatised that state of the man seized by ambition, 'a proud covetousness, or a dry thirst of honour, a great torture of the mind', as Burton was later to define it. In coveting the throne, and plotting the death of Duncan, Macbeth is like those Burton describes as 'seeking that, many times, which they had much better be without; ... with what waking nights, painful hours, anxious thoughts, and bitterness of mind, *inter spem metumque* [i.e., between hope and fear], distracted and tired, they consume the interim of their time.' Burton's analysis, however, was confined to the perpetually unsatisfied aspirers, always seeking to rise, and swelling in the end until they burst or 'break their own necks.'[22] Macbeth achieves his aspirations, gains the throne, all at one throw, or so it seems when he kills Duncan, before the end of Act II; but Shakespeare's concern was to probe further in the last three acts into what happens then, into the way he becomes a prisoner of his own imagination, bound into doubts and fears, and is able to achieve release from these only at the appalling cost of losing his capacity to care. In daring to do all that may become a man, he destroys the best part of himself; and in showing the process by which Macbeth comes to realise this, Shakespeare makes his most searching analysis of the effects of ambition.

NOTES

1 *Charles Lamb on Shakespeare*, ed. Joan Coldwell (New York, 1978), p. 35.
2 *Macbeth*, ed. Kenneth Muir (1951), Introduction, p. lvi.
3 Willard Farnham, *Shakespeare's Tragic Frontier* (Berkeley and Los Angeles, 1950, reprinted 1963), p. 79.
4 Matthew N. Proser, *The Heroic Image in Five Shakespearean Tragedies* (Princeton, 1965), p. 52. Proser is interested in the inadequacy of such a comment to explain Macbeth's deeds, and he too finds the centre of the play's complexity in Macbeth himself, emphasising the manliness required of the soldier-hero, and describing the action in terms of a conflict between conscience and desire; for him Macbeth moves 'toward enacting without moral reservation – the ethic of pure desire' (p. 74).
5 Lascelles Abercrombie, *The Idea of Great Poetry* (1925), p. 178; see also R.A. Foakes, 'Macbeth' in *Shakespeare Select Bibliographical Guides*, ed. Stanley Wells (1973), pp. 190–3.
6 *The Wheel of Fire* (1930), pp. 171–2. In his fine account of *Macbeth*, relating it to Marlowe's *Doctor Faustus*, Wilbur Sanders takes off from Abercrombie and Wilson Knight in trying to 'avoid separating the act of judgment which *sees through* Macbeth, from the act of imagination which sees the world *with* him', and finds, in the courage and honesty of his bearing in facing 'the realities of his situation' at the end, an important positive element, in a 'tremulous equilibrium between affirmation and despair'; see *The Dramatist and the Received Idea* (Cambridge, 1968), pp. 299–307.
7 Bertrand Evans, *Shakespeare's Tragic Practice* (Oxford, 1979), p. 221.
8 *Ibid.*, p. 215.
9 *Ibid.*, p. 219.
10 Richard David, *Shakespeare in the Theatre* (Cambridge, 1978), p. 95; David, in contrast to Abercrombie, Proser, Wilson Knight and Sanders, thinks that after the early part of the play 'there is little for Macbeth to do but decline' (p. 92), and praises Laurence Olivier's performance in the part for the sense it conveyed of 'enormous undeveloped capabilities', as opposed to Ian McKellen's playing of it, which did nothing of the kind.
11 *Holinshed's Chronicle*, ed. Allardyce and Josephine Nicoll (1927, reprinted 1969), p. 208.
12 John Russell Brown, in *Shakespeare's Dramatic Style* (1970), pp. 162–9, has a full and interesting analysis of this speech emphasising especially the function of the antitheses in it in showing Macbeth losing 'his present bearings, and the ability to act'.
13 *Holinshed's Chronicle*, p. 210.
14 *Ibid.*, p. 211.
15 *Shakespearean Criticism*, ed. T.M. Raysor, 2 vols (1930; revised

1960), II.221 (a lecture of 1813), and I.65 (notes made for a lecture given in 1819).

16 Coleridge noted that Lady Macbeth showed 'No womanly, no wifely joy at the return of her husband' (*Shakespearean Criticism*, I.65).

17 *Holinshed's Chronicle*, p. 207.

18 While this is, I think, true, it could be misinterpreted as an over-simplification; it needs to be said that at the point when we realise the extent of her complicity in the deed, in laying ready the daggers of the grooms, she shows a moment's vulnerability:

> Had he not resembled
> My father as he slept, I had done't   (II.ii.12-13)

Although she can abstractly talk of dashing out the brains of her own babe (I.vii.58), when faced with such a deed she cannot bring herself to do it. Her mettle is not so 'undaunted' as she leads Macbeth to suppose.

19 Cited in E.K. Chambers, *William Shakespeare A Study of Facts and Problems*, 2 vols (Oxford, 1930), II. p. 338.

20 See Dennis Bartholomeusz, *Macbeth and the Players* (Cambridge, 1969), pp. 133-4, and A.C. Sprague, *Shakespeare and the Actors The Stage Business in his Plays (1660-1905)* (Cambridge, Mass., 1945), pp. 256-8.

21 R.A. Foakes, 'Poetic language and dramatic significance in Shakespeare', in *Shakespeare's Styles Essays in Honour of Kenneth Muir*, ed. Philip Edwards, Inga-Stina Ewbank and G.K. Hunter (Cambridge, 1980), pp. 82-3.

22 Robert Burton, *The Anatomy of Melancholy*, part 2, section 1, member 3, subsection 11; Everyman edition (3 vols, 1932), I. pp. 280-2.

2

The kingdom, the power and the glory in *Macbeth*

Brian Morris

'We cannot imagine him on his knees', says Kenneth Muir of Macbeth,[1] contrasting him with that other murderer, tyrant and usurper Claudius in *Hamlet*. It is a shrewd contrast, since *Macbeth* has little to offer about prayer, repentance, or contrition, though it has much to say about guilt. Indeed, the play is hardly concerned with religion at all. There is no Church, there are no priests, God impinges but slightly on the affairs of humankind. The play is deeply involved with the supernatural, with prophecies and portents, with 'Augures, and understood relations', above all with a piercing analysis of evil, but the other side of the religious coin – sin, repentance, forgiveness, salvation and grace – is no more seen than the dark side of the moon. Macbeth's perspective is from 'this bank and shoal' to 'the last syllable of recorded time', but not beyond. In this respect the play is more like Marlowe's *Tamburlaine* than his *Faustus*, though the relationship between the three plays is more complex and rewarding to study than such a simple statement allows. Yet the glance at *Faustus* may help to enforce the truth that *Macbeth* is not sharply and continuously aware of the religious dimension in human experience; life, here, is frankly seen from man's point of view and not *sub specie aeternitatis*.

Macbeth himself makes this quite clear in I.vii when he specifically dismisses eschatological considerations from his planning:

If it were done when 'tis done, then 'twere well
It were done quickly. If th'assassination
Could trammel up the consequence, and catch

With his surcease, success; that but this blow
Might be the be-all and the end-all here –
But here upon this bank and shoal of time –
We'd jump the life to come.

(I.vii.1–7)

Despite (or perhaps because of) the complex syntactical structure of this passage, with its succession of hypothetical clauses, its repetitions and interpolations, the progress of the thought is analytic, cool and clear. As S.L. Bethell crisply paraphrases it: 'If there were no ill-consequences in this life I should be quite satisfied, for I should ignore the question of a future state.'[2] So, in this speech, Macbeth is content to dismiss death, heaven, hell and judgment from his calculation, and concentrates on the fact that 'We still have judgment here'; this 'even-handed Justice' is the stumbling-block, and his problem is how to circumvent it. He is unconcerned about the *dies irae* and the terrible judgment of God. The point is enforced in the deadly irony of what follows. Duncan's virtues

Will plead like angels, trumpet-tongu'd, against
The deep damnation of his taking-off.

Pity, like heaven's cherubim.

Shall blow the horrid deed in every eye.

The 'virtues' will arouse the 'pity' in Macbeth's contemporaries, and that would be a nuisance. The angels and the cherubim, God's ministers and messengers, are no more than similes and illustrations of the immediate political problem. This is perfectly in line with Macbeth's previous attitude to the spiritual world. At his first encounter with the Weird Sisters (I.iii) he does 'start, and seem to fear' (I.iii.51), but he is startled not by the apparition, but by what is said: 'Things that do sound so fair.' His first words to the witches are a request for information:

Stay, you imperfect speakers, tell me more.

(I.iii.70)

And when he has had time to think, and recognise them as 'instruments of darkness' (l.124) he can still ignore the terror

31

and the wonder, and concentrate on the reliability of the message:

This supernatural soliciting
Cannot be ill; cannot be good.   (ll.130-1)

All this may strike us as too cool and calculating by half, but it is certainly the way Shakespeare presents his hero: a man to whom the rewards and terrors of eternity are unimportant. Macbeth, indeed, seems to 'count religion but a childish toy, And hold there is no sin but ignorance.' [3]

This impression is not vitiated by the play's final scenes. When the death of his Queen is reported (V.v), Macbeth is moved to meditate on life and death, but his vision is limited to the earthly realm. The poor player, who struts and frets his hour upon the stage, is then 'heard no more'. The tale is full of sound and fury

Signifying nothing.   (l.28)

This, as Bethell comments, 'Expresses in Shakespeare's terms the hopelessness of the hardened sinner, to whom the universe has now no meaning', and it 'merely implies the atheism . . . which has resulted from his gradual hardening in crime.'[4] The final scenes of Act V show Macbeth valorous and defiant, but without one whit of concern for his immortal soul.

This is not to deny the presence in the play of what L.C. Knights has called 'images of grace and of the holy supernatural'.[5] He points to Act III, scene vi, where Lennox and another Lord discuss how Macduff has fled to 'the Pious Edward', 'the Holy King', who has received Malcolm 'with such grace'. Lennox invokes 'some holy Angel' and the other Lord adds 'I'll send my prayers with him' (which prepares the way for the long, still, holy and contemplative scene in the English court, IV.iii). Knights singles out one passage in III.vi which has a peculiar power:

That, by the help of these – with Him above
To ratify the work – we may again
Give to our tables meat, sleep to our nights
Free from our feasts and banquets bloody knives
Do faithful homage and receive free honours –
All which we pine for now.   (ll.32-7)

This is certainly, in tone and movement, very different from the 'banquet' scene which precedes it, but it must be pointed out that the specifically religious reference is conventional and muted. The stress is on peace on earth, and goodwill amongst men, but the periphrasis of 'Him above' is a far cry from the Christ whose incarnation was believed to bring about that peace, and who, at his second coming in glory, will judge both the quick and the dead. The reticence, the hesitancy, of 'Him above' is typical of the references to holiness and godliness in the play. 'The pious Edward' is never allowed on stage, and IV.iii, which is, admittedly, the strongest and most extended presentation of goodness in the play, presents the cause of God only in an oblique, allusive and inferential way. Macduff says that Malcolm's mother was a woman of prayer:

> the Queen that bore thee,
> Oft'ner upon her knees than on her feet,
> Died every day she liv'd. (ll.109–11)

But that is our only glimpse of her. Even the last lines of the scene, when action is resumed, are periphrastic:

> Macbeth
> Is ripe for shaking, and the pow'rs above
> Put on their instruments. (ll.237–9)

Are these 'Powers' literally 'that order of Angels which God, in his providence, has deputed to be concerned especially with the restraint and coercion of demons' (cf. II.i.7–9, and Muir's note), or is the reference more general? It is difficult to be sure. The point is, surely, that the presentation of goodness and holiness in *Macbeth* is muted and peripheral. The tyrant is eventually overthrown by human powers, in hand-to-hand combat, where the presence of God is neither invoked nor declared, though it may be assumed. It is nothing like the end of *Richard III*, where Richmond is identified as God's retributive agent. To that extent, and while not wishing to minimise the imagery of grace and goodness in any way, I would argue that the play focuses on the rise and fall of a temporal tyrant, whose religious experience is presented as minimal. Macbeth does not so much oppose God as ignore him.[6]

This may become clearer if we examine Macbeth's attitude

to the concept of Omnipotence. The *locus classicus* for the Christian expression of this must be the peroration of the Lord's Prayer, as recorded in St Matthew's gospel: 'For thine is the kingdom, and the power, and the glory, for ever. Amen.'[7] There is, as Touchstone might have said, much virtue in your *for*. The seven preceding petitions are presented to God *because* he is the source of all potency and is alone able to grant any request. Kingdom, power, and glory, then, sum up and encapsulate in a triple image the ability of the Almighty to do whatever he wants and grant whatever he will. Much has been written on the theological significance of the triple image,[8] but it may be readily and simply applied to its microcosmic equivalent, the earthly kingdom ruled over by God's vice-regent the King, reigning in glory and exercising power.

Macbeth seeks not the kingdom of God but the kingdom of Duncan. Yet he is supremely uninterested in the land itself. Scotland is not a presence in *Macbeth* as England is in Shakespeare's Histories. This is evident from the very faint frame of geographical reference, and Shakespeare's obvious dramatic intention not to evoke strongly any sense of place. When the play opens the witches, who have come from nowhere, resolve to meet again 'Upon the heath', and the following scene is likewise given no specific location. This has puzzled editors. Muir comments:

> Theobald and Capell, followed by most modern editors, deduced from I.iii.39 and from Holinshed that Sc.ii was laid at Forres. But Macbeth – assuming he is Bellona's bridegroom – was fighting at Fife (I.ii.49) which, as Wilson points out, is 100 miles from Forres, and could not be in two places at once. The two battles have been run together in place as well as in time. . . . But not even an audience of Scotsmen would notice the geographical difficulties.

Only two place-names are mentioned in the scene, Fife and Saint Colme's Inch; the emphasis is on the rebels with their Kernes and Gallowglasses, the Norweyan banners which flout the sky, and the valour of Macbeth and Banquo. This is typical of the play's refusal to evoke particular places. When King Duncan approaches Macbeth's castle, he could be anywhere:

34

This castle hath a pleasant seat; the air
Nimbly and sweetly recommends itself
Unto our gentle senses.

                                                    (I.vi.1 – 6)

In this salubrious spot our eye is drawn upwards to 'The
temple-haunting martlet', to the 'jutty, frieze, Buttress . . .
coign of vantage', but never outwards to the landscape with
its hills, its forests, its cattle, its people and all the con-
stituents of a commonwealth. Shakespeare rigorously abstains
from evoking any but the most enclosed and claustrophobic
locations. People meet in castles or just outside them, on
heathland or in unspecified places, and the dramaturgy offers
only the scantiest preparation for the necessary changes of
place. Shakespeare's Histories are full of scenes which end
with directions like 'Away with me in post to Ravensburgh',
'Now to London / To see these honours in possession', or

      some twelve days hence
Our general forces at Bridgenorth shall meet.
Our hands are full of business. Let's away.

Places are important in political planning; there is a sense of
the necessity for urgent movement to the outposts of empire
if rebellion is to be contained. *Macbeth* knows nothing of
this. There is no consideration of what Ulysses in *Troilus
and Cressida* calls 'the specialty of rule'; indeed, there is no
real political dimension to Macbeth's thinking. Above all,
there is no sense that for him the nation, the kingdom, has
any value in itself. Of its inhabitants we see only the upper
class, and many of them are flat and shadowy presences –
Lennox, Ross, 'another Lord'. There is no counterpart in
the play to Burgundy's speech in Act V, scene ii of *Henry V*,
describing at full length the lovely visage of 'Our fertile
France', and making it a prize worth fighting for. Macbeth
has no map, as Tamburlaine has and King Lear has, to chart
his movements or his boundaries, and for the central scenes
of the play the kingdom of Scotland seems a barren tract,
ungoverned and unpeopled. As indeed it is, for its inhabitants
have, we are told, fled to England to escape the tyranny, and
it is in England that we glimpse the only vision the play per-
mits or an ordered and governed state. Act IV, scene iii shows
the Scottish nobles in the English court, and it is there that

Malcolm learns the arts of government. The theme of the
ruler educated in exile is one which recurs regularly in
Shakespeare's later plays.[9] Timon has to leave Athens in
order to find himself; both Antony and Octavius learn their
lessons in Egypt; Florizel and Perdita are educated abroad, in
the pastoral world of the shepherds, and Prospero has to be
exiled by his usurping brother before he can gain the political
wisdom necessary to govern his Dukedom. In *Macbeth* the
kingdom of Scotland is born again in King Edward's England.
The Scotland which Macbeth rules is bereft of its people, an
eggshell, containing only his enemies or his victims. It is a
kingdom in which he has no interest.

If the kingdom, the control and governance of land and
people, means little to Macbeth, glory means even less. The
word occurs only once in the play, and then in a scene
which is almost certainly not by Shakespeare, the Hecate
scene, I, II.v:

> And I, the mistress of your charms,
> The close contriver of all harms,
> Was never call'd to bear my part,
> Or show the glory of our art.   (ll.6-9)

This sense of the *display* of power or honour was not un-
familiar to Shakespeare, as any concordance will witness. He
was especially concerned with it in the Histories:

> Ha, majesty! how high thy glory tow'rs
> When the rich blood of kings is set on fire!
>   (*King John*, II.i.350-1)

> I see thy glory like a shooting star
> Fall to the base earth from the firmament!
>   (*Richard II*, II.iv.19-20)

> But I will rise there with so full a glory
> That I will dazzle all the eyes of France.
>   (*Henry V*, I.i.278-9)

The images in this random sample are of hawk, star, and sun,
characteristic of majesty, and examples could be multiplied.
Majestic glory is what Tamburlaine envisages:

Is it not brave to be a king, Techelles?
Usumcasane and Theridimas,
Is it not passing brave to be a king,
And ride in triumph through Persepolis?

Macbeth does not ride in triumph through anywhere; triumph
is not his métier. Nor does he long for the crown as the
symbol of glorious majesty with any hydroptic thirst. There
is nothing in the play like the heavenly vision of that Duke of
Gloucester who is to become Richard III:

I'll make my heaven to dream upon the crown,
And whiles I live t'account this world but hell,
Until my misshap'd trunk that bears this head
Be round impaled with a glorious crown.
(*3 Henry VI*, III.iii.168–71)

Macbeth knows nothing of the glory of kingship, and, indeed,
it is remarkably absent from the whole group of Shakespeare's
major tragedies. It is as if he has explored and exhausted the
vision by the time he had written *Henry V*, and perhaps the
turning-point occurs in Act IV of *2 Henry IV*, where the
Prince anticipates his wearing of the crown, this 'polish'd
perturbation! golden care!' (l.23), and learns from his father

How troublesome it sat upon my head.   (l.187)

The tragedies seem to expand this insight, and there is no
glorious king in *Macbeth*, or *Hamlet*, or *King Lear*, and no
king at all in *Othello*. It is significant that, after the discovery
of Duncan's death, there is but one brief scene before Macbeth's appearance as King in III.i. There is no royal funeral
(cf. *1 Henry VI*, I.i), there are no councils to decide the
succession, no offering of the crown (cf. *Richard III*, III.vii),
and no coronation. The interim is occupied with the related
story of flights and portents and auguries of ill. Act III opens
with Banquo's foreboding soliloquy, and then follows the
stage-direction:[10]

*Sennet sounded. Enter Macbeth as King, Lady [Macbeth as
Queen] Lenox, Ross, Lords, and Attendants.*

Some sort of processional entry seems to be suggested by this

direction, but it is not mandatory, and this moment marks
Macbeth's nearest approach to any kind of regal glory. His
language is uncertain:

> To-night we hold a solemn supper, Sir,
> And I'll request your presence.   (ll.14-15)

Banquo's reply, 'Let your Highness / Command upon me',
indicates that Macbeth has instantly failed to meet the needs
of the new decorum, and as the scene develops he moves
uneasily between the royal 'We' and 'I'. His speech enforces
our sense of his lack of command. It is full of questions: 'Ride
you this afternoon?', 'Is't far you ride?', 'Goes Fleance with
you?', 'Attend those men our pleasure?', 'Have you consider'd
of my speeches?'. This is the usurper's interrogative mode,
not the imperative of a king. The scene is full of rumour and
uncertainty ('We hear, our bloody cousins are bestow'd / In
England and in Ireland'), stratagems rather than orders are
the instruments of state, and Macbeth's overwhelming need
is not to display glory but to obtain security:

> To be thus is nothing,
> But to be safely thus.   (ll.47-8)

This is a remarkable echo of Richard III's feeling at the very
moment he, another usurper, ascends the throne:

> But shall we wear these glories for a day;
> Or shall they last, and we rejoice in them?   (IV.ii.5-6)

Macbeth seems not even conscious that there are 'glories'. A
sense of insecurity haunts the following scene (III.ii). There
are phrases like 'Unsafe the while', 'restless ecstasy', and they
are summed up in Lady Macbeth's epigrammatic couplet
before Macbeth's entry:

> 'Tis safer to be that which we destroy,
> Than by destruction dwell in doubtful joy.   (ll.6-7)

From this scene on, there are no moments of glory. Macbeth
is totally subdued to the need for securing his position. The
only processions are those of the revengers of their country's
wrongs, who mass in England and march towards Dunsinane.

Macbeth is increasingly isolated and dishonoured, reduced to the iron core of his nature as an heroic warrior. After the banquet scene we may call his name Ichabod, for 'the glory is departed'.[11]

Power is what Macbeth seeks least of all, if by power we mean the possession of control or command over others, or anything to do with influence or authority.[12] He is, at all the significant points of the play, more acted upon than acting. In the opening scenes his active military exploits take place off-stage and are reported by others. When he appears his new title, Thane of Cawdor, is placed upon him; he does not have to act to achieve it. The Weird Sisters are, from his point of view, a chance encounter, and he proposes no action:

> If chance will have me King, why, chance may crown me,
> Without my stir.
>
> (I.iii.143–4)

When, after consultation with his wife, he eventually takes the decision to commit regicide there is no mention of the benefits in power which will accrue. At the very moment of decision Macbeth has no thought for the future; he is obsessed with the quality of the act itself:

> I am settled, and bend up
> Each corporal agent to this terrible feat.
> Away, and mock the time with fairest show;
> False face must hide what the false heart doth know.
>
> (I.vii.79–82)

This is not the utterance of a potential tyrant, hungry for command and control over the destinies of others; it is self-directed, self-absorbed, a moment of moral meditation. When he is King, Macbeth never exercises his regal power to do anything except preserve his own position. A glance at *Hamlet* enforces this point, since almost the first thing that Claudius, the usurper does, is dispatch ambassadors, exercise diplomacy in court affairs, issue orders and give permissions about matters of state. This dimension is wholly lacking in Shakespeare's presentation of Macbeth. He himself seldom uses the word 'power', and it is left to Lady Macbeth, once, late in the play, to refer to the sway and domination he has achieved:

What need we fear who knows it, when none can call our
power to accompt?

(V.i.36-7)

Even this insight is achieved only in the extremity of nightmare.

Power is, however, what Macbeth inadvertently achieves,
and because he did not particularly seek it and does not
understand it, he wields it unskilfully. He lacks both Tamburlaine's rage for dominion and Claudius' delight in manip-
ulating it. It was a false move on his part to kill Duncan's
grooms himself; the murder of Banquo and Fleance is botched,
the killing of Macduff's wife and children is politically
unnecessary, gratuitous and counterproductive. Above all,
it was a careless exercise of power to allow Malcolm to escape
to England. Macbeth's failure to understand the 'Realpolitik'
of his position, his casual and ineffective acts of violence, his
lack of planning, all stem from his inability to comprehend
the nature of the power which inevitably fell upon him as a
result of the act of regicide. He does not understand it because he did not particularly seek it.

Yet the play is, partially, a study of power. In this
respect it moves from the edges, not from the centre. Apart
from any supernatural energies they may command the
witches exercise the power of influence by the quality of
their prophecy and suggestion. Duncan, before and after
death, displays a power of goodness, the force of which
Macbeth recognises and takes into his calculation:

> Duncan
> Hath borne his faculties so meek, hath been
> So clear in his great office, that his virtues
> Will plead like angels, trumpet-tongu'd.

(I.vii.16-19)

This prophecy is taken up in the later scenes of the play as
the 'powers' (the word nearly always occurs in the plural)
gather head in England and advance inexorably to cleanse
the infected Scotland of the tyrant's stain. But, in terms of
initiating action, the most decisive single power in the play
belongs to Lady Macbeth. Her influence over her husband is
total, and she, almost alone in the play, is quite clear about
what she wants:

Glamis thou art, and Cawdor; and shalt be
What thou art promis'd.   (I.v.12–13)

She assumes full responsibility for the conduct of events:

> and you shall put
> This night's great business into my dispatch;
> Which shall to all our nights and days to come
> Give solely sovereign sway and masterdom.
>
>   (I.v.64–7)

It is significant that Macbeth does not take up this seductive
hint of future royal power; he says only 'We will speak
further.' At and after the murder she, like her husband, is
utterly subdued by the event, and there is no 'sovereign
sway' for her in the later acts of the play. Her role becomes
supportive, reassuring and creating confidence for Macbeth.
Power, once gained, provides no pleasures for her; it generates
only remorse and regret. At the centre of the play's exploration of the nature of power lies the insistence that
what is 'high' must be 'holy'. This is not the central thrust of
the narrative, nor is it the main course of the dramatic action,
but it is the underlying moral truth, and to this extent it
is a moral, though not a religious, play.

Although the 'Godlike' attributes of the kingdom, and the
power, and the glory are not in the forefront of Macbeth's
seeking, in the first three acts of the play we are perpetually
conscious of a great drive, onward and upward, an impetus
towards some achievement which, it is felt, will provide at
least temporary satisfaction of the devouring inner urge. The
word traditionally used to describe this aspect of the hero's
nature if 'ambition', and Bradley's account of this quality
has often been ignored but seldom challenged:[13]

> he was exceedingly ambitious. He must have been so by
> temper. The tendency must have been greatly strengthened
> by his marriage. When we see him, it has been further
> stimulated by his remarkable success and by the conscious-
> ness of exceptional powers and merit . . . his passion for
> power and his instinct of self-assertion are so vehement
> that no inward misery could persuade him to relinquish
> the fruits of crime, or to advance from remorse to
> repentance.

41

This has been generally accepted, but we may now feel inclined to dispute whether a phrase like 'his passion for power' accurately describes Macbeth's inner imperative. His ambition is not for power, but for status. As we have seen, his desire is not for command over others or for some position from which he can decisively influence the onward course of events, but for personal distinction, recognised and conceded by his society and epitomised by a particular social rank: kingship. This is perhaps the simplest, purest and most naked form of ambition. He does not specifically hunger and thirst after the title and the accoutrements of a king; he simply recognises (instinctively) that a king stands at the top of the ladder, the first link in the great chain, and towards this position of eminence, with the minimum of reflection or meditation, he aims. To use the play's own word, what Macbeth seeks is 'greatness'.

The words 'great', 'greatness', ring like a bell through those early scenes of the play in which Macbeth is concerned. He himself sees the witches' prophecy in these terms:

> Glamis, and Thane of Cawdor!
> The greatest is behind. (I.iii.116-17)

This is picked up and reiterated by Lady Macbeth in I.v, when she associates greatness with winning, with success, with 'height', as she reads her husband's letter and glosses it:

> They met me in the day of success . . . my dearest partner
> of greatness . . . by being ignorant of what greatness is
> promis'd thee . . . . Thou wouldst be great; / Art not
> without ambition . . . what thou wouldst highly . . .
> wouldst wrongly win . . . great Glamis.
> (I.v.1-19)

The word deepens into prophetic irony immediately afterwards, when the messenger enters with tidings of Duncan's arrival:

> Give him tending:
> He brings great news. (ll.34-5)

When Macbeth himself appears the word turns yet again, by its ambiguous association with 'worthiness' in a kind of ironic adjectival sandwich:

> Great Glamis! Worthy Cawdor!
> Greater than both, by the all-hail hereafter!   (ll.51–2)

And a coda recapitulates theme and development when Lady Macbeth tells him to 'put / This night's great business into my dispatch'.

As Macbeth soliloquises on the consequences of regicide in I.vii, he muses that all might be well if Duncan's 'surcease' could bring with it 'success', and there is, as Muir notes, an Empsonian ambiguity in that word, combining as it does the senses of 'prosperous issue' and 'succession'. But it is far from clear, at this point, precisely what rewards and pleasures Macbeth envisages for himself. We are given a hint later in the scene, when he tells Lady Macbeth 'We will proceed no further in this business', and gives as his reason:

> I have bought
> Golden opinions from all sorts of people,
> Which would be worn now in their newest gloss.
>   (I.vii.32–4)

But he adds, as if half-anticipating the grim issue, 'Not cast aside so soon.' By Act III the gloss has faded, and the central scenes of the play are informed not by ambition for status (it has been achieved), nor by any quest for an extension of 'greatness' (perhaps in terms of pomp and ceremony), but by the restless search for what can only be called 'security of tenure'. The dramatic action swings on that phrase

> To be thus is nothing,
> But to be safely thus.

It is not until Act V that we glimpse, and then fleetingly, what must have been Macbeth's vision (scarcely ever defined) of the rewards accruing to 'success'. In a scene strangely reminiscent of *Richard III*, V.iii (where Richard, alone except for the minor character Ratcliff, sums up the hopelessness of his position in a soliloquy), Macbeth dismisses one servant, summons another, and while waiting for him to arrive, says:

I have liv'd long enough. My way of life

Is fall'n into the sere, the yellow leaf;
And that which should accompany old age,
As honour, love, obedience, troops of friends,
I must not look to have.   (V.iii.22-6)

Honour, love, obedience, golden opinions, these are the con-
comitants of status, the fruits of 'greatness', and these are
the ultimate and only aims of Macbeth's ambition. They
may seem few and petty, but Macbeth is neither the first nor
the last of Shakespeare's heroes to find that the pleasures of
great office lie almost wholly in the imagination of them. A
coronation is a climax.

The reason for the vague and limited quality of Macbeth's
ambition is not far to seek. Richard S. Ide[14] aptly directs our
attention to the fact that, at the turn of the seventeenth
century, the heroic soldier of Elizabethan drama was transformed into the tragic hero of the Jacobean stage. His study
of *Othello, Bussy, Antony and Cleopatra*, the *Byron* plays,
and *Coriolanus* charts the changes in fortune the military
man underwent from the simple exemplar of heroic virtue
to the complex tragic protagonist who is both servant and
victim of violence. Ide offers no study of *Macbeth* but the
play surely has its place in his sequence, and without offering
any large analysis it may be noted that in no previous play
has Shakespeare so uncompromisingly presented his hero as a
soldier. When first we hear of him (I.ii) he is 'brave Macbeth',
'Valour's minion', 'Bellona's bridegroom, lapp'd in proof';
this whole scene is little more than a paean of praise to his
personal qualities as a fighting man. Neither the Captain nor
Ross describes the generalship of Macbeth, or his tactics
against the rebels, or his charismatic command of his troops.
Each is concerned to emphasise his personal prowess as a
fighting machine:

Point against point, rebellious arm 'gainst arm.   (I.57)

In this respect the analogies are more with *Coriolanus* than
with *Antony and Cleopatra*, in that Macbeth is described in
terms of a single, simple heroic quality to the exclusion of all
else. The same point is made, in the same terms, and at length,
in I.iii, when Ross says:

The King hath happily receiv'd, Macbeth,

The news of thy success; and when he reads
Thy personal venture in the rebels' fight,
His wonders and his praises do contend,
Which should be thine or his. Silenc'd with that,
In viewing o'er the rest o' th' self-same day,
He finds thee in the stout Norweyan ranks,
Nothing afeard of what thyself didst make,
Strange images of death. As thick as hail,
Came post with post; and every one did bear
Thy praises in his kingdom's great defence,
And pour'd them down before him.   (ll.89–100)

In the narrative development of this short play such luxuriant description is redundant, superfluous; its purpose is to enforce and emphasise the equation between success and personal killing power in this heroic soldier. Killing the enemy is what Macbeth does best. And at the climax of the play, in the short scenes of Act V, it is personal valour in military combat that characterises his heroic nature; when all else is stripped away it is his essential quality: 'At least we'll die with harness on our back', he says, and 'I cannot fly, / But, bear-like, I must fight the course', and, finally, 'lay on, Macduff'. It is to just such a simple, soldierly intelligence that the idea of status is so attractive. Military life depends upon a hierarchy of command and obedience, a clear, uncomplicated subordination of one man to another; in a word, it depends upon rank. Superior rank, promotion by the correct sequence of gradations, is precisely what the witches offer Macbeth. It is the temptation most apposite and appealing to his particular way of life. It is offered formally, with due verbal obeisance to the projected status, and in almost liturgical syntax:

All hail, Macbeth! hail to thee, Thane of Glamis!
All hail, Macbeth! hail to thee, Thane of Cawdor!
All hail, Macbeth! that shalt be King hereafter.

                                                    (I.iii.48–50)

The ritual, ceremonial mode of utterance is important; it pays rhythmic tribute to the significance of social distinction.[15]
    As this prophecy begins to work itself out (I.iii) Macbeth sees it as a series of steps, 'Glamis, and Thane of Cawdor! / The greatest is behind' (I.iii.116–17), and in the following

scene when Duncan announces the succession formally and hierarchically:

> Sc   Sons, kinsmen, thanes,
> And you whose places are the nearest, know
> We will establish our estate upon
> Our eldest, Malcolm.   (I.iv.35-8)

Macbeth sees the new fact as both step and stumbling-block:

> The Prince of Cumberland! That is a step,
> On which I must fall down, or else o'erleap,
> For in my way it lies.   (I.iv.48-50)

These steps to kingship are ironically recapitulated in reverse order immediately after the murder:

> Glamis hath murder'd sleep; and therefore Cawdor
> Shall sleep no more – Macbeth shall sleep no more.
>   (II.ii.42-3)

Once the crown has been achieved, however, these images of status and distinction degenerate and disappear. In persuading the two murderers (III.i) Macbeth sets up a curious canine hierarchy, when they assert 'We are men':

> Ay, in the catalogue ye go for men;
> As hounds, and greyhounds, mongrels, spaniels, curs,
> Shoughs, water-rugs, and demi-wolves, are clept
> All by the name of dogs.   (III.i.91-4)

But in Acts IV and V, as his followers desert him, distinctions of rank become meaningless. Left with only a handful of servants, he realises like Richard, Duke of Gloucester, 'I am myself alone.'[16] As the deserted Antony faces the assembled forces of Caesar, as Coriolanus stands alone against Romans and Volscians, so Macbeth opposes his single, personal soldiership against the ordered, ranked army of his enemies. He dies 'in character', practising his trade, and this gives him both pathos and nobility. At no point in the play is there anything like the realisation which comes to Shakespeare's other soldier-hero: 'Othello's occupation's gone' (III.iii.361).

Seen only in terms of its ideals and aspirations, *Macbeth* might seem a shallow, even a shabby, play. Its hero is ambitious for nothing more than social and professional status, he lacks any sense of the glory of kingship, he fails to comprehend the uses of power, and his kingdom is of no interest to him. To see the play so, and only so, would be to chart its physical and social structure and to ignore its ethical, imaginative dimension. But it is necessary to emphasise the social structure to enforce the point: *Macbeth* is not the tragedy of ambition, it is the tragedy of guilt.

There are significant studies of guilt in *Julius Caesar, Hamlet, Measure for Measure*, and elsewhere, but only in *Macbeth* does Shakespeare present such an excruciatingly particular case-study. Macbeth is a soldier, professionally trained to kill his king's enemies and notably successful in doing so. In his moment of triumph he is supernaturally incited to advance his career and secure the ultimate preferment by killing his king. Means and opportunity present themselves, and the precise method is provided by his totally supportive wife. Yet this one simple, additional killing is almost as difficult for him as it is for Hamlet. Any soldier is alert to the difference between killing and murder, and Macbeth would have assented to the words spoken by Iago:

> Though in the trade of war I have slain men,
> Yet do I hold it very stuff o' th' conscience
> To do no contriv'd murder.
>
> *(Othello*, I.ii.1–3)

Macbeth is in no doubt that this would be 'contriv'd murder', all the more heinous in that the intended victim is his king. Maynard Mack, Jr, has pointed out[17] how often Shakespeare concerns himself with the crime of regicide. But *Macbeth* stands alone in the narrowness, intensity, and clarity of the murderer's analysis. And this is true both in anticipation of the act and in retrospect. Macbeth never attempts to justify his action by any appeal to the national interest, or *raison d'État*, or the upward thrust of his personal *virtù*. He never claims that he has any right to the throne, nor does he assert that Duncan is a usurper, weak, or in any way inadequate. His clear and undeceived moral intelligence labels the act as utterly evil, and he feels pervasive, dislocating guilt at even the idea of it:

My thought, whose murder yet is but fantastical,
Shakes so my single state of man .
That function is smother'd in surmise,
And nothing is but what is not.

(I.iii.139–42)

As long ago as 1930 G. Wilson Knight[18] noted that this last
line is 'the text of the play. Reality and unreality change
places.' The intensity of Macbeth's sense of guilt finds release
only in the creation of a phantasmagoric world of visions
and images which, through the central acts of the play,
overwhelms the simpler, more restricted, soldierly world in
which his ambitions are pursued. Just as the king has 'two
bodies'[19] so Macbeth has two minds: the prosaic, unpolitical
military intelligence, and the powerful, creative visionary
imagination, fuelled by guilt. In the one, he acts; in the other,
he is tortured. In the end, the haunted vision brings about the
self-destruction of the military man.

Montaigne, in the 'Apology for Raymond Sebond',[20]
provides a key to this inner world of Macbeth's imagination:

> Dares not Philosophie thinke that men produce their
> greatest effects, and neerest approaching to divinity when
> they are beside themselves, furious, and madde? We
> amend our selves by the privation of reason, and by her
> drooping. The two naturall waies to enter the cabinet of
> the Gods, and there to foresee the course of the destinies,
> are furie and sleepe. This is very pleasing to be considered.
> By the dislocation that passions bring into our reason,
> we become vertuous; by the extirpation which either furie
> or the image of death bringeth us, we become Prophets
> and Divines . . . . Our vigilancie is more drouzie then sleepe
> it selfe; our wisdome lesse wise then folly; our dreames of
> more worth then our discourses.

Macbeth 'does murther Sleep', and his dreams are waking. As
early as I.iii he summarises the insights available to the
ravaged conscience:

Present fears
Are less than horrible imaginings. (I.iii.137–8)

This provides the play's characteristic vision, of a kind

48

anticipated by Brutus in the earlier play, *Julius Caesar*:
(II.i):

> Since Cassius first did whet me against Caesar,
> I have not slept.
> Between the acting of a dreadful thing
> And the first motion, all the interim is
> Like a phantasma or a hideous dream.
> The Genius and the mortal instruments
> Are then in council; and the state of man,
> Like to a little kingdom, suffers then
> The nature of an insurrection.   (II.i.61-9)

The 'hideous interim' in *Macbeth* centres on the vision of the
dagger in II.i, where the debate in Macbeth's mind is as
to whether the weapon is real or 'but a dagger of the mind'.
The phantasm becomes a stage presence, and the dramatic
spectacle is complicated by the 'real' dagger which Macbeth
draws. The inversion of reality and appearance, and the
values attaching to them, is illustrated by Macbeth's general-
isation:

> Mine eyes are made the fools o' th' other senses,
> Or else worth all the rest.
>   (II.i.44-5)

The uncertainty in this, the idea that one testimony may be
as valid as another, anaesthetises the moral conscience
sufficiently to permit this special killing to be done. Thereafter, the phantasmagoric world is the stage on which the
agonies of guilt are enacted. As his wife observes, Macbeth
keeps alone:

> Of sorriest fancies your companions making.   (III.ii.9)

In his isolation (for he has gone the way where there are no
friends) he fights a losing battle against himself:

> But let the frame of things disjoint, both the worlds suffer,
> Ere we will eat our meal in fear and sleep
> In the affliction of these terrible dreams
> That shake us nightly. Better be with the dead,
> Whom we, to gain our peace, have sent to peace,

49

Than on the torture of the mind to lie
In restless ecstasy.   (III.ii.16–22)

The banquet scene, with its fear and confusion – the Ghost
of Banquo being seen by Macbeth and the audience, but by
no one else – culminates in yet another phantasmal vision
of disordered reality, induced by guilt:

It will have blood; they say blood will have blood.
Stones have been known to move, and trees to speak;
Augurs and understood relations have
By maggot-pies and choughs and rooks brought forth
The secret'st man of blood.
                                                       (II.iv.122–6)

All this disables action, vitiates power, and prevents government. By the time (the end of IV.i) Macbeth can close up
the 'interim' and make 'The very firstlings of my heart
... The firstlings of my hand' (ll.147–8), it is too late. The
irony of

        And even now,
To crown my thoughts with acts, be it thought and done
                                                       (ll.148–9)

lies in the fact that, by this time, events have assumed a
momentum of their own. Macbeth, deserted, isolated, sustained only by the richness of illusion, is swept towards the
abyss. The final phantasms are weaker, less colourful –
'Life's but a walking shadow, a poor player' (V.v.24) –
as reality reassumes command: Birnam wood comes to
Dunsinane, and Macduff 'was from his mother's womb /
Untimely ripp'd' (V.viii.15–16). Macbeth's bid for 'greatness'
is foiled by the fecundity of his moral imagination, its
disabling and inhibiting images generated by guilt.
    Yet it is guilt without remorse. In the Christian context,
as we know from Bunyan's *Grace Abounding to the Chief
of Sinners*, and a host of similar testimonies, the sense of
guilt leads to conviction of Sin, and the burden of Sin brings
about contrition and repentance, and repentance sues for
Grace and forgiveness. There is nothing of this in *Macbeth*.
The play remains firmly in the realm of morality and never
ventures into the territory where Grace can be the sinner's

salve. Macbeth has no such utterance as:

O, my offence is rank, it smells to heaven.
(*Hamlet*, III.iii. 36)

In his own mind and imagination he has offended mightily against his fellow man, but he never envisages that by Sin he has grieved God's heart of love.

Macbeth's inability to register the religious dimension of human life narrows and blinkers the scope of the play's vision. But this very narrowing focuses attention on a particular quality which is, I believe, found nowhere else in Shakespeare. The play's concern with hospitality has often been noted: the duties of a host to his guest are important both to Macbeth and Lady Macbeth, the decorums of rank and address are sedulously respected, ritual and ceremony abound — from the royal banquet to the pseudo-litrugies of the witches and the stately, rhetorical interview between Macduff and Malcolm in IV.iii, which has all the grave formality of a royal audience. Courtesy, in the Aristotelian or Spenserian sense, is the highest moral value in the play, or at least its most central and respected value. Courtesy is easily and widely identifiable in the Comedies, but what gives the tragedy of *Macbeth* its unique tone is the association between courtesy and extreme violence. We see it in the final encounter between Macbeth and Macduff, but it is there from the beginning, most notably in the account given by the Captain of the way in which Macbeth killed the rebel Macdonwald:

For brave Macbeth – well he deserves that name –
Disdaining Fortune, with his brandish'd steel
Which smok'd with bloody execution,
Like valour's minion, carv'd out his passage
Till he fac'd the slave;
Which ne'er shook hands, nor bade farewell to him,
Till he unseam'd him from the nave to th' chaps,
And fix'd his head upon our battlements.
(I.ii.16–23)

Why, in the heat of battle, with his brandished steel smoking, *should* Macbeth pause to shake hands and bid farewell to the man he was about to disembowel, behead and impale?

51

Nowhere in Shakespeare is there a comparable example of military civility. In *Macbeth* it is characteristic of the play's exploration of the unnatural encounters between killing and politeness; it is one of the play's 'strange images of death'. Courtesy, in its secular mode, stands proxy for piety.

NOTES

1 *Macbeth,* ed. Kenneth Muir (Arden Shakespeare, 1977 reprint, p. xliv).

2 Quoted in Muir, *op. cit.*, p. 36.

3 Marlowe, *The Jew of Malta*, Prologue, pp. 14-15.

4 S.L. Bethell, *Shakespeare and the Popular Dramatic Tradition*, pp. 74 and 98, quoted in Muir, *op. cit.*, p. 153.

5 See *How many children had Lady Macbeth?* (Cambridge, 1933) reprinted in *'Hamlet' and other Shakespearean Essays* (Cambridge, 1979).

6 A nice example of Macbeth's theological naivety is furnished by the description of prayer in II.ii, immediately after the murder. Macbeth asks 'But wherefore could I not pronounce "Amen"?' (l. 31). Any priest could have told him. It was not 'blessing' he needed, but confession and repentance.

7 Matthew, 6, 9-13. Cf. Luke, 11, 2-4, which is shorter and has no doxology. The doxology was probably added in early times, since it occurs in the Didache (assigned by some to the 1st century, but now generally thought to be later). See *Oxford Dictionary of the Christian Church*.

8 See F.H. Chase, *The Lord's Prayer in the Early Church* (Cambridge, 1891).

9 See G.K. Hunter, 'The Last Tragic Heroes', in *Later Shakespeare* (*Stratford-upon-Avon Studies*, 8, eds John Russell Brown and Bernard Harris, 1966), pp. 11-28.

10 The reading is that of F1 (1623). The addition in square brackets is as in Alexander's edition, but all editors agree substantially.

11 1 Samuel, 4, 21.

12 See *OED*, sb.^{2} I, 2 and 4.

13 A.C. Bradley, *Shakespearean Tragedy* (1904, ed. 1963, p. 294.

14 Richard S. Ide, *Possessed with Greatness: the heroic tragedies of Chapman and Shakespeare* (1980).

15 Cf. the rhythms and repetitions in that section of the *Gloria* which begins 'O Lord God, Lamb of God, Son of the Father'.

16 *3 Henry VI*, V.vi.83.

17 Maynard Mack, Jr, *Killing the King* (1973).

18 G. Wilson Knight, *The Wheel of Fire* (Oxford, 1930, 1949 reprint), p. 153.

19 Ernst Kantorowicz, *The King's Two Bodies* (Princeton, 1957). See Maynard Mack, Jr, *op. cit.*, pp. 6 ff.;
20 Montaigne, *Essayes* (trans. John Florio, 1603), 'The Second Booke', Chapter XII. The relevance of this passage to *Macbeth* was first discussed by Professor J.P. Brockbank, in an unpublished lecture at the University of York, 1968.

3

'A new Gorgon': visual effects in *Macbeth*

D. J. Palmer

The faculty of sight has special significance in *Macbeth*. Not only do 'sightless substances' assume visible shape and bloody spectacles appal us, but we are made as aware of what is veiled from our eyes (for instance, the murder of Duncan) as of what is seen. There are degrees of visibility, and the language of the play, with its powerful appeal to the visual imagination, mediates between the seen and the unseen. The inner world of Macbeth's visionary awareness, expressed through his soliloquies, and the off-stage world reported by the play's many messengers, contain images that extend the play's concern with sight beyond what is visible on the stage. This verbal imagery and the recurrent references to the eye itself as a vulnerable agent, prone to deception and confronted by what it hardly dare look upon, add the power of suggestion to the play's visual impact.

Just as the linguistic structure of *Macbeth* contains ironic repetitions and reiterative patterns of imagery, so too does its use of spectacle. There are visual as well as verbal echoes, creating dramatic meaning through parallels and contrasts. For instance, the play begins and ends in battle, although only in the final battle does fighting take place on the stage. At the beginning, the stage-image of Duncan 'in his great office' takes precedence over the actual sound and fury of battle, as, attended by the princes and nobles, he receives news of the defeated rebels and dispenses honours to his loyal thanes. The bleeding Captain, the first of the play's messengers and the first of its sanguinary figures, is a sight, like the tale he tells, more heroic than horrific. There is a distinction between blood shed in a just cause and murder,

54

and an ironic recapitulation of this image of the wounded Captain reporting to his King occurs when the First Murderer is seen informing Macbeth of Banquo's death ('There's blood upon thy face.' ''Tis Banquo's then,' III.iv.13), a point which gains emphasis if Macbeth in the later scene is wearing the royal insignia first worn by Duncan. The final clamactic battle is more spectacular than the first. We see the drums and colours of the opposing forces, and instead of the bleeding Captain's news of the rebels' defeat, a messenger brings word to Macbeth that Birnam Wood is moving towards Dunsinane. As battle is joined, a rapid sequence of entries and exits and stage-combats culminates in the image of the victorious Malcolm, attended by the same nobles who were seen with his father in the play's opening scenes, with Macbeth's severed head (on a pole, according to Holinshed) visually recalling the justice formerly executed by Macbeth himself on the traitor Macdonwald.

The outdoor location of these opening and concluding scenes is dramatically significant and should be visually apparent. The action of the play moves from battlefield and heath into the confines of Macbeth's castle, as evil closes in. Lady Macbeth's first appearance, alone, is the first scene set indoors, and as she takes charge of the stage she also takes charge of the impending situation. Far from suggesting security, the sense of moving into an interior world is that of oppressive confinement, or sometimes of violent intrusion. The cave in which Macbeth conronts the 'secret, black and midnight hags' is therefore a stage-image of particular significance (Hecate refers to it as 'the pit of Acheron', III.v.15). The movement from these dark, enclosed worlds out into the open again in the final scenes is liberating and restorative.

Another pattern of visual repetition is formed by the two feasts in the play. Macbeth is host on both occasions, but the first, in honour of Duncan, takes place off-stage and is represented only by the processional entry at the opening of I.vii: 'Hautboys, torches. Enter a *Sewer*, and divers *Servants* with dishes and service over the stage.' This brief pageant, both functional and emblematic, serves to express the festive values of fellowship and community which Macbeth will destroy, and indeed no sooner has the procession passed over the stage than Macbeth enters to meditate on 'the horrid deed'. Its sequel is the coronation feast in III.iv, another travesty of social concord, as the ghost of the murdered

Banquo makes its unwelcome appearance. The interrupted feast, with the guests departing in confusion and disarray, spectacularly confirms the words of Lady Macbeth: 'the sauce to meat is ceremony; / Meeting were bare without it' (III.iv.36–7).

An ironic visual counterpart to this feast, with its spectral visitation, is the Cauldron Scene, of which G. Wilson Knight has written, 'Here we watch a devil's banqueting, the Weird Women with their cauldron and its hideous ingredients. The banquet idea has been inverted.'[1] This scene is the climactic point of the play's use of spectacle: the cauldron itself is an image traditionally associated with hell,[2] and each of the three Apparitions in turn rises and descends from within it. The presentation of these sights by the witches to Macbeth is a diabolical parody of the emblematic pageants and allegorical masques with which royalty was greeted and honoured in Shakespeare's day, often at a banquet. Like the shows in such court entertainments, each of the Apparitions directly addresses the principal guest, offering counsel and flattering assurance. On this occasion, however, the Apparitions take the shapes that Macbeth should fear most: the traitor's severed head, the babe 'from his mother's womb / Untimely ripp'd' and the lineal heir to the crown who bears the tree from Birnam Wood to Dunsinane. This is followed by a sight which does appal Macbeth but which ironically incorporates what is a complimentary allusion from the point of view of a Jacobean audience: 'A Show of eight *Kings*, and *Banquo* last; the last king with a glass in his hand.' This tribute to the ancestry of King James with its implication that his line will last for ever is in keeping with the usual function of this kind of spectacle. The 'entertainment' is completed with the witches' 'antic round', a dance we can suppose similar to that performed by the witches in the anti-masque of Jonson's *Masque of Queenes* (1609): 'a magicall Daunce full of praeposterous change, and gesticulation, but most applying to theyr property: who, at theyr meetings, do all thinges contrary to the custome of Men, dauncing, back to back, hip to hip, theyr handes joyn'd and making theyr *circles* backward to the left hand, with strange, phantastique motions of theyr heads and bodyes.'[3]

As Macbeth's second encounter with the witches, the Cauldron Scene echoes their first meeting on the heath only to emphasise the differences. Instead of being accosted by the witches, and betraying fear at their words, it is now Macbeth who seeks them out, aggressively demanding to know the worst. Prophecy now takes visible shape, and the general effect of the contrast is to suggest an intensification of evil. Whoever was responsible for the introduction of Hecate, the scene in which she first appears, III.v., balances the play's opening scene as each prepares for an encounter with Macbeth. The addition of Hecate is in keeping with the hellish associations of the cave and cauldron, and with the sense that we are closer here than at the beginning of the play to spirits of greater power than the witches themselves. Moreover, although modern editors provide Hecate with an exit before Macbeth's entry in the Cauldron Scene, the First Folio does not. Her presence is not essential and she does not speak after Macbeth has entered, but as a presiding figure, visible to the audience though unseen by Macbeth (as the Ghost of Banquo in the feast scene appears to Macbeth but not to the other characters), she would add to the spectacular as well as the ironic effects of the scene. Hecate, after all, is a goddess, not a grotesque hag, and a spectral counterpart to that other Queen of Night, Lady Macbeth.

A catalogue of all the visual echoes in the play would also include the two Doctors, the English doctor who describes the miraculous powers of healing possessed by the saintly Edward the Confessor, and his counterpart, the Doctor who in the following scene looks on with the Gentlewoman as Lady Macbeth sleep-walks: 'More needs she the divine than the physician' (V.i.72). Lady Macbeth's sleepwalking is itself a visual and verbal repetition, a re-enactment of former sights and acts. The compulsive rubbing of her hand, for instance, ironically recalls her words after the murder of Duncan, 'A little water clears us of this deed' (II.ii.67). In her trancelike state, with her open but expressionless eyes, she creates a visual effect more like that of a ghost than of a living woman.

The visual impact of the play is not confined to its spectacular tableaux and shows. Facial expression and physical gesture are important means of visual expression in any play, but *Macbeth* is remarkable for the frequency with which these are specified in the text. Generations of commentators, for instance, have stressed the significance of Macbeth's initial reaction to the witches and their prophecies, as Banquo describes it: 'Good sir, why do you start, and seem to fear / Things that do sound so fair?' (I.iii.51-2). As well as prescribing a particular expression to the actor like an implied stage-direction, Banquo's words draw the attention of the audience to Macbeth, who is silent himself. Similar examples include Lennox's exclamation on the entry of Ross, 'What a haste looks through his eyes! / So should he look that seems to speak things strange' (I.ii.47-8), lines which amplify the otherwise featureless stage-direction, 'Enter *Ross*.'

Banquo gives a very graphic indication of the appearance and gestures of the witches:

> What are these,
> So wither'd, and so wild in their attire,
> That look not like th'inhabitants o' th' earth,
> And yet are on't? Live you, or are you aught
> That man may question? You seem to understand me,
> By each at once her choppy finger laying
> Upon her skinny lips. You should be women,
> And yet your beards forbid me to interpret
> That you are so.
>
> (I.iii.39-47)

Since the audience can see for themselves what Banquo so precisely details, this account seems theatrically superfluous. It suggests, however, that Shakespeare thought it important to establish the resemblance of the witches to grotesque old women, whatever their true nature. Holinshed describes them as 'three women in strange and wild apparell', though he goes on to refer to the opinion 'that these women were either the weird sisters, that is (as ye would say) the goddesses of destinie, or else some nymphs or feiries.' Shakespeare clearly specifies the traditional figures of English witch-lore.

The treachery of the first thane of Cawdor prompts Duncan to reflect, 'There's no art / To find the mind's construction in the face' (I.iv.11-12). To the audience, however, the actors' expressions are the means of showing 'the mind's construction'. Macbeth in particular is required to give himself away, as it were, by his look. Lady Macbeth's first exhortation of her husband on his homecoming is:

> Your face, my thane, is as a book where men

May read strange matters. To beguile the time,
Look like the time; bear welcome in your eye,
Your hand, your tongue; look like th' innocent flower,
But be the serpent under 't.

(I.v.59-63)

In the first half of the play, however, Macbeth's face is more often registering horror and fear, at first when alone, as in the soliloquy when he 'sees' a dagger. A contemporary account of Garrick's performance of this moment emphasises the effect of his expression and gesture: 'who ever saw the *immortal actor* start at, and trace the imaginary dagger previous to Duncan's murder, without embodying, by sympathy, insubstantial air into the alarming shape of such a weapon?' Another such moment occurs when Macbeth joins his wife after murdering Duncan, and all the hideousness of the murder itself is concentrated in the gesture and gaze that must accompany the words, 'This is a sorry sight' (II.ii.20). Garrick again illustrates the point: 'The wonderful expression of heartfelt horror when he showed his bloody hands, can only be conceived and described by those who saw him.'[4]

Macbeth's capacity to conceal the true self in looks and bearing when in public is immediately put to the test at the discovery of Duncan's murder. Only a few moments after he has left the stage in a dazed awareness of guilt and fear, he must reappear to receive Macduff and Lennox:

Macduff: Is the King stirring, worthy Thane?
Macbeth: Not yet.

(II.iii.43)

In this scene, it is possible to find in Shakespeare's text signs of Macbeth's rather unconvincing and uncertain attempts at feigning the reactions of amazement and outrage which the other characters express as genuine. He certainly does not convince his fellow thanes. He is seen more completely as the confident dissembler in the preparations for Banquo's murder, bidding the unsuspecting victim, 'Fail not our feast' (III.i.27), then inciting the two Murderers, and, most ironically, urging Lady Macbeth (who knows nothing of his plans) to show special favour to Banquo at the feast, 'And make our faces vizards to our hearts, / Disguising what they are' (III.ii.34-5). Macbeth's hardening in evil can be traced in his growing ability not to betray himself to others in look or gesture, and this the actor will communicate to the audience by the very looks and gestures used.

Macbeth's reaction to the Ghost of Banquo in the feast scene is therefore all the more effective because it shatters in public the mask he is becoming practised in wearing. The visual effect of the scene depends above all upon what is registered on the faces of those on stage. Horrifying as the sight of the spectre is, what Macbeth finds unbearable is not the ghoulish object in itself, but the fact that it gazes directly and accusingly at him, as these lines tell us: 'Thou canst not say I did it; never shake / Thy gory locks at me' (11.50-1); 'If thou canst nod, speak too' (1.70); 'Thou has no speculation in those eyes / Which thou dost glare with' (11.95-6). Equally, Macbeth's eyes are fixed upon the Ghost's face; however, horrified, he 'dare look on that / Which might appal the devil' (11.59-60), outfacing rather than shunning the sight. This suggests a stronger nerve than he possessed in the scene with his wife after the murder of Duncan, and indeed after the Ghost makes its first exit, Macbeth regains the self-control to feign assurance to his guests and actually pledges a toast to Banquo. The traditional stage-business of dropping his cup, or else hurling it from him, on the Ghost's reappearance, seems entirely appropriate; it is also another instance of the way in which verbal and visual imagery are linked, recalling as it does the 'poison'd chalice' of Macbeth's soliloquy in I.vii.

Since the Ghost is not seen by the other characters on the stage, their expressions will register, in varying degrees, amazement at Macbeth's distraction. An account of an actual performance of the scene makes clear what it demands in the way of gesture and expression, and in particular how much of its total visual impact depends on Lady Macbeth. I quote from another contemporary description of a Garrick production:[5]

> This admirable scene was greatly supported by the speaking terrors of Garrick's look and action. Mrs. Pritchard showed admirable art in endeavouring to hide Macbeth's frenzy from the observation of the guests and drawing their attention to conviviality. She smiled on one, whispered to another, and distantly saluted a third; in short she practised every possible artifice to hide the

transaction that passed between her husband and the
vision his disturbed imagination had raised. Her reproving
and angry looks, which glanced towards Macbeth, at the
same time were mixed with marks of inward vexation and
uneasiness. When at last, as if unable to support her feelings
any longer, she rose from her seat, and seized his arm, and
with a whisper of terror, said, 'Are you a man!' she
assumed a look of such anger, indignation and contempt
as cannot be surpassed.

Arguably, Lady Macbeth's smile of reassurance ('Think of
this, good peers, / But as a thing of custom', 11.96–7) is a
more blood-curdling sight than the Ghost itself.

Macbeth becomes increasingly inured to horrors and so
accustomed to suppressing and masking his natural feelings
that in the latter half of the play they seem to wither away.
In the Cauldron Scene, neither the witches nor the Apparitions hold any terrors for him, and it is not until the 'Show
of eight *Kings*' that he is appalled, but what to him is a
'horrible sight' is to us a congratulatory pageant. After the
Cauldron Scene, Macbeth does not appear again until V.iii,
but the deadening of his capacity to react seems to have
repercussions in the treatment of looks and gestures as the
play draws to its conclusion. For instance, when Ross breaks
the news of the slaughter of his wife and children, Macduff's
immediate response is indicated in Malcolm's line, 'What
man! Ne'er pull your hat upon your brows' (IV.iii.208).
Macduff hides his face at first, as if his grief is quite inex-
pressible. The gesture is, of course, just as expressive as any
imaginable look, but it is a notably different way of registering emotion. In the Sleep-walking Scene, although her words
and actions convey what the Doctor calls 'a great perturbation
in nature', Lady Macbeth's face is expressionless: her eyes
are open but 'their sense is shut.' The effect adds greatly
to the eeriness of the scene.

We are prepared for the Macbeth of the play's final scenes
by Caithness's report, 'Some say he's mad, others, that
lesser hate him, / Do call it valiant fury' (V.ii.13–14). When
he reappears in V.iii, the brusque physical activity of his
preparations for battle creates a sense of manic energy. The
text indicates that he is helped on with his armour as he
gibes sardonically at the Doctor, a visual image which
suggests his violent agitation and his lust for action, as well as

recalling Caithness's image of him in the previous scene, 'He cannot buckle his distemper'd cause / Within the belt of rule' (V.ii.15-16):

> Throw physic to the dogs - I'll none of it.
> Come, put mine armour on; give me my staff.
> Seyton, send out. Doctor, the thanes fly from me.
> Come, sir, dispatch. If thou couldst, doctor, cast
> The water of my land, find her disease,
> And purge it to a sound and pristine health,
> I would applaud thee to the very echo,
> That should applaud again. - Pull't off, I say, -
> What rhubarb, senna, or what purgative drug,
> Would scour these English hence?
>
> (V.iii.47-56)

The frenetic bustle is punctuated by moments of still reflection on the emptiness of life, moments that reveal how bankrupt he is of feeling, most notably when he receives the news of his wife's death (recalling Macduff's reaction to the report of his slaughtered family). The Macbeth of these concluding scenes is himself a grim and fearsome figure, and at the end the head of 'this dead butcher' is there to transfix us with its sightless gaze.

Many of the play's entries and exits are visually expressive moments. Exactly how characters should arrive and depart, and how those they join or leave should react, are matters for the director and players to discover. But the context often strongly suggests that such moments create significant stage-images. I have already referred to the explicit comment on the 'haste' with which Ross enters in I.ii, and many of the play's numerous other messengers will bring their news similar urgency, breaking unexpectedly upon the scene. The First Murderer who reports Banquo's death to Macbeth in III.iv is given a mere 'Enter' in the Folio stage-direction, but in 1767 Edward Capell added 'to the door', a phrase which has been adopted by most subsequent editors of the play and which indicates how furtively he appears and waits at the door until Macbeth crosses to him. This 'door' itself might acquire powerful visual associations if it is also that through which Macbeth leaves to murder Duncan ('as his host,

/ Who should against his murderer shut the door, / Not bear the knife myself,' I.vii.14–16), through which he re-enters after the murder, and to which he leads Macduff ('This is the door,' II.iii.49) after the latter and Lennox have been admitted by the Porter. Another entrance must serve as the 'south entry', which the Porter likens to 'hell-gate', and it might be this which is later used by the Ghost of Banquo and by Macbeth in the Cauldron Scene, where his entry-cue is the Second Witch's line, 'Open, locks, whoever knocks' (IV.i.46).

To conclude each of Macbeth's two encounters with them, the Witches 'Vanish', according to the Folio stage-direction. This presumably indicates the use of the trap, through which the cauldron and the three Apparitions also rise and descend. However it is managed, the disappearance of the Witches is an exit startling enough to draw astonished comment from Macbeth and Banquo and one that visibly, or perhaps invisibly, demonstrates their unnatural powers. Equally ingenious is the first entry of the Ghost of Banquo in the Feast Scene, though in this case the ingenuity is one of timing rather than stage-machinery. By having the Ghost enter several lines before it is seen by Macbeth, Shakespeare heightens the audience's horrified anticipation and ironic awareness. Its appearance to the audience, followed by Macbeth's delayed recognition and the inability of the other characters to see it, is a visual arrangement which conveys a sense of the spectral as much as the ghastly figure itself. Indeed, here and elsewhere (as certain recent productions have shown) excessive attempts at producing gruesome spectacle can spoil the effect, which depends partly on the visible reactions of others on stage and partly on the audience's imagination.

Macbeth's own entries, particularly in the opening acts, are often charged with dramatic intensity and with ironic impact. On his first appearance, prepared for by the Witches in the opening scene and then by the successive accounts of his prowess in battle, he has one line to speak, recalling the equivocal play of the Witches upon 'foul' and 'fair'. The moment, visually and verbally, is like a frame in which he stands, poised briefly before us until Banquo sees the Witches. Some of his subsequent entries have a similar effect, possessing this quality of the suspended, intensely charged, moment. His second appearance is cued by Duncan's comment on the previous thane of Cawdor, 'He was a gentleman on whom I built / An absolute trust' (I.iv.13–14). Such ironies are un-canny, beyond mere coincidence, intimating the ominous and fateful. His next entry is his return from the wars to his wife, who is eagerly awaiting him. Whatever looks they exchange, whatever embrace seems appropriate, will visually underline the darker implications of their reunion, their intimacy that of conspirators.

Entries and exits register strong impressions in the scenes immediately before and after the murder of Duncan. After the brilliant festive torches borne in the processional entries of I.vi and vii, the single torch held by Fleance as he and Banquo open II.i is a puny light, insufficient for them to recognise Macbeth as he approaches, himself attended by a torch-bearer. These single torches, like that which Fleance carries again on his entrance with his father in III.iii, do not merely inform us that night has fallen; they suggest what little protection there is against the forces of darkness. In-deed, in the latter scene, it is the light of the torch which betrays Banquo to his murderers and Fleance escapes when it is extinguished. (In the Sleep-walking Scene, the taper held by Lady Macbeth, although she sees nothing, is a visual echo that emphasises the pathos of her appearance, a 'brief candle' guttering in the dark.) To revert to II.i, the departure of Banquo and Fleance followed shortly by Macbeth's dismissal of his servant, takes the torches off and leaves Macbeth alone, more intensely alone than if he had entered an empty stage to wait for the bell that is his cue for murder. His exit after his soliloquy concludes the scene on the highest pitch of tension so far reached in the play.

The entry of Lady Macbeth which follows sustains that tension, for there is evidently no break in the time-sequence and her words make us aware of the proximity of the murder off-stage. Macbeth's re-entry, therefore, must be a stunning sight. A description of Garrick's performance of this moment might not entirely suit modern theatrical taste, but it does convey the sense of visual opportunity which the actor must exploit by look and gesture:

The door opened and Macbeth appeared, a frightful figure of horror, rushing out sideways with one dagger, and his face in consternation, presented to the door, as if he were pursued, and the other dagger lifted up as presented for action. Thus he stood as if transfixed, seeming insensible to everything but the chamber, unconscious of any presence else, and even to his wife's address of 'my husband'.

However the entry is made, with whatever motion and expression the actor feels to be right, it will be to create an appalled and appalling sight. This is a changed Macbeth, but there need be no change in his appearance except that which can be expressed by the actor's face and body. It is not until six lines after his entry that Macbeth speaks of the 'sorry sight' of his bloody hands, and the delayed revelation of that spectacle, as he unclenches his fists that still grasp the daggers, is another concentrated visual effect. The hasty exit of the couple, prompted by the insistent knocking at the gate, requires Lady Macbeth virtually to take her stupefied husband from the scene. Her words in the Sleep-walking Scene, 'Come, come, come, come, give me your hand' (V.i.65), suggest an appropriate action to convey in their exit an image of their partnership sealed in blood.

The discovery of the murder precipitates a rapid sequence of entries and exits, generating an effect of confusion, shock and suspicion. Macduff, who proclaims the dreadful fact (visually, his entry as from Duncan's chamber is part of the pattern of messengers bringing urgent news), also takes immediate charge of the situation; his prominence in this scene first establishes his importance in the play. Apart from Macduff and Lennox, the characters appear in night-attire, roused by the alarum bell. Banquo's words, 'When we have our naked frailties hid, / That suffer in exposure, let us meet' (II.iii.125–6), not only give the textual indication of this but voice as well the sense of vulnerability and unpreparedness which their state of undress depicts. The murder of Duncan leaves them all insecure.

There are other entries and exits later in the play, not so far mentioned, of strong visual impact and significance. For instance, only a few lines after Macduff's grimly ironic farewell to Banquo, 'Adieu, / Lest our old robes sit easier than our new' (II.iv.37–8), there occurs in the following scene the entry of the coronation procession, in which Macbeth wears the borrowed robes of majesty. After enquiring of Banquo what his movements are to be before supper, Macbeth dismisses everyone except a Servant; the Folio's stage-direction, 'Exeunt *Lords*', obscures the fact that Lady Macbeth also withdraws at his injunction. In performance, however, her exclusion from his company makes her exit striking evidence of the change in their relationship. Without her knowledge, he now plots the killing of Banquo with the two Murderers, so that when he enters to her in the next scene, their rejoining is heavily underscored by the unwitting irony of her solicitous greeting, 'How now, my lord! Why do you keep alone, / Of sorriest fancies your companions making' (III.ii.8–9). The spiritual gulf between Macbeth and his wife is echoed in the separation of Macduff from his wife and children; no sooner have we seen the violent entry of the Murderers who kill Macduff's son on the stage and pursue Lady Macduff to dispatch her off-stage, than Macduff himself enters with Malcolm, safe in their English exile. There is one other entry which must not be overlooked in this survey, if only because it creates a visual effect quite different from the prevailing concern with horror and fear. This is the appearance at the beginning of V.vi of Malcolm and his army with their 'leavy screens'. What is to Malcolm a tactical device for disguising the strength of his forces, and to Macbeth the scarcely credible fulfilment of the prophecy of a seemingly impossible event, appears to the audience to identify Malcolm's army with the reassertion of the natural order, as if the land itself has risen against Macbeth. It is an emblematic tableau, yet another instance of a visual image drawing its expressive value from the play's verbal imagery of growth and fertility, and it endows Malcolm's cause and that of Macduff with more than personal significance.

An audience can be made as conscious of not seeing something of dramatic importance as it is of what it actually witnesses, and in this respect *Macbeth* is as remarkable for its unstaged events as for its many sensational sights. I have commented more than once on the play's use of messengers; reported action is a means of focusing upon the repercussions of an event. It can be used when the event itself is difficult or impossible to stage for obvious practical reasons, as for instance when Ross and the Old Man, in the aftermath of Duncan's murder, recount strange disturbances of the natural order: a falcon killed by a mousing owl and Duncan's horses 'contending 'gainst obedience' (II.iv.17). But frequently in the play reported action is not a substitute for the staged event: Macbeth's letter to his wife describes his encounter with the witches as we have seen it, the First Murderer reports to Macbeth the killing of Banquo and Fleance's escape, staged only a few moments previously, and Ross brings to Macduff news of his slaughtered family after we have seen the Murderers at their work. In other cases, however, the play withholds important events from our eyes, and the unseen thereby creates its own effects.

In choosing not to stage to our view Macbeth's victories in battle over Macdonwald and the Thane of Cawdor at the beginning of the play, Shakespeare follows his customary practice of delaying the first entry of the tragic hero until he has established an image to arouse anticipation. That image, of course, will prove ironic, when 'Brave Macbeth', the hero of the hour, is first seen showing signs of fear and then thoughts of murder. Macdonwald and the Thane of Cawdor are themselves part of the irony and, since we do not see them, their shadowy existence as portents of treachery is the more ghostly. To borrow Ross's words, Macbeth might be said to confront them both 'with self-comparisons' (I.ii. 56), since the justice he executes upon Macdonwald, severing the traitor's head from his body, will in turn be executed upon him by Macduff, after Macbeth has become another Thane of Cawdor in more than name.

We do not see Duncan after his reception by Lady Macbeth in I.vi, when he disappears into the castle. His murder is veiled from our eyes, although we are in a sense present while it is committed, sharing Lady Macbeth's awareness of what is taking place off-stage but close to hand. Instead of distancing the deed from us, therefore, the effect is to intensify its sacrilegious horror. Kings are murdered on the stage elsewhere in Shakespeare: Henry VI and Richard II suffer such a fate. But the murder of Duncan as a dramatic event is a crime invested with profound spiritual significance, and when Macduff sees what has been done and bids Lennox 'Approach the chamber, and destroy your sight / With a new Gorgon' (II.iii.69–70), it is not merely because the old man had so much blood in him. Macduff's reaction after the event serves to emphasise the artistic reasons for not staging the event itself.

After the murder of Duncan, Macduff recedes from view though not from awareness. He tells Ross in II.v that he will return home to Fife instead of attending Macbeth's coronation and in the Feast Scene Macbeth's suspicions are aroused by this absence. The audience is further reminded of his disappearance when news is given of his flight to England: he is now felt to be even more out of sight. Since we are not shown Macduff revealing his intentions or plans to escape, the effect is to screen his flight from us. This dramatic effect is appropriate to Macduff's need to keep his own counsel amidst the suspicions and rumours, spies and murderers, that Macbeth's rule brings to Scotland. The effect is reinforced when we see Lady Macduff protesting bitterly to Ross at her husband's desertion, as if she is unaware of his reasons for leaving the country. When we see Macduff again, his trustworthiness is being tested by Malcolm.

Finally, the deaths of Lady Macbeth and Macbeth are both off-stage events. The Sleep-walking Scene prepares us for the end of Lady Macbeth: she concludes her part on the stage, as she began it, alone, despite the presence of the Doctor and the Gentlewoman. By not staging her death, Shakespeare makes it a reported event to which Macbeth reacts with a speech of sombre gravity but without any sense of personal loss or grief; since we do not see it, we are also open to Malcolm's suggestion at the end of the play that she took her own life. Macbeth's own death is also obscured from our view, despite the stage-direction of the Folio, 'Enter Fighting, and *Macbeth* slaine.' This stage-direction might be taken to indicate that Macbeth is seen to receive a fatal wound in his fight with Macduff, but he does not die on the stage. Four lines later, Macduff is reported missing by Malcolm, and the Folio stage-direction a little further on, 'Enter Macduffe, with Macbeths head', does not make sense if Macbeth's body is lying on the stage. To deprive the tragic hero of the customary death in full view of the audience is certainly a notable departure from dramatic convention, and it is one of several features of *Macbeth* that recall *Richard III*. If the effect involves a certain denial of sympathy, at least our last image of Macbeth alive is appropriately that of a man fighting against the odds, and the sight of Macbeth's head brought in by Macduff is a fitting conclusion to the play's visual horrors.

NOTES

1 *The Imperial Theme* (1931), p. 138.
2 See G.K. Hunter, 'The theology of Marlowe's *The Jew of Malta*' in

Dramatic Identities and Cultural Tradition: Studies in Shakespeare and his Contemporaries (Liverpool, 1978), pp. 92-4.

3 C.H. Herford, P. and E. Simpson, eds, *Complete Works of Ben Johnson*, 11 vols (1925-52), vii. 301.

4 Quoted in D. Bartholomeusz, *Macbeth and the Players* (Cambridge, 1969), p. 58.

5 *Ibid.*, p. 69.

6 *Ibid.*, p. 63.

Part 2

The play
in the theatre

4

Macbeth and Lady Macbeth in the eighteenth and nineteenth centuries

Marvin Rosenberg

A curious thing happened to Macbeth and his Lady on their way to the twentieth century.

In 1800 they could not easily have recognized their theatre selves of a century later. Their earlier characterizations had been shaped by the special cultural fashions of the eighteenth century, and by the manipulation of those fashions on the stage. The patterns that emerged were generally similar throughout Europe; and what happened in the British theatre can be taken, at this time, as generally representative.[1]

Begin with that great actor and master manipulator of Shakespearian texts, David Garrick. His version of *Macbeth*, that dominated England's stage in the decades before 1800, cruelly constricted the implications of the play. It was not all Garrick's fault. He had inherited, from the Restoration, oppressive relics of Davenant's musicalized version of *Macbeth*, in which Shakespeare's ominous Weird Sisters had been danced by the then emergent women actresses, titillating audiences unfit for Shakespeare's austere tragedy. Had Davenant only taken the Folio's hints for III.v and IV.i, and merely intensified with his larger choruses the malevolent implications of the witches' singing and dancing, their sinister contributions to the structure of the play might have been preserved. Alas, the Sisters became, instead, inoffensively foolish - finally comic - broomsticked witch-cartoons, un-thinkable as serious tempters to murder.

But in Garrick's time Macbeth needed more than ever to be lured - if not indeed driven - to do his killing. For the bloody tyrant was transforming into the familiar contem-porary image of a man of sensibility - a hero who in anguish

73

did wrong virtually in spite of himself. By now all the other great, tragic Shakespearian heroes had been, by textual cutting and interpretative adulteration, bleached of their darker ambiguous undersides: nice old Lear, in the Tate version holding the stage, lives happily forever after with a Cordelia married to Edgar; Othello, expurgated, is piteously, tenderly murderous in word and deed; Hamlet's behaviour is largely purified, with many of his truest, truant lines gone, including most of what Garrick called the fifth act 'rubbish'. But these were relatively innocent heroes compared with Macbeth; how could the grim Scots regicide be made into an honourable murderer? Especially now, when the Weird Sisters no longer seriously represented an uncanny stimulus to – if not awakening of – his terrible ambition? If they could not tempt him, and he was himself too honourable to embrace murder, some compelling spur from outside had to be found.

It was found – notably in England – in the persons of two mighty, marvellous actresses who, with the aid of textual cuts and carefully shaped characterizations, lifted the power of Lady Macbeth over her husband to such dominance that the blame for his virgin venturing into murder became almost entirely hers. In many European theatres similar titanic Lady Macbeths would surface, the British actresses serving as patterns of the characterization.

First in prominence was Hannah Pritchard, who towered even physically over her Macbeth, Garrick – as we can see in the familiar Zoffany picture of the two frozen in the moment after he has returned from killing Duncan. Pritchard, even without her soaring head-dress, looms larger and more determined, fearsome; the smaller Garrick poises uncertainly on his toes, fearful. The contrast is even richer in the Fuseli picture that depicts Garrick, the daggers in his hands, horribly frightened, while the massive, controlled, almost smiling Pritchard, a finger to her lips, coolly quietens him. A verbal painting of the pictured moment emphasizes her ruthlessness, as opposed to his humanity. At 'Give me the daggers', she seized them

> from the remorseful and irresolute Macbeth, despising the agitation of a mind unaccustomed to guilt, and alarmed at [his] terrors of conscience, [presenting] a picture of the most consummate intrepidity of mischief.

Pritchard's 'angry Hecate' showed 'a mind insensible to compunction', inflexibly bent to gain her purpose. She was praised for her 'apathy' (unfeeling callousness), for her 'horrible force of implacable cruelty'. When Macbeth dared to resist her initial urgings to murder, 'her whole ambitious soul came forth in fury to her face, and sat in terror there.' When Banquo's ghost unmanned Macbeth in the banquet scene, after her 'angry and reproving looks', she 'seized his arm, and . . . assumed a look of such anger and terror as cannot be surpassed.'

In the sleep-walking scene, most later ladies would project at least a touch of remorse; no observers report this of Pritchard. Her handwashing was classically controlled: she touched one palm with the fingertips of the other hand, while suffering momentary flashes of horror. Cuts in the text accommodated her fearsome image: thus she did not appear, in Act II.iv, to 'faint' at Macbeth's description of the murdered grooms – Garrick was afraid audiences would laugh at the 'hypocrisy' of so formidable a figure pretending weakness.

Oppressed by such a mate, Garrick's Macbeth had – and needed – little will of his own to commit regicide. This fitted the actor's conception of Macbeth's nobility, given in a curious essay[2] ascribed to Garrick himself:

> An experienced general crown'd with Conquest, innately ambitious and religiously Humane, spurr'd on by metaphysical prophecies and the unconquerable pride of his Wife, to a deed horrid in itself, and repugnant to his nature.

Such a Macbeth had to spend much of the play in grief and shame. One unconverted correspondent complained of this to Garrick:

> You almost everywhere discovered dejectedness of mind . . . more grief than horror . . . heart heavings, melancholy countenance and slack carriage of body . . . . The sorrowful face and lowly gestures of a penitent which have ever a wan and pitiful look . . . quite incompatible with the character.

But for the general, the characterization was a success; Garrick was praised for his Macbeth's 'humane' side – his sensibility, his sufferings: 'his pensively preparatory attitudes . . . the propriety and gracefulness wherewith he touches the soft falls of sorrow, terror, and compassion.' He brooded long before he went to kill Duncan; and after, shaken, his 'distraction of mind and agonizing horrors were finely contrasted to [Pritchard's] seeming apathy, tranquillity, and confidence.' We hardly need these details of Garrick's 'honourable' characterization to appreciate his 'defence' of Macbeth, if we examine his textual cuts, small and large, that clearly give a soft focus to his regicide. A minor cue: in the crucial I.vii speech ('If it were done when 'tis done'), when Macbeth considers the murder of his royal guest, Garrick cut 'If th' assassination / Could trammel up the consequence', as if the very word of murder should not yet fall from his lips. Other entire scenes were cut, or butchered, to protect Garrick's image: the whole brutal assault on Lady Macduff and her babes was eliminated, as was Macbeth's casual killing of young Siward – these moments too clearly conveyed Macbeth's dark side. Worst of all was the 'poetic justice' wedged into Macbeth's death scene, turning the heroic intransigence endowed him by Shakespeare into prosy sentimental piety – and providing by hindsight a dismal perspective on the shallow 'innocence' of the whole characterization:

> 'Tis done. The scene of life will quickly close. Ambition's vain, delusive dreams are fled, and now I wake to darkness, guilt and horror. I cannot bear it. Let me shake it off – 'Two' not be; my soul is clogg'd with blood — and cannot rise. I dare not ask for mercy. It is too late, hell drags me down. I sink, I sink - Oh. - my soul is lost forever. Oh.

After Pritchard came Sarah Siddons; after Garrick, John Philip Kemble, in the same patterns. Because they were true artists, Siddons and Kemble found their own ways into the roles, but they were still aware of the times and they brought into the early nineteenth century the familiar, acceptable characterizations: fierce, eagerly murderous wife; noble, reluctantly murderous husband.

Siddon's own comments, as well as those of her admirers, reveal how deliberately she played the 'female fiend of Scotland'. She did write that, plausibly to corrupt a character as brave, amiable, and honourable as Macbeth, she would have liked to project Lady Macbeth's dark evil in the guise of an innocent-appearing, fair-haired woman, with 'all the charms and graces of personal beauty . . . fair, feminine, nay, even fragile'. In this she was prophetic of Ladies to come, as we will see; but she herself could not embody her vision. Her audiences would not let her. They wanted, not the pretended dove, but the unmistakeable hawk:

> [Her] idea of a delicate and blonde beauty . . . the public would have ill-exchanged for her dark looks and eagle eyes.

Thus Hazlitt described her Gothic image:

> Her turbulent and inhuman strength of spirit, [her] unrelieved fierceness, [yielding] no intercourse with human sensation or human weakness. Vice was never so solitary and so grand. The step, look, voice of the Royal Murderess forces our eye after them as if of a being from a darker world, full of evil, but full of power – unconnected with life, but come to do its deed of darkness, and then pass away.

Siddons read Macbeth's letter with 'the apathy of a demon'. When she invoked the murdering ministers, one observer was certain that 'Till then . . . a figure so terrible had never bent over the pit of a theatre.' She drove her Macbeth, usually Kemble, to Duncan's murder with 'horrible purpose, . . . fixed posture, determined eye and full deep voice of fixed resolve', her expression 'slow, severe and cruel'. When she returned from leaving the daggers by the sleeping grooms, she wore the ghastly horrid smile of a 'triumphant fiend',

> The daring fiend whose pernicious potions have stupefied Duncan's attendants, and who even laid their daggers ready – her own spirit, as it seems, exalted . . . in eager expectation of the results of her diabolic diligence.

Siddons had been fearful that audiences, hypnotized by Mrs Pritchard's Lady Macbeth, would not readily accept a new interpretation. But the first part of her portrayal was formidable enough to satisfy; and she felt sure enough to bring a new dimension to the later parts of the play. She could still not 'faint' after Macbeth's tale of killing the groom; but her comments indicate an image of awakened vulnerability once she had become queen, and hostess to the thanes:

> Dying with fear, yet assuming the utmost composure,
> ... with trembling nerves, having tottered up to the
> steps of her throne, ... Lady Macbeth entertains her
> wondering guests with frightful smiles, with over-acted
> attention, and with fitful graciousness .... Whilst writhing
> under her internal agonies, her restless and terrifying
> glances towards Macbeth, in spite of all her efforts to
> suppress them, have thrown the table into amazement.

Siddons theorized a deeper layer in Lady Macbeth, and a further one in the sleep-walk. She wanted audiences to accept her idea that, fierce as she was, her nightmare could yet include a touch of remorse as well as horror. She envisioned this:

> [a] wasted form, with wan and haggard countenance,
> her starry eyes glazed with the ever-burning fever of
> remorse .... Her ever-restless spirit wanders in troubled
> dreams ... and whether waking or asleep, the smell of
> innocent blood incessantly haunts her imagination.

In her own time Siddons was indeed seen as restless here, in radical contrast to Pritchard's still figure; but in the next generation, as acting styles changed, she would be remembered as almost unmoving:

> She looked like a living statue ... Her grand voice, her
> fixed and marble countenance, and her silent step, gave
> the impression of a supernatural being. Nothing so solemn,
> so awful, was ever seen upon the stage. Yet it had one
> fault – it was too awful. She more resembled a majestic
> shade rising from the tomb than a living woman,
> however disturbed by wild fear and lofty passion.

It was this formidable virago against whom Kemble's gentlemanly Macbeth played at the turn of the nineteenth century; and inevitably he was smothered by her power. Siddons had so frightened the actor, Alexander Pope, who was playing Macbeth, that he only recovered his manliness after Lady Macbeth's death. Another player was said by Boaden to

78

'sink under' Siddons. Kemble was a greater actor, but G.J. Bell, the most careful observer of his acting with Siddons, described him as playing:

> only a co-operating part . . . I can conceive Garrick to have sunk Lady Macbeth as much as Siddons does Macbeth . . . . She makes [him] her mere instrument, guides, directs, and inspires the whole plot.

Sadly enough, Kemble had had the good sense to realize that Shakespeare intended the Weird Sisters to help provoke what was murderous in Macbeth, and the actor wanted to bring back the sinister trio, but public opinion would not have them, and so his external compulsion had to come largely from his Lady.

But change was in the theatrical air. As Mrs Siddons's Lady Macbeth had reached a character depth beyond Pritchard, so newer actresses would seek further dimensions. Kemble, probably with some grateful relief, played against one such in 1808, a Miss Smith. She was even praised, in *The Cabinet*, for some departures from the Siddons's pattern; although inevitably blamed for 'faults . . . the most material of which was a notion of tenderness at times, and a querulous sensibility [improper for] Lady Macbeth's cool, deliberate and inflexible resolution.'

By this time a German actress, Rosalie Nouseul, had outgrown the stereotyped monster-Lady, and had demonstrated – generally to the dismay of conventional German critics – that Lady Macbeth could be an affectionate wife, rising with resolution to partner her husband in his first crime, rather than to engineer it. English Lady Macbeths would move slowly in the same direction, at first against critical resistance, then with some critical support. Edmund Kean, the next great star after Kemble, eased the way for his Ladies by finding in his Macbeth more innate responsibility for the regicide's murderous career. Kean was working toward the stretching dialectic that is in the character, as his biographer, Hawkins, observed:

> A marvellous compound of daring and irresolution, ambition and submissiveness, treachery and affection, superstition and neglectfulness of the future, a murderer and a penitent.

So Kean's partly self-generated criminality took some of the
burden from his Ladies of having inhumanly to goad him to
crime. Thus one Lady Macbeth, a Mrs Hill, was charged
with being '*bit* . . . by the present mania for new readings'
because she was 'the most jovial, open-faced, and unsuspecting-
looking Lady Macbeth we ever saw.' The 'originality' of
another of Kean's Ladies, Miss Campbell, was found similarly
troubling: 'We have . . . but one Lady Macbeth' – Siddons –
a review insisted. Miss Campbell

> had none of the dignity, none of the masculine energy,
> none of the unrelenting cruelty, none of the devouring
> ambition which belongs to the cool murderess. She
> seemed to coax and wheedle her husband to the
> commission of the crime, instead of pouring her bold
> spirit into his milky nature.

This Lady Macbeth was always a mere woman, not unsexed,
nor filied from top to toe with direst cruelty.

As critics in Germany slowly warmed to the humanized
Lady, so critics in England, helped by innovative actresses,
began to discover the character's soft 'femininity'. Two in
particular were pivotal. First, Walter Maginn, happy in his
championship of an unorthodox view, now saw Lady Macbeth
somewhat as Macbeth had been seen before:

> Love for [Macbeth] is, in fact, [Lady Macbeth's] guiding
> passion. She sees that he covets the throne, that his
> happiness is wrapped up in the hope of becoming a king;
> and her part is accordingly taken without hesitation.
> With the blindness of affection she persuades herself that
> he is full of the milk of human kindness, and that he
> would reject false and unholy ways of attaining the
> object of his desires. She deems it, therefore, her duty to
> spirit him to the task . . . . Her sex, her woman's breasts,
> her very nature oppose the task she has prescribed
> herself; but she prays to the ministers of murder . . . and
> she succeeds in mustering the desperate courage that
> bears her through.

The second major critical influence on the changing image of
Lady Macbeth was George Fletcher, who was perhaps directly
influenced, as Maginn may have been indirectly, by innovative

theatre characterization. The actress whose modulation of the role impressed him enough to earn a footnote in his essay, which defended Lady Macbeth in Maginn-like terms, was Helena Faucit. She was an interestingly transitional figure between the Siddons's and post-Siddons's characterizations. She had no doubt about Lady Macbeth's strength:

> I could not but admire the stern grandeur of the indomitable will which could unite itself with 'fate and metaphysical aid' to place the crown upon her husband's brow.

But even this conception was not fierce enough for conservative criticism, as represented in, of all places, the *Lady's Newspaper*, with the complaint:

> She expresses care, anguish, and a fiendish vindictiveness with force. This, however, does not accord with our notion of the character, which requires the subtle hardihood and terrible immobility that the greatest actresses have hitherto given . . . . Perfect self-possession and an utter absence of susceptibility are the true characteristics of this wicked woman . . . . She is an odious as well as a criminal woman, who could hardly be personated by the most feminine and delicate of our actresses, and the effort to throw tenderness into the part seems to us absurd.

But Faucit deepened the wedge into the hidden vulnerability of the Lady, mainly by conveying persistently her sense of womanly, wifely devotion to her husband, her encouragement for him before Duncan's death, her care for his distraction afterwards. One significant step in her softening of the characterization was that she could carry off the 'faint' after Macbeth's description of the dead grooms without seeming hypocritical. Siddons had also meant to humanize Lady Macbeth after the initial crime, yet when Macbeth reminded her that Banquo and Fleance were still obstacles in his way, she instantaneously urged their death; in contrast, Faucit's 'naturally generous' Lady responded wearily with 'wonder and dread'.

This element in Faucit's interpretation may have moved the critic Fletcher to enlist on the side of the Lady as loving wife: certainly he approved of her newer, more-dimensioned image, an

> essentially feminine person . . . together with that energy of intellect and of will, which this personation equally demands, [enabling] her to interpret the character with a convincing truth of nature and feeling, more fully thrilling than the imposing but less natural, and therefore less impressive grandeur of Mrs. Siddons.

Fletcher's zeal to justify Lady Macbeth's 'femininity' prompted him to shift the blame for criminality from her shoulders to Macbeth's – who then became the only begetter of the killing of the king. Here again he was following Maginn. Macbeth was now seen as bloodthirsty, selfish and callous. Kemble's portrayal was attacked by Fletcher for distorting Shakespeare's creation: 'the remorsefully reluctant . . . repentant criminal is continually substituted for [Shakespeare's] heartless slave of more selfish apprehensiveness.' Macbeth was not a sensitive poet, but a 'poetically whining' villain, speaking from a morbidly irritable fancy. Because Lady Macbeth devotedly loved him, she desperately invoked the murdering ministers in an intense effort 'to silence the "still small voice" of her human and feminine conscience.'

Theatre and criticism were now well on the road toward discovering how much of Macbeth's motivation came from within, and how much from external stimulation other than his wife's. For one thing, the lure of the supernatural was reinstated – against popular and critical resistance at first, but finally triumphantly – with the reappearance, in often spectacular staging, of the sinister Weird Sisters. In some cases the gnarled Sisters would be complemented, in IV.i, by three sweet-looking girls as the Folio's 'other three' witches accompanying Hecate, but the effect intended now was spooky wonder rather than amusement.

Macbeth's role was substantially enlarged by his communion with the other world. Of the many notes Shakespeare sounded in the character's polyphony, Macbeth's sensitivity to the uncanny must often beat strongly: the Sisters at last cue him to his murderous course, and their seeming assurances tempt him on until finally entangling him mentally. Kean, searching out the multiplicity of Macbeth, seems to have been the first to eliminate the broomstick rubbish in favour of sinister enticement; but Macready, by mid-century, had absorbed into his characterization Macbeth's experience of the uncanny. The first confrontation with the Sisters shook him deeply; he moved through the play as if always alert to the resonance of a world beyond, and was sometimes almost trance-like. He was praised for conveying the impression of 'looking at nothing'; *The Times* noted 'the glassy eye, the dreamy expression, the uncertain gait, the lapses and trances of thought, all mark one who feels himself a passive instrument in the hands of fate.' Half-possessed,

> he seemed to reel through a visionary region where he must stumble on, urged by a mysterious power which he cannot resist and cannot fathom, through a dark, unriddled, portent-laden future.

Given this force on his behaviour, his Lady had not by herself to compel Macready's Macbeth to murder. Even when he acted against interpretations held over from the old Lady-monster pattern, like the ferocious American Charlotte Cushman's, he asserted Macbeth's semi-autonomous way to crime. He allowed the new Ladies, like Faucit, to play the more devoted, 'feminine' side of the characterization, and help lead his Macbeth to murder for his sake more than for their own.

Ladies would appear who, assuming the softer face of the loving wife, would in fact be monsters in disguise. Such a one, for instance, was the Italian Ristori, as 'fiendishly' ambitious for herself as any predecessor, but always behind a silk-smooth façade of concern only for her husband. But the momentum of character-exploration in the last decades of the nineteenth century was toward the image of the Loving Wife virtually sacrificing herself to her husband's witch-awakened ambition; and the century ended with some spectacular examples.

Outside of England, the most remarkable of the new breed of Lady Macbeths was Sarah Bernhardt. But she lacked as her opposite the English Macbeth who complemented ideally the most famous of the softer Ladies: Henry Irving was the Macbeth, Ellen Terry his Lady.

In Terry, Siddons might have recognized her own unrealized image of the character: 'Fair, feminine, nay, even fragile'. Except that Siddons had imagined this image as a mask for

Lady Macbeth's shrewd manipulation of her honourable husband – rather the way a later nineteenth-century American Lady, Clara Morris, eased her Macbeth into crime. For Ellen Terry 'femininity' was the true core of her characterization – pitted against a husband quite unlike Siddons's gentleman Macbeths.

Terry was indeed fair, with wonderful red-gold tresses framing her face. Her blondeness was startling to many critics, more used to the dangers implicit in dark hair; one Philadelphia review observed, 'Most of the harm in the world is done by soft, yellow-haired women.' Terry was also most 'feminine', in being gentle, tender, and caressing – except when impelled to stiffen her Macbeth's will by whipping herself into urgency. Then she was no longer 'fragile': she assumed the royal manner and authority that are reflected in her Sargent portrait, where she is every inch a queen. Reviewers marvelled at the contrasting notes in her characterization:

> Such a red-haired, splendid, fearless, stimulating, unscrupulous woman. . . . Feminine [her characterization] is; wifely it is. Powerful it is; [she] seizes Macbeth in a vice, and uses it and him by sheer force. . . . Halfway between the grim ferocity of Cushman and the beguiling suavity of Clara Morris . . . , we observe for the first time the stormy, dominant woman of the eleventh century equipped with the capricious emotional subtlety of a woman of the nineteenth century, . . . [Hers] is the Lady Macbeth Shakespeare would have drawn had he had an Ellen Terry in his company . . . . We can really accept this clinging and cajoling enchantress, whose enkindled ambition affects her with a temporary paralysis of conscience.

This 'soft' interpretation apparently came in a direct line from Faucit, for her copy of Fletcher's criticism had found its way to Terry, who in turn left her notes on the margins. Terry had a great deal to say about the character, much of it having to do with its polarities:

> *I* can only see that she's a Woman – *A mistaken* Woman and Weak – Not a Dove – of course not – but *first of all a Wife.* I don't think she's *at all clever* . . . . She seems

shrewd, and thinks herself so at first, but oh how quickly she gets steeped in wickedness beyond her comprehension . . . . I by no means make her a gently lovable woman, as some of them say. That's all pickles; she was nothing of the sort, although she was not a fiend and did love her husband.

Ellen Terry's 'husband' took a good deal of loving: Henry Irving. He it was who seems to have handed on to Terry Fletcher's criticism which had not only defended Lady Macbeth, but had insisted on Macbeth as the primary villain in the couple's murderous career.

By this time, in the later nineteenth century, psychologists, plumbing into repressed motivation, could see Macbeth's traumatic introspections as 'neurasthenic', and so German actors were portraying him (as many other actors would, worldwide, in the 1900s). Romantic, heroic Macbeths could still hold the stage, as in Beerbohm Tree's highly poetic interpretation; but Irving's spectacular scoundrel evidently satisfied some need of the the time. Over a period of years it pleased audiences both at home in England and in America.

Irving's Macbeth was meant to be a cowardly, ambitious blackguard, who had thought of murdering Duncan long before the play begins. Irving played Fletcher's notion that Macbeth was not poetic by nature, but indulged in fine-sounding words – e.g. 'pity, like a naked, new-born babe' – because he enjoyed weeping sentimentally. So, in Macbeth's pronouncements of loyal sorrow at Duncan's death and Banquo's absence, Irving sounded a touch of the same resonance of covert hypocrisy that had won him applause in his triumphant Iago. Similarly, his Macbeth provoked his wife to urge him to the crimes he had already thought of and needed support for. He would be horribly frightened by Banquo's ghost. Critics, unhappy with Irving's conception, damned him for making Macbeth only a cowardly villain, but other observers sensed the power, nervous energy, and intelligence which emanated from this Macbeth at the crisis of the action; and though he blanched at the supernatural, against flesh and blood enemies he fought fiercely to the death.

The great achievement of nineteenth-century Lady Macbeths was to discover dimensions of humanity in the 'monster' characterization of the early 1800s, and to provide a spring-board for actresses in the twentieth century. Similarly, Macbeth grew from honourable murderer toward the many-sided man-husband-soldier-regicide-king-sorcerer-poet-tyrant-butcher-mourner-tragic hero still being explored in the theatre today.

NOTES

1   A detailed account of the international evolution of interpretations of the play's main characters is available in my study, *The Masks of Macbeth*, University of California Press (1978). In that book may be found references to actors and actresses discussed in this chapter.
2   *An Essay on Acting*, in which will be consider'd the Mimical Behaviour of a certain Fashionable Actor (1744).

5

Macbeth: 1946–80 at Stratford-upon-Avon

Gareth Lloyd Evans

During the second half of the twentieth century the ebbs and flows of the fortunes of theatres and theatre organisations have been documented on a far more extensive scale than ever before. Film, tape, photocopy, speed-typing and the ubiquitous nosings of the media have all contributed to the production of huge graphs and charts of the world of theatre.

The precious and vivid memories of observers like Georg Lichtenberg which vivify study of eighteenth-century theatre are inevitably compounded of speculation, fancy and the tenuous subjectivity of imagination – the waywardness of these is only too apparent to the present writer who has witnessed all the productions under review both as professional critic and private theatre-goer. The caprices of memory might seem out of place in our time when the proof or disproof of individual experience of performance lies waiting to be unwound from camera or tape-recorder.

Yet there is a sense in which nothing can replace the wayward evidence of memory, especially when it is excited by sympathy and disciplined by knowledge. A thousand silicon chips working in a thousand engines of mechanical record cannot body forth the reality of what happened to a particular observer at any given performance of a play. Technology can turn out a very detailed map, but no amount of contour lines, hachuring, shading and fathom marks can show the height, depth, width and temperature of a theatrical experience.

The copious records[1] will show that since 1946 the Royal Shakespeare Theatre has staged *Macbeth* in only eight different productions, but that this numerically low frequency disguises wide exposure – Australian, European and British tours and production runs both at Stratford and London – and that some of the most distinguished players and directors were employed in the process. MacOwan, Quayle, Gielgud, Byam Shaw, Hall, Nunn, Tearle, Richardson, Olivier, Porter, Scofield and McKellen represent to a close degree the very best in Shakespearean acting and production since the Second World War, while Robert Harris and Nicol Williamson should not go unremarked.

What the records do not show is something which only the pressure of constant theatre-going and subjective experience can reveal – that the sinuous often bewildering movements of style, the sometimes self-conscious blueprinting of policy in the Memorial (to become the Royal Shakespeare in 1960) Theatre since the war are embodied far less in the productions of *Macbeth* or indeed any of the other Tragedies (except Hall's *Hamlet*) than in its productions of the Histories. They have been better served than the Tragedies both in quality of production and (in general) in standard of acting, and it seems to have been easier for this theatre to accommodate the Histories to the prevailing, sometimes obsessive, policy of the 1960s and 1970s of 'making Shakespeare speak to the twentieth century'.[2] It is perhaps less difficult to exploit ironies of social, political and human behaviour between Then and Now than to file the Tragedies, with their complex temporal and psychological patterns, in the modern idiom.

Productions of *Macbeth* in this period show very little of the company's broad lines of policy and stylistic development – indeed they seem, when set deliberately in the full context of the period, rather lonely, isolated one-off affairs – but perhaps we should be content to be able to record one great performance (Olivier's) and one of notable distinction (McKellen's) in 34 years. Indeed, perhaps it is more than we should expect – it is nearly 50 years since Gielgud created a commensurate Hamlet and in the period under review the RSC has produced no Hamlet of more than flickering grandeur.

Where *Macbeth* is concerned it would be impossible to devise a set of actors whose interpretation differed so much in nature and quality than those at Stratford. Godfrey Tearle created a Thane that was predictably grand and civilised, Richardson simply failed dismally, Scofield's was consistently out of sorts with its surrounding production, Porter's had the dullness of intellectual clarity almost totally devoid of emotional vibrancy and Nicol Williamson, again predictably, confused eccentric behaviour with perceptive acting.

The period began with Michael MacOwan's 1946 production, which harboured the young Paul Scofield as Malcolm, Valerie Taylor as Lady Macbeth and a palpably versatile Hugh Griffith as the First Witch. MacOwan seemed to have conceived of the play in genteel terms and his Macbeth, Robert Harris, was nothing if not curiously polite in aspect and notably well-educated in tone and delivery. The brutality of Macbeth's ambition, his spiritually clemmed imagination, the animal courage of his despair had very little house-room in the production or the performance – one critic referred to its being concerned with 'essentially sophisticated people'.

In memory it has the visual aspect of a private performance in a large Jacobethan interior. It was very much in 'modern' dress and setting, and its modernity was of Shakespeare's own time. The permanent set employed many (too many) stairs and steps; there was an impression of restless up-and-down movement from the highly civilised study which dominated centre stage and was, for *afficionados*, a very passable version of the conjectured Elizabethan inner stage. It had also a large upper gallery.

Despite the refined architecture of the set a good deal of stage-smoke was released – probably of necessity to facilitate the difficult task of disguising domesticity as heath and cavern.

Robert Harris spoke Macbeth's language with clipped gentility and intelligence, but his presence lacked power. Evil was absent and was replaced by head-shaking regret for a moral miscalculation which was deeply vexatious but not profoundly disturbing. 'His devil', wrote one critic, 'was a home-sick angel, human-hearted, never reconciled to the murky hell of his own deeds.'[3]

Valerie Taylor was unable to thicken and enrich this thin brew. Her acting was consistent in echoing Harris's refined appearance and speech, but inimical to Lady Macbeth's huge acquisition of guilt. Her sleep-walking scene became a kind of penance for a bad social *gaffe* and completely neglected to depict the sickening reality of a mind turned and twisted by a memory which is a relentless shadow-version of her husband's imagination. The scene had some significance for collectors, however, – it was done from the wings without what has become the statutory candle.

This production sent few signals into the memory, but one should be recorded. Scofield's shouted 'Oh, by whom?', as his Malcolm heard of his father's murder, was one of the unexpected moments of theatre which direct an audience to attend – an unusual acting quality was announcing itself.

In outward show the next production, in 1949, was categorically different. The *Birmingham Post* critic described its appearance as 'Caledonia stern and wild'.[4] This was compounded of two steep and narrow stone staircases flanking a huge crag which served little purpose beyond a large wasting of space. More to the point, however, although the set and costumes were wild and woolly, eleventh-century and primitive, the interpretation and acting were, in their way, no less genteel than in the previous production. It was stag-at-bay imagery in Surbiton.

Some critics saw a far graver and more reverend miasma about it and one felt 'There were times when this Macbeth looked Apostolic and even Christlike.'[5] Certainly Godfrey Tearle's bearing and facial expressions bodied forth a kind of noble radiance, but the aura was less holy than decent. This was a performance which placed all its bid for conviction on the audience's expectation from Tearle of fine speaking, fine glancing, fine mien.

It is necessary to remember that, in 1949, English classical theatre was still embroiled in the star system – a system which still perpetuated the post-restoration tradition that whatever role the star played – good or evil – was not allowed, indeed conspicuously not allowed, to expunge a certain high decentness, nobility, and a well-spoken, larger-than-life image of the idol. Tearle was a star and, willy-nilly, his Macbeth was destined to be remarked not for its fidelity to Shakespeare's Thane but its adherence to traditional expectations.

Tearle's advance towards accepting the promptings of his ambition was suitably reluctant: his pre-murder musings were understated, as if unworthy of his noble notice; his post-murder reflections had a flowing lucidity about them – he caressed the words as if their poetry were more important than their dramatic implications and for him perhaps it was.

One critic wrote of his speaking with flowing words 'like a lover'.[6] The performance, indeed, relied less on interpretation than enunciation.

And, since one bright star cannot easily accommodate the too-near presence of other luminaries, there was nothing surrounding Tearle which challenged his presence. Diana Wynyard at first encouraged hope by giving us momentary glimpses of a face-slapping termagant but her countenance as Lady Macbeth radiated sweetness and light and sadness from first to last – evil was in abeyance.

Three years later Ralph Richardson under John Gielgud's direction did nothing to rescue the history of recent productions from mediocrity. The season was an artistic disaster for this intellectually wry and emotionally spry player simply because there seemed to have been a comprehensive ignoring of the fact that, though he is master-actor in prose, his voice, gestures and mien give him no rendezvous with high poetry. His great Falstaff achieved its distinction less from his physical presence than from the rolling, sibilant, rich conjugations of vowel and consonant in his speaking of Falstaff's prose.

Richardson's natural habitat as an actor seems to be in roles where the resources of language are being used at the frontiers of eccentricity – one remembers, for example, the chilling crack of the voice in that curiously self-conscious line – 'Light thickens and the crow makes wing to the rooky wood' – but he seems temperamentally unsuited either to the sonorities of impassioned dramatic poetry or to the subtle limpidities of lyricism. He is essentially a witty actor and as such can encompass many roles where the emphasis is on ironically expressed intellectuality. But the role of Macbeth is neither witty nor intellectual, and it demands more from voice and imagination than Richardson was either able or prepared to give.

One senses that Richardson himself was aware of his distance from the requirements of the part. Two characteristics of his interpretation gave the impression of being substitutes for what might be termed the real thing. His Scots accent seemed to be an imposed and *ersatz* alternative to ferocity, and his frequent recourse to a staring immobility, described by one critic as a 'man sleep-walking',[7] and by

Tynan as achieving a 'point of paralysis',[8] was perhaps Richardson's version of Macbeth's frozen captivity in the caverns of his own imagination.

Fleeting moments were memorable – his grief at his wife's death, his horror at his blood-stained hands, as if they themselves bled rather than were the instruments of another's bleeding. Such few moments when the observers' imaginations were caught and held did not belong entirely to Richardson. Margaret Leighton battled hard to find a dark spirit in Lady Macbeth: on the whole she was low-key in voice and presence, but in the sleep-walking scene she got her noises and rhythms attuned to the language and embodied, for a few moments, the mixture of loss, abandonment, fear and self-pity in this bitch.

Siobhan McKenna conquered the most difficult of minor roles – her Lady Macduff refused to allow the sentimental aura generated by Shakespeare's hideous stage-child to fog her performance. She played with defiant and touching spirit. Even more, her death, far from being merely the conventional corral of pathos and cruelty, was a most terrible emblem of the comprehensiveness of Macbeth's murderous work.

It was, and still is, impossible not to wonder how much direction Gielgud had given Richardson. It is, of course, purely speculative to suggest that it was not much, but on the evidence of the rest of the production one inclines to that view. It seemed underdirected, lacking subtlety, variety and cohesion. The initial sense that we were about to experience a production visually uncluttered and therefore amenable to an emphasis on strong acting and speaking soon dissipated. The classically severe black-velvet curtains that surrounded the stage soon became mournful accompaniments to a production that lacked variety of movement and setting, that gave no hint of an explanation other than the tediously obvious one as to why Macbeth's followers were dressed in tattered robes while those of the avenging hosts were neat and well-pressed.

Yet another three years were to pass before, in 1955, Stratford attempted the play again. Expectations were high for Glen Byam Shaw's production with Laurence Olivier and Vivien Leigh and, for many, great hopes were surpassed, though the pleasures in the memory must not be allowed to obscure the fact that it did not, by any means, receive total critical acclaim. Olivier has always seemed to earn respect rather than the kind of emotional rapport with theatre-goers that, for example, Gielgud has enjoyed. This has had the effect of increasing the demands of expectation for Olivier's performances – more is expected and there is less leeway in the allocation of merit. Gielgud's Prospero, for example, received but the mildest of critical rebuke for its marked physical ineptitude and he received full remission for his accomplished speaking of the role. On the other hand, Olivier's Macbeth, his filmed Hamlet and, later, both his Coriolanus and Othello were subjected to reservations which, sometimes, descended into carping dismissiveness.

But Stratford in the spring of 1955 had what turned out to be its last overwhelming experience of the presence of stardom. It is recorded that, in the early days of the century, the return of Benson and his company gave the town an *en fête* air that barely relaxed during the festival season. Something similar happened in 1955 and this, in turn, generated the yeast of legend, story and gossip – the Thane's costume was being woven in some unimaginably remote Scottish croft; he had rejected the first costume provided because its 'feel' was not right for him and a theatre minion had been dispatched post-haste in a Hebridean direction to procure another; the Macbeth curse had struck yet again and the star had irrecoverably lost his voice one week before opening.

There was a great deal of speculation about the supporting cast with the dominant opinion being that Olivier would Wolfit his way through it surrounded by the ineffectual low fires of mere supernumeraries. This was not so. Experience was well-blended with unknown quantity. Ralph Michael could be relied upon to create a strong Banquo, Geoffrey Bayldon, a stalwart of the Birmingham Repertory Theatre and, therefore, replete with know-how, was Duncan. Maxine Audley had already acquired something of a name for classical poise – some felt that she should not have been allocated to Lady Macduff but should play Lady Macbeth. Indeed, apart from Keith Michell and Patrick Wymark (both successful as Macduff and the Porter respectively), the biggest unknown quantity, in a sense, was Vivien Leigh. Opinion divided itself between those who felt she was not in the same league as

Olivier and those who felt that his very presence as her husband had, in the past, obscured what was a remarkable talent.

Thus the scene was set by fact and fiction. It seems now a different age and a different clime. Perhaps it was. It must be remembered that 1955 was within five years of the beginning of the end of the 'star' system in Stratford. Peter Hall, in the 1960s, was to change, irrevocably, not only the artistic direction of the theatre, but the whole ambience of the status of his company and its relationship with the public. In many ways Olivier's Macbeth marks the beginning of the end of a theatre-world that had persisted since the time of Shakespeare.

In some cases the percolating rumours about the production seemed to have an essence of truth in them – the story of secrecy, for example, about Olivier's preparations for his role which, it was said, would bring about an interpretation of surpassing surprise, has a rationale in the known fact that he and Vivien Leigh rehearsed a good deal separate from the rest of the company; the hints of dark incompatibility between the director and Olivier were distorted versions of a conflict of opinion about the role of Malcolm between the actor, Trader Faulkner and Byam Shaw – a conflict in which Olivier seems to have supported Faulkner.

Other more theatrically rich intimations of the preparation can be detected in the account by a supernumerary of Olivier's rehearsal practice of filling in any gaps in his memory of his lines with rhythmic noises – a king of formalised gobbledy-gook. Perhaps this is given credence in its sequel which is that when Olivier had mastered his lines the resulting sound and rhythm pattern was exactly that of the gobbledygook version. This report may well be seen as finally falling into the essence of truth when one recalls the nature of Olivier's speaking of the roles of Henry V, Hamlet and Othello (in the filmed versions), and of this staged Macbeth.

There is a very strong impression in his communication of these roles that he is speaking from a kind of musical score of his own where each word bears the force of a musical note. It is, almost invariably, a score which is written for wind instruments rather than (as with Gielgud) the tense limpidities of strings. Again it is much more in evidence in speeches where Olivier is given a liberty by the text to exercise one of his most obvious verbal characteristics – the use of onomatopoeia. His 'drown the wind', 'trumpet tongued', 'creeps in this petty pace' and 'crow makes wing to the rooky wood' (among many other examples) were astonishing tonal impersonations of the words' indentities and characters.

Glen Byam Shaw's production, with few dissenting voices, was regarded generally as an unsatisfactory complement to Olivier's acting. It perpetrated what had seemed to become a permanent characteristic of *Macbeth* sets – an excess of narrow staircases. But, unlike the Tearle version, there was no attempt at Gaelic primitiveness in visual presentation. Indeed there was a faintly Disneyesque imagery. The witches' cavern was garishly fantastic; pointed arches, rising a shade too much for verisimilitude, gave Glamis the eeriness of a super-natural dream-castle; the various pieces of offal used for the witches' brew were cacklingly displayed in precise detail; the apparitions induced laughter by their bizarreries. All in all the production lacked imaginative aptness and control.

Neither had Shaw induced complementary performances from a company which contained a number of experienced players. Trader Faulkner's Malcolm had benefited neither from the actor's contention with the director nor from the support of Olivier that he is supposed to have had. Ralph Michael's Banquo was an adequate acting-foil to Olivier without being a character in itself. Maxine Audley emoted with theatrical largesse, but the best of her Lady Macduff was in her scream of terrified anguish.

Two players alone met the challenge of what Faulkner called Olivier's 'dangerous presence'[9] – Keith Michell as Macduff and Patrick Wymark as the Porter. The former's contribution to the England scene was notable, not only for destroying the prevailing notion that it is tedious and fit for cutting only, but also for its unsentimental anguish – his speaking of 'one fell swoop' restored a line, which had been made hackneyed by insensitive speaking, to its status as an image of death. Wymark remembered the simple trap that awaits the actor playing the Porter – the temptation to confuse comic relief with daft behaviour. Wymark ensured that there was frost on our smiling and was as surely porter of hell-gate as he was drunken guardian of the gates of Glamis.

The absence of unanimity about Olivier's performance and about Shaw's production also encompassed Vivien Leigh's Lady Macbeth. The characteristic which received most con-sistent critical comment at the time was the timbre of her voice. She had succeeded in dropping it an octave lower than usual and the best of her performance was in the chilling hollowness of her speaking. Yet what remains in memory is her facial beauty – a feline symmetry of bone – which paradoxically both enhanced and devalued her attempt at the part. The sheer delicacy and fragility of her white countenance encouraged apprehension for the fate of a woman out of her moral depth, but her inability or refusal to change her expression cut expectation of a moving performance very short. She could not be 'unsexed' because, visually, she was already curiously sexless in her pale Dresden look, and her voice, too, lacked passion. She lacked convincing committal to evil intent, for her eyes were devoid of calculation, and her final fear was, so to speak, skin-deep rather than a shudder of the soul. Even a favourable notice (and there were several), which found her 'sleep-walking' scene to be 'true and exact', seemed to put hard brakes on its approval by adding 'and thoroughly upsetting'[10] – a bathos of insufficiency.

Criticisms of Olivier's performance were characterised by a large amount of puzzlement about the nature of his interpretation and, frequently, about where he had faltered. The remark of James Courtenay in the *Stratford-upon-Avon Herald*[11] neatly sums up a prevailing opinion – 'Olivier [was] the most unexpected Macbeth of our time.' Olivier confounded many by not conforming to a traditional image of the character. For one critic he was not 'heroic', for another he was not 'bestial' enough, yet another felt that his speaking of the 'noble poetry' was flat. Milton Shulman in the *Evening Standard* sought to rationalise and wrote that 'The fault probably stems from Sir Laurence Olivier's decision to concentrate on the philosopher rather than the butcher in Macbeth.'[12]

That was a way of describing it but, arguably, it still missed what Olivier seemed to be seeking to do. This, in hindsight, seems to have been an attempt to avoid the conventional dark violence, the access of butchery, the Grand Guignol of supernatural soliciting, the verbal pyrotechnics, which had characterised so many Macbeths of the near and far past. Olivier sought to convey the one characteristic of the character and, in a sense, the play, which has often been described and reflected upon, but never named, by many scholars and critics – the raising of unanswered questions by the play and within the character: How much had Macbeth thought on kingship before meeting the witches? How reluctant is he at heart to murder Duncan? What is the force, relatively, of the influence of the witches and of his wife on him? Why does Lady Macbeth faint? Why do Malcolm and Donalbain fly so precipitately? Why does Macduff leave his wife and children to their fates? Is Malcolm testing Macduff in the England scene or are we required at least to suspect come truth in his self-portrait? And so on. It is easy to declare that we can give answers to these questions, but the truth is that the play does not. *Hamlet*, so long regarded as the repository of most queries in Shakespeare, in fact gives first place to *Macbeth*. The name of the characteristic is ambiguity. The play is ambiguous in many respects and its chief character is an ambiguous creation. He seems, for a good deal of the action, not to know what he is himself or which side he wishes to walk on – dark or light? Which side should he walk on? – he is unsure even about that.

Olivier captured this ambiguity. But this is not to be 'philosophical' as Shulman opined, for there is nothing philosophical about Macbeth – images haunt him, not ideas. Moreover, Olivier's style of acting is inimical to the creation of philosophical men. His Hamlet (Shakespeare's nearest approach to a 'philosophical' character) was a portrait of a man of action immobilised by reflection, grief and disgust, not of one wrestling with intellectual and moral concepts.

Olivier created an overwhelming sense of growing spiritual fatigue in a man haunted by some of the very questions the play leaves us wondering at. In the first Part, and including the murder of Duncan, the performance was dominated by an air of distraction. His 'I have done the deed' (II.ii 14) was spoken with flat unbelief, but his consorting with the air-drawn dagger was that of an agonised man who had almost expected to see it. The ambiguity of his spiritual condition was shown with menacing pathos as he turned 'Tarquin's ravishing strides' (II.i.55) into a reluctant all-but-shuffling gait while his hands pushed downwards at the stones begging their silence. As Bartholomeusz noted – 'Olivier seems to have caught unerringly the sensitiveness intermingled with the evil in Macbeth.'[13]

In some ways his performance was an exercise in the gradations of spiritual fatigue which throbbed out of the incompatibilities at war inside him. The reluctant, muted, physically drained would-be murderer of Part one became the dark eye-socketed, occasionally ranting, weary but physically unstoppable killer of Part two. The change was marked in the scene following Duncan's murder when he appeared in a dark robe tied at the waist, having something of the appearance of Rasputin. His performance, as it ran the gamut of *mal d'esprit*, did not, however, jump from positive to negative – that is from early assurance (programmed by Lady Macbeth's injunctions) to final desperate resolve leading to resignation. This man was defeated from the word go because he could not find himself – but what a defeat it was!

Olivier had a short jet-black beard, his eyes flashed black, his hair, thick and rich, glowed black. His imperial crown added to the danger which his visage promised. It looked, with its hint of sword-like pinnacles, more like a weapon than an emblem of royalty, and Olivier employed its inanimation as if it were part of his own body. He wore it (and this was particularly noticeable in the scene with the two murderers) at a very slight tilt. Students of Olivier's way with classical tragedy might well have expected this superbly disciplined visual confirmation of the reality that, for this actor, the tragic always walks within one theatrical ell of the absurd, the bizarre, the darkly foolish.

Visually, this was the most menacing and, in its facial contours, the most handsome of modern Macbeths, but one non-visual feature consorted so naturally with what one saw that no commentator has ever noted it. Olivier had the ghost of a Scots accent which he used with superb judgment of tone and effect – in marked contrast to Ralph Richardson. One notable example of its use was in the phrase ''Twas a rough night' (II.iii.59). He spoke it side-stage right – as far away from Duncan's death chamber as he could get and from which any moment the appalled Macduff would emerge. If there had been a pillar, one felt that Olivier would have leant against it in utter fatigue. As it was, he stood listening to Lennox's alarmed accounts of the wild weather of the preceding night with his head shaking up and down slightly in silent confirmation. When Lennox stopped speaking there was a very short but awful pause: Olivier's head stopped shaking, he looked towards Duncan's chamber and with slight elongation of the vowel in ''Twas' and a rasp on the -r-, he spoke the line as if it were a curse.

Great performances by the same actor have a habit of arcing across from one to another as if similar elements in them suddenly discharge flashes of the actor's basic source of acting. The stance, the head-shaking, the pause (though not the tone of) ''Twas a rough night' struck into our imaginations like lightning. In that same season of 1955 he was to create another great performance, that of Titus Andronicus: Titus was to stand in that self-same place, with his back to the wall, grieving upon the death of yet another son and croaking that he had no more tears to shed.

But these examples also reveal something else which conspicuously identified Olivier's way with a text. He seems to seek out, and invariably succeed in finding, phrases, half-lines, apparent debris on the great tide of Shakespeare's iambics, and to collect it into a form that gives its existence a relevance. In the scene with the two murderers, his address to them, which includes the references to dogs, there occur three words which some actors have been known to cut, some to slur, others self-consciously to use as if they were introducing an after-dinner speech. They are 'well, then, now' (III.i.74) – not, one might have concluded, among Shakespeare's greatest encouragements to dramatic inspiration in an actor. Olivier played the scene with jocund menace and the overall impression was of two animals frozen by fear into immobility while their embodied fate dallied with them with words that bewildered, then insulted, then joked, then threatened, then encouraged them. Visually the scene's pattern was of Macbeth restlessly advancing towards them and their disposition to back away. But with 'well, then, now', that pattern was broken. Olivier stopped in his hypnotic movements, eyed them mockingly, lifted up his arms and with each index finger pointing at a murderer said 'well' questioningly. Each finger then crooked as, after a pause, he said 'then' and the movement and tone suggested he wanted them to move nearer to him. They remained still, however, and his 'now', after another pause, was a commanding and frightening imperative. This verbal equation which produced fissionable material out of apparently verbal rubble, produced a silence in the audience that beggars description.

Documentations of this performance contain other examples of this remarkable exploration of a text whose effect was to synthesise all elements in it – high and low verbal tension, poetry and prose, plain and decorated – to the end of intensifying the dramatic impact of character. The 'roundness' of Olivier's greatest performances, whether in

Shakespeare or elsewhere, comes largely from his ability to penetrate a text with an unfailing sensitivity to dramatic truth and relevance – he uses what he finds.

If one is inclined to celebrate Olivier's Macbeth as a great performance it is because not only was it based on a courageous head-on acceptance of the ambiguities of the character, but exhibited all of his qualities as an actor being used at their finest.

When Olivier is in this kind of form he is capable even of turning accident into theatrical profit – a capability which is a testimony to his speed of reaction and often to his physical control. One vivid memory is of an occurrence which almost certainly only one night's audience witnessed – a repetition might well have proved physically damaging. On the second appearance of Banquo's ghost, the director's stage-direction called for a leap by Macbeth on to the banquet table. In one performance he slipped as he leapt on the table which wobbled and scattered its load of utensils and stage-food. Incredibly Olivier kept his balance and eyed the unrehearsed chaos in such a way as to naturalise it. Incredibly he had turned a mishap into one emblem of the reality of chaos and loss of reason in which the banquet scene is played out. No living actor has – and perhaps none dead had – Olivier's ability to feel, to nose out, to grasp at the actualities of theatre, wherever and under whatever circumstances they exist, with unerring intuition, skill and audacious nerve.

After Olivier perhaps it was only right that the perturbed spirit of the play should be allowed a long rest. Seven years later, in 1962, Eric Porter and Irene Worth played the leading roles.

The production and the acting had a kind of worthy dullness about them and it almost seemed as if Olivier had left little for anyone to do except, as Porter did, to present a clear, uncluttered 'reading' of the role. Porter, as actor, often gives the impression of being a frustrated teacher. His authority is less a theatrical than a personal one, his address had pedagogic firmness without dramatic fire. He is excellent at displaying a character possessed of mental shrewdness, but he seems to lack the will or disposition to display the workings of imaginative processes – he would make an excellent Torvald but Dr Rank would elude him. He is unsurpassed at

100

depicting the cunning *nouveau* middle-class rich of the Victorian industrial epoch and the Galsworthian successful man of trade.

His Macbeth, like so many of his Shakespeare roles, became a lecture *expliquée* and this impression was increased in that director and actor both seemed to regard Macbeth as a very rational, intelligent man who, presented with an opportunity to fulfil a well-thought-out ambition, proceeded to do the correct things in order to achieve his ends. Even the witches seemed less supernaturally inclined than part of an inevitable series of occurrences, which he dealt with in cool order, avoiding the moral turpitude involved almost fastidiously. The moral element in the play, in fact, entered very late, and then in a curiously negative way, in that, having attained his ambition, Macbeth found he was holding an empty crown, signifying nothing – damnation was a mere miscalculation.

Porter's most moving emotional area is anger – this made his Macbeth of the penultimate scenes more credible and effective than the earlier ones. His wife's death he greeted less with grief than with wild anger at the temporal inappropriateness of her passing – and, surprisingly, this reaction increased the sense of their mutual isolation. His 'Tomorrow and tomorrow' soliloquy was spoken with furious irritation: the idiot in charge had committed an irrational act in creating the universe, but this realisation offended Macbeth rather than drove him to despair.

Because of his overmastering anger, physical fatigue rather than spiritual destitution dominated him. His dispossession of arms and followers, his death (on stage) encouraged more sympathy for him than for many other Macbeths whose sufferings have seemed deeper-seated. The critic of the *South Wales Evening Argus* found the right words – it had 'intensity', 'remorseless logic' and 'complete theatrical integrity'.

Irene Worth lacked conviction. There was a certain homely glibness in her speaking. She seemed to be in no sense aware (perhaps because her husband wasn't) of the moral enormity of what she helped to bring about. *The Times* critic said that her sleep-walking scene 'had the pathos of a stupid person unhinged and she talks of daggers as if they were kitchen knives.'[14]

This Macbeth, in all respects, went off at half-cock. The set was indeterminate but veered towards impressionism. One critic spoke of a 'simple stage with converging planes' and of 'dramatic light changes',[15] but another likened the set to a 'shingle beach . . . dominated by a ramp . . . and, it would seem, the inverted denture of a whale. It is lit with an endearing flippancy.'[16] This lack of critical agreement appears time and again in the notices – emblems of a production that, perhaps, was stultified from the beginning by memories of what had been done with the play before the seven-year silence began.

As if it were a deliberate visualisation of Peter Hall's published conviction that *Macbeth* is the product of a Christian society, that it is 'littered' with Christian imagery, that it is about 'the nature of evil . . . and what happens when I do a murder', his 1967 production opened with a quite sensational statement of purity, virtue, innocence, snatched away to show the evil lying beneath. A great white sheet – an angel's wing? – hung over the stage and, just before the appearance of the witches, fluttered away, flapping into extinction. Its disappearance revealed a blood-red carpet like a heath with clotted heather. One felt that if one pressed one's hand in it blood would ooze out. It was backed by red granite-seeming cliffs and, at times during the action, sections of it were removed to show an arid bone-white expanse – as if it rested on a bleached skeleton.

The witches seemed to emerge from beneath this bloody carpet, bearing an inverted crucifix. This bloody carpet and the crucifix were central to Hall's production. He has frequently given interviews or lectured on his productions and has been generous in his statements of aims and problems. He declared that he felt he might be entering a period in his life in which religion, something he had eschewed before, would play a significant role. Macbeth for him was the 'metaphysics of evil'.

He had assembled a very strong cast with Elizabeth Spriggs as a witch and Ian Richardson as Malcolm. His choice of Paul Scofield as Macbeth encouraged great expectations. Stratford was ready for Macbeth; the memory of Olivier was less sharp, and Porter had left no enervating challenge. Scofield, a classical actor with huge experience, seemed an obvious choice.

Hall's conception was, as it were, total and the proof of

this lay in the extent to which it engulfed secondary as well as primary characters. For example Hall and Richardson agreed that 'Malcolm is not the sweet, young, good, holier-than-thou hero that everybody thinks he is. . . . The power to have women, money, to "uproar the universal peace" and to "pour the sweet milk of concord into hell" . . . suggests that deep down inside he has a slight conscious knowledge of something bad like that in himself.'[17]

But the curse that gives the stage-history of *Macbeth* a Gothic piquancy struck Hall's production with, one suspects, far deeper and wider effect than the wounding pricks of the near-past (a sword that narrowly missed blinding Keith Michell, a fall that badly hurt Irene Worth). At a crucial point in rehearsal, Hall fell seriously ill and the opening was much delayed. It is idle to speculate on the specific effects of his illness but certain aspects of the production suggested a deep disruptive penetration. The production's pace was slow, the lighting was capricious, the grouping sometimes seemed *ad hoc*, and some effects (notably Banquo's ghost) were awkwardly achieved. These are significant enough, but there was one other major deficiency which, one suspects, might well have been exacerbated by Hall's illness, although, given its nature, it could never have been removed.

Hall's conception of the play's Christian status was at variance with Scofield's – for there seems little doubt that the latter, too, saw the play in that same context without drawing the same conclusions. Hall saw Macbeth's ambition as a flagrant violation of Christian moral standards and his actions as an inevitable consequence of his committal to evil – 'the play is about when I *do* do a murder. The evil which is released.'[18] Scofield's Macbeth was, however, an embodiment of lapsed virtue. The difference between Hall's blood-boltered production in which Christianity was 'a grace note not a *leitmotif*'[19] was conspicuously emblematised in the fact that the witches invariably produced the Christian cross inverted while Scofield carried his sword over his right shoulder (up to the first meeting with Duncan) in the manner of a cross to be borne to Golgotha. Scofield acted as if in tortured regret for a virtuousness that was slipping away and must be recaptured: Hall directed as if goodness and virtue had long ago disappeared from the world.

Yet the difference between Hall's conception and Scofield's was the crucial feature of the production. This difference was increased simply by the kind of acting-personality that Scofield radiates. In comedy his face has the look of a clown with a secret and deep sadness, in tragedy what we see is a saint in torment or torture. His Macbeth was a Sir Thomas More with a conscience and martial instincts.

Moreover, his speaking only increased the sense of a man less concerned with what he is doing than with its astonishing moral turpitude. We heard and saw a Macbeth isolated less by his imagination and his deeds than by his conscience – so, it lacked passion, anger, violence, even doubt. It was completely dominated by agonised self-speculation.

Scofield's speaking of his Shakespearian roles, and notably Macbeth, is characterised by an enormous impression of intelligent reflection, of weighings of meanings, of hesitations about too glib or obvious a committal to a particular tone or nuance. This gives his relationship to Shakespeare's language a quite unique quality of worried intimacy – we seem to be overhearing him in what seems a painfully cerebral task of discovering all of its meaning. Unlike Olivier, who dares all on one note, or Gielgud, who soars and swoops in a flight whose direction and destination is carefully vectored, no Scofield performance seems to be a final result; it is as if we overhear him in yet one more attempt to unravel complete and total meaning. His pausing often seems excessive and eccentric because, one feels, his mind has come across yet another possibility and he must stop to weigh and wonder.

It was noticeable in *Macbeth* how this process forced him to eschew the rhythm of single lines. He worked in short phrases, single blurted and blunted words. The effect was to keep the audience tense with expectation at what would come next – not from the actor's body (for Scofield the physical is secondary to the verbal) but from his throat and lips. He emphasised sibilants, 'he's here in double trust' (I.vii.12); he whispered a great deal, ''Twere well / It were done *quickly*,' (I.vii.1–2); he rose or dropped a register with almost sensational ease and effect,'but *(high)* . . . judgment *(low)* here *(high)*' (I.vii.7–8); his pauses were often long and daring like the one before, 'Not bear the knife myself' (I.vii.16).

He revealed something of Olivier's onomatopoeic ability, as in 'light thickens' (with the second word pronounced as if it had three n's); 'clutch thee' he pronounced as if the first word were tied tight about his throat; 'abuse the curtain'd sleep' he spoke with a very deliberate isolating of the vowel sounds to increase their different sound values.

The *Macbeth* which opened in 1974 held two major surprises. The first was the casting of the tragic hero and the second was the close proximity of the director's to Hall's 'Christian' version.

Nicol Williamson was not everyone's idea of a natural choice for Macbeth. An actor of many technical accomplishments, he had acquired a name more for a particular brand of unpredictability than for the depth of discipline required for a major Shakespearian role. Yet, in a sense, perhaps it was inevitable that, in one respect at least, the successor to Peter Hall as artistic director of the RSC should have wished to make a radical gesture. Trevor Nunn, with a handful of splendid personal productions to his credit, and at least an equal number by others under his directorate, still had not established a clear set of fingerprints, a trade mark, on this company which categorically was different from Hall's. Perhaps Nunn, in choosing Williamson, was more radical than he knew, for in hindsight, Williamson can perhaps be seen as the forerunner of a truly 'contemporary' style of acting which has characterised the end of the 1970s and the beginning of the 1980s at Stratford. In future this may come to be seen as an early sign of Nunn's handprint on this theatre. It is a style perpetrated and developed (if that be the apt word) by Alan Howard and Jonathan Pryce, and its characteristics have percolated, and are percolating, through the lesser hosts both in Stratford and elsewhere.

It is introvertive to such a degree as sometimes to seem to ignore the presence of others on the stage. The actor 'recites' to his colleagues rather than engaging them in dialogue. Nervy physical movement – restless, often permissively ungainly in appearance – is unceasing. His speaking of dramatic poetry conspicuously avoids the benedictions of rhythm and the other resources of poetry; and, in the prose, punctuation's logic is overlooked. In this style, the voice seems deliberately to avoid grace-notes and seems intent on a kind of harshness of tone and expression – often, indeed, it seems to be produced by methods that run contrary to all established modes of voice-production and stage-speaking (and, it may be added, of medical safety).

A simplistic opinion may declare this style as the epitome of the 1970s' philosophy of 'doing your own thing'. Certainly, it lacks that particular charm which implies that the actor is as much aware of his relationship to the company about him as he is of himself. There is a kind of stony-faced selfishness about it, which some might think is a reflection of the characteristic facial imagery of the 1970s. Employed with technical skill, it is often theatrically sensational in impact and it is certainly the best acting style that has yet emerged which seems custom-built to make Shakespeare 'speak to the twentieth century'. Its chief weakness is its total avoidance of everything that is meant, both in human and theatrical terms, by the word 'grace'.

Williamson's adhesion to the ur-version of this style of acting is well evidenced by Irving Wardle's comment – 'Mr Williamson stands as a secretive man who becomes more and more unreachable until by the end the events are happening only inside his head.'[20] And the access of unpredictability and eccentricity is implicit both in the phrase 'get your face hence', which he accompanies by cutting the servant's face with a knife, and in his twelve-second pause after the announcement that 'the Queen, my lord, is dead'.

But for all Williamson's eye-rolling eccentricities and Helen Mirren's undoubted natural advantage to aid her in a depiction of Lady Macbeth as almost wholly sexually orientated, and whose fall from normalcy is seen as a direct consequence of sexual deprivation following Macbeth's attempted insulation of himself after Banquo's murder, it was Nunn's production which excited the longest-lasting comment.

His adherence to Hall's conception of the play extended as far as a concentration on the realities of evil, crime and horror. Nunn's set was a dark wood interior which resembled nothing so much as a large church or cathedral – in fact it served to depict three events which do not occur in Shakespeare's play – the coronations of Duncan, Macbeth and Malcolm. Atmospheric organ-playing accompanied the flickering of four massive candelabra'd candles.

Indeed, the imagery seemed in all to be a mixture of Christian and Black Magic: the blind Duncan's crown was topped by a cross, the witches carried inverted crosses, and hung (at their first entrance) from a chandelier. One notable directorial innovation was the bringing in and displaying of Duncan's body – on seeing it Lady Macbeth collapsed: a neatly achieved visual justification for her fainting.

Nunn miscast his Macbeth and Lady Macbeth and, in so doing, achieved a curiously freakish result. But there was a relentlessly careful, detailed and impressive evocation of menace and evil in his production.

Trevor Nunn did not repeat his casting error for his second production of the play in Stratford's small Studio Theatre, The Other Place, in 1977.

The new venture was presented at a time when his small theatre had reached a high point of artistic recognition and was about to challenge the main auditorium for pride of place in artistic quality and success. It was no longer regarded as an annexe to the main house, and production after production testified to the undeniable advantages to be gained from the necessary economy and constriction which were the inevitable results of working in a very small space.

Nunn exploited this space with great discipline, and this was no dwarf version of his previous production. The set was virtually non-existent – a few wooden boxes, a bell, a rope, a few lamps were all the stage furniture used and which he surrounded with austere blackness. His one concession to 'design' was a painted circle on the floor – a relic, perhaps, of the Black Magic imagery of his previous *Macbeth*. The company was small and Nunn adopted (but did not, as several critics stated at the time, invent) the practice of players sitting around the playing area watching those parts of the action that did not involve them and springing into illusion when their cue arrived. At this time this process was not the slightly twee self-conscious cliché of stage-technique it has since become.

The acting surrounding the Principals – Ian McKellen and Judi Dench – was, by far, the strongest of the period under review: notably John Woodvine's physically tough, slightly calculating, near flash-point Banquo; Roger Rees's intelligent, handsome, spiritually exhausted Malcolm, totally aware of the knife-edge he trod between Macbeth's murderous existence and Macduff's unknown motivation; and Griffith Jones's Duncan, saintly in look, grave and deliberate in speech – every inch the good king, yet in the first encounter with Macbeth seeming to be very vulnerable to age and to the obvious political eying and weighing of the court around him.

Judi Dench's Lady Macbeth was so far superior to her modern predecessors that it was easy to forget, if one knew, that she had publicly expressed a determination that she would never be asked to play the role after what sounds like a ludicrous experience on tour with the play in Africa.[21] The blackness of her enveloping robe and turban-like head-cover was relieved only by the pallor of her face. Her relative youthfulness, the caressing huskiness of her voice, and the curiously sensual chubbiness of her face all suggested sexual potency. But the pallor, the terror which her eyes could show, and the fact that both her voice and her face are capable of shifting into hardness and coldness, immensely increased the dimension of her playing.

She was a dangerous but determined amateur in crime; an unknowing but eager meddler in supernatural soliciting; a novice, but a quick learner, in the art of disguising her emotions. When she sank to her knees in her later wild anguish her gown swirled large and looked like a huge black surrounding stain. If Olivier collected together all the ambiguities and paradoxes of Macbeth, Judi Dench assembled the parsimoniously scattered bits and pieces of character-evidence, and made of Lady Macbeth what she so often fails to be in performance – a venomous but vulnerable and credible human being.

Ian McKellen has always seemed to have to conquer a prevailing idea that he is slightly too young to play the Shakespeare roles he has attempted in a career which is far longer than most theatre-goers realise. Saving his grace, he was no longer very young when he played Macbeth, but there was admittedly about his performance a youthful litheness of body, speech and mental quickness which suggested the green time of life. His Macbeth had, physically, a tigerish spareness – though McKellen is far from being scrawny and delicate – and an alertness which had a strongly dual characteristic.

It is perhaps a unique and noticeable feature of McKellen's acting that it not only seems watchful of everything about it but is also watchful of itself – he is doubly alert. This eminently suited the depiction of Macbeth's terrible *caravanserai* inside his own imagination: the effect was to hypnotise the audience as they, in their turn, watched this man look with horror on what was happening inside and outside himself.

McKellen is also an actor who uses his physical attributes to the uttermost: the daggers rattled uncontrollably in his shaking hand; the smile that crossed his face after his coronation was ghastly and over-large; his eyes kept pace with the litany of absurdity, so to speak, that unfolds in the 'Tomorrow' speech, and changed in expression from disgust to mocking wryness, to incredulity.

In speaking, he was not averse to the use of stammer, and he sometimes elongated a pause as if he dared the audience to stay with him – notably in the 'Tomorrow' soliloquy. If his physical acting was sometimes reminiscent of Olivier's in its audacity – though it avoided, in its stabbing movements, Olivier's tendency to ritualise movement and leave patterns in the air – his speaking displayed something, not only of Scofield's searching for comprehensive meaning, but also his surprising inflections and his espousal of pauses. Yet McKellen almost always stopped short of eccentricity of speech, risking it only in sometimes overstaying a consonant, particularly 'm', as in 'tomorrow', 'trammel', 'most need of blessing'.

This Macbeth, slim and dark-suited in modernity, looked slightly Japanese with its sleeked black hair and slightly slanting eyes. Perhaps this was more than a personal fortuitous impression, for the very production itself (as have a number of Nunn's) seemed to be attempting to express the mixture of inner reflective quietude and physical ritualism which we take to be characteristic of eastern culture. Every movement and moment appeared designed, every word seemed weighed, every statement seemed as much directed to an inner self as to a listening observer.

In the final analysis perhaps, what this production and tragic hero lacked was a sense of chaos, both internal and external, and a sense of damnation – ritual and reflection seemed to insulate this Macbeth from the ultimate despair. It was, nevertheless, a theatrical experience of immense power and skill. It achieved the kind of indelibility in the memory which, ironically, might well sentence Stratford theatregoers and actors alike to another seven years' absence from this play's rich and frightening potency.

NOTES

1 See for example, D. Addenbrooke, *The Royal Shakespeare Company - The Peter Hall Years*, (1974) and M. Mullin (ed.), *Macbeth On Stage - an annotated facsimile of Glen Byam Shaw's 1955 Promptbook*, (University of Missouri, 1976).
2 A popular cry of many theatre directors in the 1960s - the implications are enthusiastically reflected upon in an essay 'Shakespeare and the Modern Director' in *Royal Shakespeare Theatre Company: 1960-3* (1963).
3 Ruth Ellis, *Stratford-upon-Avon Herald*, 28 June 1946.
4 *Birmingham Post*, 18 April 1949.
5 *Birmingham Mail*, 18 April 1949.
6 Ibid.
7 Cecil Wilson, *Daily Mail*, 11 June 1952.
8 *Evening Standard*, 13 June 1952.
9 Mullin, *op. cit.*, p. 251.
10 Milton Shulman, *Evening Standard*, 8 June 1955.
11 *Stratford-upon-Avon Herald*, 8 June 1955.
12 Shulman, *op. cit.*
13 Dennis Bartholomeusz, *Macbeth and the Players* (Cambridge, 1969), p. 259.
14 *The Times*, 6 June 1962.
15 Ken Griffin, *South Wales Evening Argus*, 6 June 1962.
16 Gareth Lloyd Evans, the *Guardian*, 6 June 1962.
17 Gareth Lloyd Evans, 'Shakespeare and the Actors', *Shakespeare Survey*, 21 (1968), p. 124.
18 Quoted in Addenbrooke, *op. cit.*, p. 147.
19 Gareth Lloyd Evans, *op. cit.*, p. 123.
20 *The Times*, 30 October 1974.
21 'Judi Dench talks to Gareth Lloyd Evans', *Shakespeare Survey*, 27 (1974), p. 141.

Part 3

Enacting
the text

6

'Multiplying villainies of nature'

Robin Grove

Some Shakespearean Themes: the title of course is that of
L.C. Knights's splendid book (1959), and, in the world of
Shakespeare studies, work such as Professor Knights has
done is too valuable for us to dream of going back on it
now. All the same, I doubt that 'themes' draw many people
to read the plays or to watch them in the theatre. The word
suggests a more abstract interest than we actually take; and
certainly the best critics, including Knights, have been aware
of this. They would say, rightly, that it is hard in written
essays to convey much sense of just how vivid the drama is,
and harder still to keep it present to one's readers throughout
a full-length book. Perhaps inevitably, what we write about is
not Shakespeare exactly, but a more or less immobilized
literary text. So discussion even of *Macbeth* is liable to be
formed by the expectations of book-readers like ourselves:

> The main theme of the reversal of values is given out
> simply and clearly in the first scene - 'fair is foul, and foul
> is fair'; and with it are associated premonitions of the
> conflict, disorder and moral darkness into which Macbeth
> will plunge himself. Well before the end of the first act
> we are in possession not only of the positive values against
> which the Macbeth evil will be defined but of the related
> aspects of that evil . . . . All these impressions, which as
> the play proceeds assume the status of organizing ideas,
> are produced by the interaction of all the resources of
> poetic drama - action, contrast, statement, implication,
> imagery and allusion.
>
> (*Some Shakespearean Themes*, ch.VI)

There is no need to list other occasions on which something similar has been said, though seldom so persuasively. Yet is it really through 'action, contrast, statement, implication, imagery and allusion' that poetic drama mainly works? It seems to me that we experience *Macbeth* in more immediate ways. Experience it, too, as something other than 'themes' and 'values' and 'aspects' and 'ideas' – terms which direct us specifically into modes of *thought*, whereas drama like this is capable of taking the place of 'thought'. Not that it is sub-intellectual, or that we will see more by closing our eyes to the words on Shakespeare's page: quite the reverse, in fact. The common separation of 'text' (suitable for academic study) from 'theatre' is itself an impoverishment of both, since great drama prompts us to be sensuously intelligent: bodily, intuitively – it engages us as deeply as that. Yet whenever we bring our criticism nearer this ideal, we do so by closer, not looser, attention to what Shakespeare has written and shaped.

Where *Macbeth* starts, then, is the place to start. Probably, the witches chanting 'Fair is foul' is what we all remember best, but what is it that we hear and see?

Nothing like the ghost in *Hamlet*, for a start. Coleridge's famous account of that play's opening – 'the armour, the dead silence, the watchfulness that first interrupts it, the welcome relief of guard, the cold, the broken expressions as of a man's compelled attention to bodily feelings' – conveys the eeriness Shakespeare can send through detail after detail of common physical life. 'Even the word "again" has its *credibilizing* effect.' But the witches have no such reality. They are not 'characters' exactly – not even conventional scene-starters, like Marcellus and the rest – so much as disembodied voices. A couple of editors have supposed that the balcony of the Globe was used, so the actors might appear to hover over the stage; but however the scene was played, its rhyming chant half-dehumanizes what we hear – which anyway is alien enough: [1]

When the hurly burly's done,
When the battle's lost, and won.

To human participants a battle is either lost *or* won (nobody is on both sides at once), whereas these voices toss the outcomes disorientingly together. Besides, it hardly matters which of the three is speaking, since they sound more like one being than like several, if they are human at all. But then, they are witches, creatures who would turn the world inside-out, to make fair simply foul; and if the effect is strange, then so it has to be, for to proclaim No is Yes causes bewildering collisions in the mind. A 'reversal of values', 'a kind of metaphysical pitch-and-toss' – L.C. Knights's description catches the self-annulling contradictions of their language, bent on thwarting ordinary life and sense.

All the same, we might wonder if the witches are so disturbing. It is usual to claim they are, and to speak of the evil, the menace and so on represented by this opening scene. Yet, however ready we may be to take the thematic hint, the effect of the poetry here and now is surely half-comic and banal. How can metaphysical implications be taken seriously, voiced in rhythms like these? What the witches pass back and forth among themselves is a childish-sounding stock-in-trade. They speak gloating doggerel, in fact. And just as they won't make much flesh creep with that, neither will they with supernaturalism like this:

I come, Gray-Malkin.
> Paddock calls.
> > Anon.

Notes on witchcraft, how feared and where practised, will hardly strengthen the poetry here, not even appeals to James I's known interest, or to the beliefs of the 'average Jacobean'. For the Jacobean Mind held various opinions, as the Modern Mind does too, and concerning witchcraft was capable of being sceptical, the King himself (who changed his views after his *Daemonologie* was published in 1597)[2], being inclined to hold it 'but a mere conceit'. So we are under no obligation to suppose that Shakespeare's play was written out of or directed to credulity, and what we make of its 'Weyard' women must be a matter of critical judgment and comparison, as always. If evocations of evil are in question, then Goneril and Regan, Volumnia, Lady Macbeth herself, daunt us far more than these creatures.

But there is one thing the witches do have, and that is a potent music of their own. From the first line, their sing-song nags in the brain. It is not great poetry; that is just the point; language trivialized to the witches' doggerel will not carry serious meaning's ordinary weight, and to make human meanings feel spurious and banal is what they aim to do. Opening the play, they claim its ground from the start, and the self-assured ordinariness, almost, with which they set about inverting sense is obscurely shocking, as one writer says. 'They have managed to put themselves forward as the chorus; at first they do represent what is normal in the play, and so are terrible. For if the witches are what is normal in the world, the world is hell, nor are we out of it.'[3] So, malevolent, and weird, yet banally commonplace: it is an unnerving combination, and its workings spread an inner destruction through the play.

I don't mean that this is because the witches succeed in tempting Macbeth. Tempting is hardly what they do: they merely declare what the future *will be*. But their voices get into the mind, and that is what makes the difference. It's as though in the primitive region of the play such voices are in the air, part of the blowing northern cold of a wilder climate, inhospitable, murky, where fog and darkness come down, light thickens, days close in threateningly - a bleak half-savage place: Scotland, not England, Wilbur Sanders argues in a recent essay[4] - and to this environment, pervading it like the weather, the witches' sing-song music belongs. Three high whining syllables start it off. 'When shall *we three meet* again?': the ugly sound is not carelessness on Shakespeare's part, but a way of setting in motion 'Shakespearean themes', of a different kind: audible motifs - in which the germ of the tragedy lies.

> we three meet
> done   and won   the set of sun
>   Upon the *heath*
> There to *meet* with *Macbeth*

We are close to the possibilities of something like a musical score. But that exaggerates. Language cannot be sounds alone, it is meaning as well, whatever the witches claim; so the analogy with music remains analogy, nothing more.[5] As such, though, it helps us realize what is being done by the opening scene, for while verse of this quality is without power to create large significances, or even 'character' humanly speaking, it does have the capacity a phrase of music might, to express a nature, which is the essential thing after all.

116

Essentially, it is the means whereby these creatures perform the nature *they* have inside the play's imaginary world.

They are wind-hags perhaps, as Richard Flatter calls them;[6] certainly the sound of their voices suggests it, sawing, wailing, in a cheerlessly mocking to and fro, as they echo vowels between them ('again', 'vain') and vanish into 'air' as eerily as they came.

> Fair is foul, and foul is fair,
> Hover through the fog and filthy air.

A last drawn-out cry on the word, and they are gone. But wind-witches or not, the rhythmic back-and-forth of their speeches penetrates the play. In fact the music of the opening, degraded and trite though it is, works *as* dramatic music with a directness that conceptualizing seldom has. There is even a further hint of how the full score of the scene might have been played, since the lineation of the First Folio is almost certainly a mistake. What was printed is pointlessly unmetrical, and makes poor sense as well:

> 1   I come, *Gray-Malkin.*
> *All Padock* calls anon: faire is foule and foule is faire

whereas the usual modern emendation removes both these blots:

> 1   I come, *Gray-Malkin.*
> 2   *Paddock* calls.
> 3   Anon.

and in doing so it virtually necessitates a change in performance too; for the voices now form a dialogue in which each hag is answering her familiar. Thus a cat's cry summons the first witch, a toad's the second; and when the third witch replies 'Anon', Davenant's stage-direction of 1666 records what perhaps had been happening in the theatre since Shakespeare's time, inserting 'A Shriek like an Owl'.[7] Three inhuman cries, three answers to them: the to-fro of the witch-music is extended, beyond even language here.

It was Coleridge who called the 'lyric' that opens *Macbeth* 'the key-note of the character of the whole play'. Usually, it is safe to suppose that 'key-note' is a dead metaphor which no one need bother to inspect. In this play, however, there is more to the term than that. Coleridge himself hardly follows his own suggestion far, but audibly enough after the chantings of scene 1 the King and his followers are allowed only one brief interlude before the witches' music starts up again, spreading deeper into the action of the play. Its doggerel is doggerel still, but begins now to lead us into a whole tonality of malice, petty yet naggingly spiteful:

1   Where hast thou been, sister?
2   Killing swine.
3   Sister, where thou?
1   A sailors wife had chestnuts in her lap,
    And mounch'd, and mounch'd, and mounch'd.

It leads us into an insistent rhythm also, difficult either to stabilize or to escape:

2   I'll give thee a wind.
1   Th'art kind.
3   And I another.
1   I my self have all the other,
    And the very ports they blow.
    All the quarters that they know,
    I'th' Ship-man's card.
    I'll drain him dry as hay:
    Sleep shall neither night nor day
    Hang upon his pent-house lid.

This is scarcely Evil in any adult sense of the word, but neither is it 'atmosphere' or 'background'. It *is* the drama – a transaction between the stage and us, whereby the witches' nature is voiced and embodied and trodden out in a ritual or round, 'about, about', until, having honoured their three familiars ('Thrice to thine, and thrice to mine, / And thrice again'), and enforced and reinforced the pattern of the spell, the preparation is complete, onstage, and in our, the audience's, rhythmic consciousness too.

Peace, the charm's wound up.

So, 'Enter *Macbeth* and *Banquo.*'

But now stranger patterns show. The witches' music, un-
heard by Macbeth, is none the less the first thing *we* hear
from *him*, when he enters on words that chime exactly with
those the 'Weyard women' spoke two scenes before.

So foul and fair a day I have not seen

he says; and with that, our dismissively sceptical judgments
have to be revised. The witches are more powerful than we
had thought. This doesn't mean they cease to be grotesque;
sensibly examined, they are never as frightening as superstition might expect. But even while the sensible mind is
noticing how nastily ridiculous they are, a deeper, auditory
imagination is at work. For embodied by the actors and
correspondingly realized in us is a distinctive rhythm, and a
tonal quality to go with it. The mind, or the securely thought-
ful judgment, is not going to be shaken by what the witches
say, but bodily imagination may be, and it may tell the
deeper truth, that our response to such evocations is not
wholly under intelligence's control. If in us, then, the absurd-
compulsive chanting goes about, about, so much the worse
is it to be met by Macbeth's first words. His will and judgment
have not even been put to the test, yet already the witches'
music has somehow got into his head.

An echoed phrase, a repetition, is not enough to damn the
man. Between this and murder is a gulf indeed. But to understand where Macbeth's murderousness comes from has always
been hard, and the most resorted-to explanation is that it
was slumbering in him anyway: secretly, he wanted to be
King. That makes an ordinary kind of sense, only it is not
quite what Shakespeare shows. He gives us a man saying
'foul and fair' instead, and an unfolding pattern of which
that is part. Put aside the standard accounts of the play as a
tragedy of Ambition, therefore. Shakespeare intimates that
self-destruction is more mysterious, and more commonplace.
Macbeth struggles with conscience only after he has found it
possible, in 'thought', to murder the King; and it is to the
sides of his already moving 'intent' that he applies the spur of
vaulting ambition. To him, if he can but bring himself to
believe it, foul *is* fair already.

In other words, what the murder comes from, so the
drama seems to show, is some equivocation or irresponsibility;

not just in Macbeth himself, but (worse still) glimpsed at the heart of things. This takes us beyond the old considerations of the hero's fatal flaw, and in any case the tragedy of a great man greatly tempted would be easier to cope with than what we actually find, which is a conscience caught into self-destruction: suddenly and without warning caught into a state of disbelief or self-undoing, where previous certainties are lost and nothing holds as it used to at some sticking-place. More than Macbeth's private affliction, the possibility is at large in the world itself, an equivocation in *it*. For 'Nature' in the play is no longer a standard to which we can appeal. If it is welcoming, it is violent too; it as readily becomes the ravined salt-sea shark as the temple-haunting martlet, and night's black agents rousing to their preys are as much part of it as the good things of day. Nor does the natural order discriminate between these opposites (as they seem to us): what *we* call Good and Evil simply occur: 'what is't you do?' 'A deed without a name.' So whatever humane statute may exist is founded in ourselves, Nature refusing that responsibility. Perhaps the desolate northern landscape of the play, bleakly indifferent to that irrelevance, Mankind, helps disintegrate the assurances bred in more comforting climates. At all events in *Thunder and Lightning* the play begins, and a see-saw chanting which, far from establishing that the witches are evil, does its best to unseat the supposition that moral qualities might be real. With that, the play's attack on certitude begins, and the treacheries of the next scene plunge us deeper still.

For when it comes to Cawdor, we never know why he rebelled. The King himself can say only that 'He was a gentleman, on whom I built / An absolute trust' – not bitter, Duncan's pause upon 'gentleman', but regretful and uncomprehending. The odd thing is that Cawdor similarly seems not to understand. What caused him to be a traitor is itself strange to him at the end. He implores pardon, his treasons are confessed with deep repentance, and he dies

> As one that had been studied in his death,
> To throw away the dearest thing he ow'd,
> As 'twere a careless trifle. (I.iv.9–11)

But in this, where is the man? Those last moments may perhaps show the true nobility some commentators claim on his behalf, contrasting them with Macbeth's unremorseful end; but it is at least arguable that the gesture is that of a man so little *in* himself that what is dearest to him can be lost as if it meant nothing really. Cawdor, it turns out, was not even recognized by the loyal general confronting him with self-comparisons, rebellious arm 'gainst arm; instead, a change-and-change-about of parts is what we seem to see, where treason gives place to frank confession, Rebel to Penitent, and death is studied up while life is tossed away 'As 'twere a careless trifle'; until in the end all comes to nothing, as though Cawdor too had been overtaken by the self-undoing reversals the first scene set in motion.

So when Macbeth enters to 'th'self-same tune, and words' as those the witches spoke, a pattern is developing all right, but not one we could elucidate through imagery to any large extent, or comprehend in symbols, allusions, and similar modes of literary thought. Even 'pattern' may suggest something less unsettling than we find, for if the play does not exist for the sake of revealing the hero's 'character', as critics some generations ago tended to suppose, neither does it invite us simply to stand back and observe. Certainly, in taking Cawdor's title Macbeth succeeds to his treachery as well. 'What he hath lost, noble Macbeth hath won', Duncan declares; so, 'dramatic irony' it is usual to note. Nothing much to do with us, then, we might be tempted to feel; these parallels, coincidences and so on are invisible to the characters (that is where the Irony comes in), but can be relished by an audience, *hors de combat*. Thus understood, Shakespeare's art confirms the spectators in their intellectuality – or to put it another way, reinforces a privileged overview, a strictly limited involvement.

Grasping the plays, however, let alone living one's way through them, is not so easy. If we had only to observe ironic parallels and contrasts, our externality would stand firm; but what exactly is it we experience here?

King. No more that Thane of Cawdor shall deceive
      Our bosom interest: Go pronounce his present death,
      And with his former title greet Macbeth.
Ross. I'll see it done.
King. What he hath lost, noble Macbeth hath won.

The rhymes mark the end of the scene, as the title passes from Cawdor to Macbeth. But can it be the case that in this moment - and from *Duncan* - we catch an echo of the witch-music heard right at the start of the play?

When the hurly burly's done	done
When the battle's lost, and won	lost . . .won
Upon the heath	death
There to meet with Macbeth	greet Macbeth

We must wonder what such echoes are doing: are they even, really, to be heard? Yet our very uncertainty about them is an essential part of the effect; and carries us outside considerations of 'character' and 'theme', to feel in our own unsure imaginations just how stabilities are set rocking, from the first scene on.

Not being able to state clearly, and so gain some mastery over, our experience - being obliged instead to undergo it, as we half-hear echoes or intuit a rhythm in part: these open, shifting, moment-by-moment presentations of possibility are the means whereby 'plot', 'character' and the rest come to us in a play. And they're reculiarly important to *Macbeth*. For identity itself is under siege in Macbeth, and in the Nature we glimpse around him what is to stop any man from similar self-undoing? Where Nature has no moral identity, that risk seems inherent in things. And so the witches spend no time 'tempting' the man at all: they simply tell him who he is - except that that means telling him he is not who he believes himself to be. 'All hail Macbeth, hail to thee Thane of Cawdor.' Bradley objected that no innocent man would have started as Macbeth does on hearing the witches' greetings, but I cannot say that his flinching strikes me as proof of 'an inward and terrifying guilt'. Rather, he is told that, without knowing it, he is both himself and someone else, and the fact comes like a blow in the pit of the self, turning the rational mind to helplessness at that old dilemma of metaphysics, the impossibility of two identities occupying the one place. For how can he be Cawdor when 'the Thane of Cawdor lives / A prosperous gentleman'? The witches make no effort to explain, but simply prophesy he will be King hereafter - at which his body starts in fearful recognition that neither present nor future self is what he had thought it to be. With dreadful swiftness he is 'rapt', hardly capable even of doubt. 'Your children shall be kings', he says to Banquo: no disbelief in that, only deep-toned wonder at what things 'shall be'.

His wonder – that it should be so – is at once the most poignant and the most dangerous response he could make.

> Whither are they vanish'd?

Into the air: and what seem'd corporal, melted,
As breath into the wind. Would they had stay'd.

In the face of that mystery, an almost reverent quietness is what we hear. But his 'went it not so?' can never last. Macbeth's nature has been dislodged into indeterminacy, and his little space of quietness is an eddy in the wake of that. The witches vanish, melting like breath, and wonder gives place to a sleep-walking giddiness as he sways on the brink of what he is going to do. Between inner and outer worlds, held a moment, he is at the crucial juncture of the play, and the long pause out of which he speaks might well be marked, if we needed the indication, by what Richard Flatter called the Nought[8] – the deliberate cease of language at the point where other, non-verbal forces are at work inside the line.

> [————————] This supernatural soliciting
> Cannot be ill; cannot be good. If ill? [———]
> Why hath it given me earnest of success,
> Commencing in a truth? I am Thane of Cawdor.
> If good? [———] why do I yield to that suggestion,
> Whose horrid image doth unfix my hair,
> And make my seated heart knock at my ribs,
> Against the use of Nature? Present fears
> Are less than horrible imaginings: [————————]
> My thought, whose murder yet is but fantastical,
> Shakes so my single state of man, that function
> Is smother'd in surmise, and nothing is,
> But what is not.

For an instant he sways between 'ill?' and 'good?', unable to choose or to reject, and then he is falling away, falling into the deed he is going to commit. He asks, not 'Will I yield?' (the question of a tempted man), but 'Why do I yield?' amazed that he is already overcome: for present fears *are* less than his imaginings while the heart knocks at the ribs and his hair seems to stir with a life of its own, as though far below the conscious mind were something in him struggling to get free. And it is not just horror that he feels at this: there is ecstasy in giving way to so dreadful a thing and heeling over into its power. From 'thought', to 'murder', he plunges in a choking spasm where surmise smothers function and 'is' is turned into 'what is not.'

In a new dimension now, and a far more potent one, the rhythms of the speech replay the to-fro of the witches' chanting. Their 'fair is foul, and foul is fair' invaded Macbeth's first speech, but repeatedly the rhythm beats through his head as though their prophecies were coming true inside him. 'Cannot be ill; cannot be good. If ill? . . . if good? My thought, whose murder; function . . . surmise; nothing is, / But what is not:' there is all the difference in the world between the opposites, and yet compulsively his imagination leaps the gap. And it is striking how often the most powerful poetry in the play comes to the gulf, gap, distance, between one state and the next: as when 'upon this bank and shoal of time, / We'd jump the life to come' (I.vii.6–7). The first acts in particular are full of metaphors suggesting something just out of reach you must strain and leap to get. But your own self is one of those things; as in some unmanageable dream-logic, the strain is felt there, in the self (felt in movements of struggling, choking, tensed against the use of Nature, until each corporal agent is bent up to this terrible feat), while at the same time it is one's self which is strained *after* – that self which must be repossessed since insurrection has so shaken its single state that the eye dreads to see what the hand will do, yet at some deeper level still that-which-will-be-done is passionately longed for all the same.

The poetry is extraordinarily complex, then. But more than poetry is involved. Verbal meanings are where we start from, by realizing how often the most basic of all verbs, the verb 'to be', appears, for that is one sign of the metaphysical struggle to grasp identity. So, 'I know I am Thane of Glamis', declares Macbeth, 'but how, of Cawdor? The Thane of Cawdor lives' – what therefore happens to 'I am'? – 'And to be King, / Stands not within the prospect of belief, / No more than to be Cawdor.' His bewilderment rings true, yet already 'I am' is straining towards 'shall be', and as it does so, the things to come are suddenly over and complete. He *is* Cawdor; there is no room for prophecy, all is ratified present fact, and what appeared the future is behind him after all. Maybe then he will be king also by no action of his own. 'If chance will have me king' (the verb again) 'why chance may crown me, / Without my stir' – but it is too late for him to say so, stirred as he is at the very thought of being crowned, his heart at his ribs, hair rising of its own accord, as the imagined crime takes on a life of its own. And so it continues, one tense leaping across another – 'if it were done, when *'tis* done' – for the murder is going to happen; in some region of his mind, inexplicably, it already has.

If there is terror in it, there is a sort of joy as well. Desires mounting up like this make us feel how huge the gap is between thought and action, but simultaneously produce the strength to leap it. There is a glorious seizing of the wish to turn it into fact, as Lady Macbeth cries 'Glamis thou art, and Cawdor, and shalt be / What thou art promised', and her voice shudders in triumphant arrival at the future it demands. No other drama I can think of makes such play with the headlong plunge of tenses. Even its opening word is 'When shall we three meet again?'; and to speak of the velocity of the first three acts is commonplace, they move at such a speed. Between one happening and the next there seems almost literally no time, as if the future had already become past. Yet the time was there for a man to choose, resist, decide; it was available all along. There *was* a gap between imaginary murder and the real thing, room for Macbeth to turn back – only he realizes that too late. And here we move beyond what is 'said' by the poetry, into the drama's non-verbal regions instead. For why is it too late? Why is it that from the first meeting with the witches, indeed, the murder is going to happen – in some deep of Macbeth's nature, it already has, and he has yielded to that 'suggestion' by which he is both terrified and entranced? Banquo, typically, sees the process as one of choice: for him, the question is whether one should or should not trust what the witches say. For Macbeth, however, it is different. To suppose him fated to kill the king would be at odds with the tragedy altogether; Shakespeare is not a Greek dramatist, we might say. But to speak of a tragedy of conscience seems almost as far from the point. Macbeth's struggle is not with his conscience, but with himself in a different sense: his identity: who he is; and he is the man who is Glamis, and Cawdor, and will be what he is promised, King. All three identities are true, and the swelling act of the imperial theme has thus begun inside him. What is alive there is something that, drugging conscience, leaves that conscience victim to forces and impulsions he can neither understand nor choose between: he yields to them, even as they shake, unfix, and smother his state of man. No doubt, to yield knowingly as he does makes him guilty of the wish, as later he will be of the deed. Yet to speak of 'guilt' as though he had freely chosen what rises inside him belittles the terror of a state in which conscience, will, identity itself, all lose the power of action, going to th' self-same tune of 'Nothing is, / But what is not' that the witches had put into the mind.

Standard notions of character, or of action for that matter, hardly help us here. The drama occurs in pauses, suspensions, felt movements of language, as well as in what the verse formally states. Of course there are dangers in claiming so. For one thing, what I am calling non-verbal effects are themselves created through language which is able to realize feelings prior to thought, sensations, intuited states, and so on. Besides, whatever else Shakespearian drama does, words as such are central. Nevertheless, with Eliot's warnings against 'musical analogies' in mind, what he says in 'The Music of Poetry' seems relevant all the same:[9]

> I know that a poem, or a passage of a poem, may tend to realize itself first as a particular rhythm before it reaches expression in words, and that this rhythm may bring to birth the idea and the image.

So it is here: some things in this play realize themselves initially as rhythm, before (or without) reaching expression in words. Subliminal might be the term we want. There are powerful, baffling continuities between what is happening within Macbeth, and what the witches say. It is still necessary, though, to emphasize the mysteriousness by which Macbeth is neither a voluntary agent altogether, nor on the other hand a pawn, and the 'Weyard' sisters neither external to him simply, nor reflections of his mind, but both, and both at once, for equivocal realities are the substance of the play. As Bradley argued:[10]

> The words of the witches are fatal to the hero only
> because there is in him something which leaps into light

at the sound of them; but they are at the same time the witness of forces which never cease to work in the world around him.

> (*Shakespearean Tragedy* (1904), Lecture IX, 2)

And even that does not adequately convey how the audience in turn is caught into this equivocating to-fro, as we take up stresses, pauses, echoes into ourselves. From the witches' words, 'at the sound of them' indeed, the tragedy stirs into life.

It is by these means that the experiences of the play are not merely talked about, or cited, but made real. There is some point in restating the truism in order to add: realized in the reader, the audience, us – for where else do they take place? But to say that our own imaginations give these experiences the reality they now have is not to claim that we see events as the characters in the work, or even its author, might. On the contrary, we make things real for *us* – which means judging, estimating, weighing any fictional world against our comprehension of ourselves and our daily world. And the easier it is to do so, the less we value its fiction perhaps. We don't see much in it, as the saying goes; that is, it has failed to challenge us with anything like the complexity of life. What *Macbeth* confronts us with, however, is genuinely hard to meet. One reason why it has the power of great tragedy is that far from being able to hold ourselves aloof from the bewilderments of its world, we find something of their reality conveyed into us. The difference is, of course, that we don't suffer the tragedy on the same footing as its participants, but rather, since our experience includes all of theirs, are enabled to 'realize' (in both senses) what the tragedy is. Because it becomes *our* experience, the tragedy can shake the mind into which it enters – it would not be of tragic stature otherwise – at the same time, though, if only because we see it whole from a standpoint no character in the drama can attain, we are not subject to its onslaughts as its own figures are. So we neither master Shakespeare's tragedy, nor are mastered by it, but empowered and prompted by the movement of the work strive to make sense of it over all.

That is not easy, though. The very length of a play as it

passes through five acts prevents our grasping it all at once, so even at best an audience is liable to find each scene fading as another replaces it on the forestage of present attention. One achievement of modern criticism therefore has been to counter this, by showing the large 'symphonic' structure which drama like Shakespeare's may have. The internal unity of the plays (expanded metaphors, said Wilson Knight) has been demonstrated so convincingly that we take it for granted mostly, not separating for analysis the characters, atmosphere, plot, but perceiving a web of interrelations in which images recur and bear upon one another. Thus the plays, seen as unities, have been held steady in discussion – a good thing to have managed to have done. Nevertheless, it has had its drawbacks. On the one hand, in some recent criticism those expanded metaphors have set and the plays hardened into static objects which commentary and interpretation surround. 'Sources' are hunted out, historical backgrounds unrolled to display what is known as Shakespeare's indebtedness to medieval thought: no one will be at a loss to list all that lies deadeningly on top of particular works.[11] Meanwhile, however, other critics make them so excitingly mobile that drama disintegrates into an asteroid-belt of metaphors and phrases. Small matter if one speech originally occurred in the fifth act, and another in the first; each serves the purpose equally, when detached from context and its pressure of time and place and speaker: for if the play *is* a unity it is hardly relevant where individual moments came from first: all can be put into orbit, to travel in the same field of interest, unsequentially and at identical speed.

Perhaps it is not redundant, then, to say this is not what the experience of the drama in action is like. On the contrary, even reading for ourselves, let alone in the theatre, we are made aware of sequence and of the time it takes. In this sense too, 'symphonic' is the relevant term, for what I have called the witch-music gathers new and more powerful resonances as it rises into the human transactions of the play – those between Macbeth and Lady Macbeth above all. In their first scene together, so intensely present are they to one another that there passes between them not dialogue alone but a whole roused activity of spirit: to convey which takes all the orchestrated momentum of the drama to this point. So an essential impetus is lost when we treat the episode in the usual fashion, breaking it into speeches, since fragmented

like the dramatic rhythm of I, v is dislocated out of the
play. True enough, Lady Macbeth's speech, 'Come you
Spirits', is unforgettable even on its own; it is true too that
Macbeth has nothing comparable to offer when he enters
two-thirds of the way through. But really the entire scene is
played between them both, from Lady Macbeth's intent
absorbing of his letter,

> *They met me in the day of success: and I have learn'd*
> *by the perfect'st report, they have more in them, than*
> *mortal knowledge*

to her rising conviction that he and she together must set on
the swelling act of their imperial theme:

> Glamis thou art, and Cawdor, and shalt be
> What thou art promis'd . . . . Hie thee hither,
> That I may pour my spirits in thine ear,
> And chastise with the valour of my tongue
> All that impedes thee from the golden round.

(lines 12-25)

A Messenger enters; but his news intensifies, does not inter-
rupt, the mounting triumph of what is being played out
between the husband and wife. Already as by instinct *her*
speeches have caught the to-and-fro cradling movements
that, far beneath conscious will and effort, have been helping
to shape his: for just as Macbeth swayed back and forth over
the soliciting of 'Cannot be ill: cannot be good', so now,
from that scene arching into this, his rhythmic movements
(his and in some way the witches' too) begin to unfold in
his wife.

> What thou would'st highly,
> That would'st thou holily: would'st not play false,
> And yet would'st wrongly win.

So Lady Macbeth. And there is more, as her sayings thicken
into still more complicated weavings and plaitings of the
mind.

> Thou'dst have, great Glamis,
> That which cries, 'Thus must thou do', if thou have it;

And that which rather thou dost fear to do,
Than wishest should be undone.

It would be no use asking if she knows what she is wanting
or echoing here. We are at a depth beyond that. Directly, as
directly as in music, we are given an almost bodily to and fro
in which the mind is not sorting out distinctions so much as
being mesmerized from within: ill/good; highly/holily;
is/is not – words in this rhythm start to lose their defining
power.

But the loosening of those bonds opens the way to the
most powerful speech so far. Across two scenes the rhythm
shared by Macbeth and his wife leads up to the Messenger's
arrival with news of the coming of the King; from which,
immediately, Lady Macbeth takes more violent energy still.
She starts on a fling of bombast:

> The raven himself is hoarse,
> That croaks the fatal entrance of Duncan
> Under my battlements.   (lines 35-7)

It's a tearing boast, and flung out this way it gives her pent-up
force an instant, impatient release, before her voice drops to
the real nature of what she feels possible within her;

> Come you spirits,
> That tend on mortal thoughts, unsex me here,
> And fill me from the crown to the toe, top-full
> Of direst cruelty: make thick my blood,
> Stop up th'access, and passage to remorse,
> That no compunctious visitings of Nature
> Shake my fell purpose, nor keep peace between
> Th'effect, and it. Come to my woman's breasts,
> And take my milk for gall, you murd'ring ministers,
> Where-ever, in your sightless substances,
> You wait on Nature's mischief. Come thick night,
> And pall thee in the dunnest smoke of hell,
> That my keen knife see not the wound it makes,
> Nor heaven peep through the blanket of the dark,
> To cry, 'Hold, hold.'
>   (lines 37-51)

From the fostering, quiet, slow pace of 'Come you spirits',

a mounting movement, the clustering and pressing forward of syllables, produce in us, as in her, the sense of thickening and hindrance, the coagulation of nature, she so passionately wants. 'Make thick my blood, / Stop up th'access': the wish becomes physiological sensation in the words; and so too those compunctious (*compungere*) prickings: such feeble pricks will never shake *her* purpose, and 'visitings' registers their delicacy with scorn. For what she is demanding is that her instincts be outraged and gratified both at once, and the strangest thing about the speech is that it turns her yearning to be un-sexed into a triumphant *sexual* outcry. In the thrusting movement of the lines, the repeated 'Come . . . come', the blatant 'fill me . . . top-full . . . Stop up . . . the passage to remorse', sensual proclivities are fulfilled, reaching to a spasm of pleasure in the climax, 'Hold, hold'.

Yet even so there is gasping emptiness in that hoarse 'cry', no contented laying to rest; there can be no peace between 'th'effect, and it', only a shuddering pounce. The body to which she summons her murd'ring ministers gains neither release nor issue, only gall and blockage and the wound which the keen knife itself cannot see in the smothering dark. Thus, rendering the ferocity of her desires, Shakespeare renders their self-mutilating unnaturalness too, beyond anything she can acknowledge. Even as the poetry gives us, shockingly, the frontal pressure of this self in the throes of its rapture, there are realizations she doesn't (cannot?) bring fully to light. 'Cruelty', for example, is a word she relishes, but is it more than a word to her – 'direst cruelty' – a mere flat moral idea? So too with 'fell purpose', or her talk of 'Nature's mischief'. Her imagination makes little of them. Intensely alive one moment, it turns dully aside the next; and the reach of her will, forming and guarding, even at this depth, what she will allow herself to see, is fearsome. For the sensation of doing things to and in *herself* is stronger than the sense of what those mortal thoughts might really be, done to Duncan or to anyone else. There, her fiercely sensual imaginings stop short. Yet just at that point they would enter, if allowed, into a world which is morally, humanly imagined: the world of sympathies, sanctions, prohibitions, to which she and Macbeth must blind themselves in order to kill the king. She will neither look upon nor find the language for it so compunctious 'Nature' is a word to sweep scornfully by; hell is nothing more than the stagiest of

131

nightmares, 'dunnest smoke', while heaven is made the impotent peeper crying out, when it's too late and the deed has happened, 'Hold, hold'.

But with that shudder into silence, Macbeth steps on stage, and the current which has been flowing between them from the beginning of the scene lifts and swells in her again.

>   Great Glamis, worthy Cawdor,
>   Greater than both, by the all-hail hereafter,
>   Thy letters have transported me beyond
>   This ignorant present, and I feel now
>   The future in the instant.
>
> *Macb.*   My dearest Love,
>   Duncan comes here to-night.
>
> *Lady.*   And when goes hence?
>
> *Macb.* Tomorrow, as he purposes.
>
> *Lady.*   O never
>   Shall sun that morrow see.

Each completes the movement of feeling the other had begun: completes, by augmenting it. For they not only answer one another, they let loose the hidden meaning in a speech, and then make reply to *that*. Emotions are caught in mid-air, exultantly ('Thy letters have transported me'), through unspoken desires, till both speakers come together in their climactic swell of purpose: 'O never, / Shall sun that morrow see.' It feels like fulfilment for them both.

Fulfilment: I think one has to give that word full value. It is in conceiving the murder and bringing it to birth that these two realize the deep powers of their nature. And 'conceiving' murder in his heart is just what Macbeth has done. Yet to produce the deed both the man and the woman are needed. Wherever the seed came from in him, Lady Macbeth carries it into reality; if she did not join her will to his, he would fail; so it takes both of them to kill the king. A monstrous parody, then, of real fertility in love? Initially that is the impression it makes, where natures are reversed, Macbeth being full of the milk of human kindness, while she pours her spirits in his ear so that he feels the swelling act within him, and his wife will chastise all that impedes the hard fruition of the crown. For every tender quality in her woman's body seems now to be turned to steel: her undaunted mettle, he declares, should compose nothing but males, and they both exult in the idea. Thus she presents her husband with the play's most terrible image, of what it is to destroy an utterly vulnerable life:

> I have given suck, and know
> How tender 'tis to love the babe that milks me:
> I would, while it was smiling in my face,
> Have pluck'd my nipple from his boneless gums,
> And dash'd the brains out, had I so sworn as you
> Have done to this.
>
> (I.vii.54‑9)

It is sensual, exquisite, as she gives herself to the smiling child, his soft gums around the nipple. And what is dreadful is not just that her deep satisfaction at it passes instantly to an ecstasy of violence, but that the ecstasy passes into her husband, provoking him, like her, to clutch the coming murder all the more. 'If we should fail?': *her* contemptuous 'We fail?' leaps up to his, and masters it in triumph. Here again, each completes the other's feeling in a mutual abandon that makes the killing seem a deed of 'blood' in both senses of the phrase.

By now, though, it should be clear that what binds these two together is not ambition or bloodlust or fear alone, it is love: married love, after all. The murder grows in the erotic pleasure they take from one another – from not just the fierceness of their natures, but their genuinely tender capacities too. For it is by making one another feel indeed how tender 'tis to love, and with what ease helpless life can be destroyed, that their strength is roused. It feeds on the vulnerability they can so deeply sense. But even that does not put the case fully. Rather, because the two of them *can* respond so deeply to what it is they kill, we are carried with them into the heart of their deed, and there judge them, not as the savage 'butcher and his fiend-like queen' (V.viii.69), but more intimately and dreadfully. They are tragic: we are made to feel their evil as unflinchingly as that. It would be easier if they *were* just a butcher and a fiend, but we are not permitted to withhold ourselves from their humanity like that. So here, from the high point of their confrontation, Lady Macbeth's will modulates and quietens, sinking back upon itself to give place to a different tone, and a very unexpected one.

Macb. If we should fail?
Lady.   We fail?
       But screw your courage to the sticking place,
       And we'll not fail:

The sticking-place is reached.

                              When Duncan is asleep.
(Whereunto the rather shall his day's hard journey
Soundly invite him) his two chamberlains
Will I with wine, and wassail, so convince,
That memory, the warder of the brain,
Shall be a fume, and the receit of reason
A limbec only: when in swinish sleep,
Their drenched natures lie as in a death,
What cannot you and I perform upon
Th'unguarded Duncan? What not put upon
His spongy officers? Who shall bear the guilt
Of our great quell.

                                        (I.vii.59-72)

It is strange to hear treachery and bloody thoughts command
so full-flowing and composed a movement. Strange, too, after
that brutal 'sticking', to hear the burdened lyricism that lies
upon the speech, bringing it to rest in the final calm of 'our
great quell'. And the moment of the murder is quieter still.
    It is not the night-scene we might expect and of which
Lennox speaks: 'Chimneys blown down .... Lamentings
heard i'th'air, screams, clamour, accents terrible' (II.iii.
53-8). In the very act of summoning himself to the bloody
business Macbeth hears his stealthy pace swallowed up by
the stones so that he moves 'like a Ghost' and his ravishing
strides imprint silence rather than sound. The night is noise-
lessly transformed. A bell rings from the inner room, the
voices cease, and we start to feel, not impending violence
oddly enough, but vulnerability. It is that of the victim all right,
but strangely that of his murderers as well - as if Duncan
lying so innocent and naked to the knife makes us apprehend
how liable to death *all* nature is. Even Lady Macbeth is
stilled as the scene lies motionless before her, suspending its
horror like a dream: [12]

    Hark, [———] peace: It was the owl that shriek'd,

134

The fatal Bell-man, which gives the stern'st good-night.
He is about it, [——] the doors are open:
And the surfeited grooms do mock their charge
With snores. I have drugg'd their possets,
That death and nature do contend about them,
Whether they live, or die.

That moment of the owl-shriek and the sleepy lift-and-fall ('Whether they live, or die') may echo the witch-music from far off, but it gives us something unlike the Lady Macbeth most actresses still play in tigerish snarls. Wondering, heavy, lyrical, the voice sounds like that of the tenderness she used to know: she thinks to have dashed it to death; it still lives on, however. For the play's most haunting paradox is that murder is never at an end: the enemy rises again, in you. And it is this that makes the murderer's sigh, 'Duncan is in his grave: / After life's fitful fever, he sleeps well' (III.iii. 22–3), a deeper thing than irony. You cannot catch with his surcease success, but neither can you, irrevocable though the killing is, ruin nature utterly. The quiet of the night, Duncan's sleeping in measureless content – *of course* such unarmoured life is under attack, but Macbeth can no more destroy it for ever than his wife can crush all the gentleness from her womanhood. Remember how she cannot kill the king when he looks like her father as he sleeps: a strange memory to occur just then, but it confounds her by the very sympathies she thought to have destroyed.

So we need not find her hypocritical when she speaks so poignantly as the play goes on. She is haunted by what she has murdered in herself. From violence she sinks to anger and alarm, from that to distraction, sleep-walking, suicide. The death she called for comes, growing inside her; but so do other qualities, and not just in her but in both. Even as they kill the King, the drugging rhythms which made it possible are transformed.

> Alack, I am afraid they have awak'd,
> And 'tis not done: th'attempt, and not the deed,
> Confounds us: hard:I laid their daggers ready,
> He could not miss 'em. Had he not resembled
> My father as he slept, I had done't. My husband?

Macb. I have done the deed: Didst thou not hear a noise?
Lady. I heard the owl scream, and the crickets cry.
      Did not you speak?

Macb.	When?
Lady.	Now.
Macb.	As I descended?
Lady.	Aye [————]
Macb.	Hark,
	Who lies i'th'second chamber?
Lady.	Donalbain.
Macb.	[————] This is a sorry sight.
Lady.	A foolish thought, to say a sorry sight.
Macb.	There's one did laugh in's sleep, and one cried
	'murder',
	That they did wake each other: I stood, and heard
	them:
	But they did say their prayers, and address'd them
	Again to sleep.

(II.ii.9-25)

Weird, breathless, fearful, it's the language of a trance, its pulse lapsing and quickening like lurching heartbeats so that both voices seem to echo in an alien world, lost. Hence the sad outcast quality of that detail Macbeth reports: 'one did laugh in's sleep . . . . I stood, and heard them.' He can no longer be one of those who answer 'Amen' to a blessing, and stage by stage he and his wife pass into a final isolation from which it's impossible they should 'wake each other'. But what makes it the more terrible as they harden themselves, force their wills to live with what they have done, and go from one butchery to the next, is that together with the violence, the greed and contempt, the coarseness with which they handle the life around them, they reach towards each other more tenderly than ever: 'So shall I, love . . . dear Wife . . . . Be innocent of the knowledge, dearest Chuck . . . . Come, we'll to sleep.' And she replies with a moving sweetness of address. It's 'Gentle my Lord' she calls him now, not 'Great Glamis' but 'My husband'; and her words grow more quiet and self-forgetting still, with 'Almost at odds with morning, which is which' (III.iv.127), and last the helpless sighing – sexual in a different way – 'Come, come, come, come, give me your hand . . . . To bed, to bed, to bed.' (V.i.64-6)

False, though, to leave the emphasis quite there. The tragedy

136

in total effect is a grim, strong, unsubduably energetic thing.
If it begins in the juggling to-fro of the witches, it goes on to
find what their equivocations might mean *humanly* speaking, when the eye is closed to what the hand will do and
conscience stifled under the blanket of the dark. The will,
mesmerized:

> If it were done, when 'tis done, then 'twere well,
> It were done quickly: If th'assassination
> Could trammel up the consequence, and catch
> With his surcease, success: that but this blow
> Might be the be all, and the end all here,
> But here.
>
> (I.vii.1-6)

o'erleaps itself and falls into vacancy – where the self should
be it finds only a nothing-something: 'th'other'. It's an extraordinary evacuation, virtually into those imbecile rhythms.
But the play goes further. The denaturing of themselves,
which both Macbeth and Lady Macbeth think they can
perform, refuses to take place. The hags' incantations work
differently in them, and instead of conscience being smothered
and ended it cries out the louder 'Sleep no more', and pity,
helpless-seeming, strides the blast powerfully, an instant
after birth. Not even gratified desire is free from the palter-
ings of the witches' tune – 'Nought's had, all's spent, /
Where our desire is got without content' (III.ii.4-5) – felt
bodily as wastage now. Looking back, they know in themselves what they earlier refused to see.

The play goes further again:

> Things without all remedy
> Should be without regard: what's done, is done.
>
> (III.ii.11-12)

It is Lady Macbeth who says so, but Macbeth who lives, and
goes on living, with the knowledge that there *is* no sweet
oblivious antidote for what they both have done. He has
killed the king and become the king, thrust Banquo into the
grave whence Banquo thrusts him from his stool; he has
triumphed over fear and conscience, only to have them rise
again. The nature he thinks to have done to death multiplies
and swarms upon him in apparitions of every kind till Birnam

Wood itself moves towards his castle. Unquailing, though, he will not repent, turn back. In the face of the worst that even-handed Justice or conscience can inflict, finally, he cries 'I will not yield' (V.vii.27) and goes to his damnation open-eyed. There's nothing noble or remorseful in that end, but tied to the stake bear-like, he does fight the course set on him – 'Throw physic to the dogs, I'll none of it' (V.iii.47) – and goes to his death with all the strength that's left.

To have driven an audience to this confrontation, without grandeur or heroism to comfort or uplift, takes daring indeed. Macbeth may kill some royalty of nature in himself, but then what's done is done, and on the further side of it remains the life one has got now. That self which yielded to suggestion once, and to fear, horror, pity, yields no longer: immeasurable the loss we might say, except that the whole tragedy has brought us to measure it. But Macbeth's final act is not emptiness all the same. The man who shrank from what the witches showed – 'Start eyes! / What, will the line stretch out to th'crack of Doom?' (IV.i.116–17) – and let himself echo the hee-haw of their prophecies in act IV, has made his terms with the world. No shrinking, he is his own man now, and he knows it: knows that these hangman's hands are his, and that time's syllables and poor players' speeches all come to the same idiot 'nothing' (V.v.28). Signifying . . .? What can it signify to him? For the Seytons and the Doctors who stand by ready with their normal wisdom, he feels (and we with him?) a shrivelling sardonic contempt, alongside the reality that is him. 'I'll fight, till from my bones, my flesh be hack'd' (V.iii.32): that grip at least is real. So too is the self he has made out of the witches' rhymes, where 'Swords I smile at, weapons laugh to scorn, / Brandish'd by man that's of a woman born' (V.vii.12–13). And the final twist of the tragedy's screw is that that, unequivocatingly at last, is the sticking-place at which he is held and killed.

NOTES

1 In this chapter the lineation and punctuation of the First Folio edition are retained. Spelling has been modernized by the editor.
2 See Henry N. Paul, *The Royal Play of Macbeth* (1950), pp. 75–130.
3 Ian Robinson, 'The Witches and Macbeth', *The Critical Review*, XI (1968), p. 102.

4   In *Shakespeare's Magnanimity* (1978), pp. 57–65. Sanders' earlier *The Dramatist and the Received Idea* has been a constant, valued stimulus too.

5   c.f. Peter Barry, 'The Enactment Fallacy', *Essays in Criticism* (1980). This is perhaps a good moment to acknowledge two other discussions: Michael Black's 'Poetry and the Linguists', *The Critical Review*, XV (1973) and the same writer's *Poetic Drama as Mirror of the Will* (1977).

6   In Richard Flatter, *Shakespeare's Producing Hand: A study of his Marks of Expression to be found in the First Folio* (1948), pp. 178–82.

7   Paul, *op. cit.*, argues for the authenticity of the stage-tradition by which these owl-shrieks punctuate important moments of the play: 'Harpier cries, 'tis time, 'tis time.'

8   Flatter, *op. cit.*, pp. 153 ff.

9   *On Poetry and Poets* (1965), p. 38.

10 *Shakespearean Tragedy* (1904), Lecture IX, 2.

11 So I argue in '*King Lear* and the Casebook', *The Critical Review*, XX (1978), from which I have drawn a couple of phrases in this paragraph.

12 Editors variously dispose the line-endings of this speech. Here, as almost everywhere, the First Folio seems the surest guide to tempo, breathing, gesture and stress, so I have followed it throughout. The comma-used-as-question-mark (see Flatter, pp. 137 ff.) or to balance the voice on uncertainties might be noted in the speech, as also the effect of Lady Macbeth's drinking. Deep pauses fill out the lines. At 'He is about it.' G.J. Bell reports that 'Mrs Siddons breathes with difficulty, hearkens towards door. Whisper horrible' (*The Nineteenth Century*, February, 1878), and at the start of the speech there is room for Harpier's shriek to be heard in the air.

7

Language and action in *Macbeth*

Michael Goldman

A writer who turns to drama from success in other forms
quickly finds that no degree of inventive richness in characterization, plot, or language can help him if he lacks two
skills: the ability to write for actors and the ability to create
action. The operation of either talent is notoriously hard to
describe, but it may be helpful to point out that the two are
related. In the theatre, our sense of action arises almost
entirely from the performance of the actors. Whatever
'action' may be, it is felt as something *playable*, an impulse
thrusting out at us from what the actors do, moment by
moment, an unbroken flow of energy carrying us forward in
time. More particularly, the actor's performance itself con-
stitutes an important part of the action of any play.

Here it is useful to distinguish among various kinds of
action, all of which contribute to what we normally refer to
as *the* action of a play; many difficulties of criticism arise
from confusing them. There are the actions the characters
perform; the action of the audience's mind in trying to interpret the events it watches; and finally the actions by which
the actors create and sustain their roles. Most discussions of
drama run the first two together and ignore the third. It is
this last kind of action on which I propose to concentrate
here. The creative action of the actor in playing his part is
best understood not as something added arbitrarily by the
performer but as governed and determined by the script, and
in this chapter I want to focus on one important feature of the
text of *Macbeth* as it tests and directs the actor's performance
in the title role. I wish to consider the language Macbeth speaks
in terms of the action its effective articulation requires.

No one, I think, would deny that the language of any great poetic drama must be studied as closely as that of a poem. But it must be approached in the light of a fact which makes the study of the language of great poetic drama far more difficult than the study of other forms of poetry. What I have in mind is that every word of a good play is designed as a performed word and must be interpreted as such if we are to understand its full function as part of the dramatist's design. If we think of an actor's performance sustaining itself through the hundreds of instants of enactment elicited by the words he must speak, we can see that the very process of delivering the lines may form an important strand of action in the play.

To begin with a very noticeable stylistic feature, Macbeth's language, like that of Hamlet and Lear, frequently presents the actor with series of words that are strikingly similar – words which may or may not be parallel in sense, but which are rendered insistently parallel by devices of style. And the movement among them which the actor must make is a testing difficulty of his performance. That is, it is a difficulty peculiar to the role, and the sense of difficulty overcome, which a successful negotiation of the passage conveys, is felt as part of the distinctive quality of performance in the role. It is not too much to say that it forms part of the role's characterization, for it markedly determines the way the character must be received by the audience.

In *Macbeth*, the typical organization of the parallel elements I referred to is very different from Hamlet's 'Bloody, bawdy, ... lecherous, treacherous, kindless villain!' or 'Tempest, torrent, and whirlwind', or Lear's 'Vengeance! Plague! Death! Confusion!' or 'Howl, howl, howl, howl!' Let me start with a very familiar example:

> This supernatural soliciting
> Cannot be ill; cannot be good.   (I.iii.130-1)

What is the relation between *supernatural* and *soliciting*? First, the sound suggests a parallelism which the sense resists – and indeed the sound resists it too, even as it suggests it. The congruence of the two words is as uneasy as it is emphatic – for all the repeated elements, the 's's, the 'l's, the 'n's and 't's, the swift polysyllables, are tangled by the *differentia*, the new sounds and altered rhythm. It has the effect of a tongue-twister. And the interplay of meanings suggested by the words reinforces the impression of movement into a tangle, a disturbing density, as does the content of the whole speech. *Solicit*, in its Elizabethan meanings, is a word of manifold suggestion, linking all kinds of persuasion - evil, neutral, and good; rhetorical, sexual, sympathetic, and manipulative. *Supernatural* only heightens the sense of doubt and attraction implicit in the word it modifies. And the speech - expressing Macbeth's rapt, doubting, fascinated interest in the apparition he has just seen - continues through a sequence of similar entanglings. Balances are set up which are quickly undermined by unassimilated residues of sound and sense, and this makes the movement from word A to word A^1 (and sometimes A^2) neither one of opposition nor simple accumulation, but of a twisting and darkening, a thickening in which the speech thrusts forward into little thickets of sound and into reflections which don't allow the speculative movement to exit, ending literally in a smothering negation:

> My thought, whose murder yet is but fantastical,
> Shakes so my single state of man,
> That function is smother'd in surmise,
> And nothing is, but what is not.
>
> (I.iii.139-42)

We may note similar effects elsewhere, as in:

> If it were done when 'tis done, then 'twere well
> It were done quickly. If th'assassination
> Could trammel up the consequence, and catch
> With his surcease, success.
>
> (I.vii.1-4)

What is the relation between *assassination* and *consequence*, between *surcease* and *success*? Both in sound and sense, they smother each other. The speech moves quickly and nervously, indeed jumpily, which probably dictates Shakespeare's choice of 'jump' for 'risk'. But the jump here is miles from the swift movement of Othello's

> Like to the Pontic sea
> Whose icy current and compulsive course
> Ne'er feels retiring ebb, but keeps due on

To the Propontic and the Hellespont;
Even so my bloody thoughts, with violent pace,
Shall ne'er look back, ne'er ebb to humble love,
Till that a capable and wide revenge
Swallow them up.

(III.iii.457-64)

In the speech just quoted, the relation of the similar parts allows us to feel word A progressing to A^1, to feel A^1 as the release, the resolution, say, of the chord struck by A. In Macbeth's speech, the jumper from A finds himself entangled in A^1. *Success* becomes a tongue-twisting pun on *surcease*; we are explicitly invited to think of *assassination* as throwing a net around *consequence*, and indeed the effect is reinforced by *trammel* and *catch*, emphatically related to each other and to the paired words they link. We feel *assassination* and *consequence*, *surcease* and *success* snatching at each other.

Such a movement into gathering thickness or darkness is of course often explicitly described by Macbeth:

Light thickens and the crow
Makes wing to th' rooky wood;
Good things of day begin to droop and drowse,
Whiles night's black agents to their preys do rouse.

(III.ii.50-3)

I need not multiply instances. We are dealing with the characteristic Macbeth-sound, a darkness, a sad heaviness, which visits the tongue in complicated fashion, a heaviness in the midst of lucidity, a heavy swiftness. Perhaps it is not fanciful, in this Scottish world, to hear in it something of a burr. But the important point is that the Macbeth-sound is not a coloration or a harmony, something properly to be described as fixed, but an action, the effect of a movement of speech which is a movement of the mind.

But we have yet to describe this action. What kind of movement is a movement through these words? What kind of action connects A and A^1, does justice to their meanings, and moves on down the paragraph? To begin with, let me provisionally characterize the verbal movement I have been describing as, in a phrase, a snatching into the thickness. I choose 'thickness' not simply because of 'Light thickens', but because it points to an underlying pattern of imagery

143

which I think is of the greatest importance in *Macbeth*. This is the motif of the thickening of fluids. I have in mind, for example, the filling of the air with rain, fog, and smoke; Lady Macbeth's blood thickening; the brew in the witches' cauldron growing thick and slab; light thickening to produce darkness; the sea turning red with blood. I think that in shaping his play of treason in the aftermath of the Gunpowder Plot, Shakespeare very strongly had in mind the kind of moral horror we ourselves have felt – though to a lesser degree, I would say – in our own times of assassination. The sudden and explosive manifestation of evil, absolute and as if out of nowhere, the sense that value, order, confidence in good proceeding can be wiped out in an instant, contributed, I think, to the kind of investigation of evil he felt compelled to make in *Macbeth*. And so he begins the play with thunder and the for-the-moment incomprehensible apparition of the witches – an explosion later echoed in the sudden darkening of Macbeth's mind, the turning of his castle into Hell, and the corruption of Scotland.

The doctrine of equivocation of course reinforced this sense of evil for Shakespeare's contemporaries, and I think the imagery of thickening fluids helps us to see the real force of the well-known motif of equivocation in the play. The destruction at one fell swoop of the entire ruling order of England, apparently averted only at the last moment; the readiness of priests of God to swear to a lie *on principle* – such discoveries must have seemed to many abruptly to open an abyss of evil possibility in the foundations of normal life. Evil, we are accustomed to say, appears in *Macbeth* equivocally – and this is undoubtedly true. But the main point here is not that evil traffics in false appearances, or that it is a perverted or negative version of the good, though both these ideas are certainly present in the play. It is rather that evil appears to Macbeth as something equivocally present in nature, a foulness violently potent in what is fair, thickening the atmosphere. Good things can convert precipitously to evil, as milk converts to gall, as the witches suddenly appear, as sleep fills with bad dreams. Indeed, sleep is presented in the play much as milk, blood, and the ceremonies of society are, as a healthful medium which can suddenly turn foul. Banquo's prayer is crucial:

> Merciful Powers
> Restrain in me the cursed thoughts that nature
> Gives way to in repose!
>
> (II.i.7-9)

The witches' prophecies have perhaps affected his dreams as they have Macbeth's waking thoughts. At any rate, even the good Banquo is aware that evil - personal evil, evil within oneself - is never more than a wink or a wish away. This sense of evil is different from any which predominates in other Shakespearean tragedies. We experience evil in *Macbeth* not as a malign external presence, nor as a rottenness undermining all things, but as a sudden thickening of a natural atmosphere.

Now, the characteristic action of Macbeth's speech is an attempt to clutch at the atmosphere he feels thickening around him - and within him. He tries to push into it, wade through it, sometimes thrust out of it. He keeps registering the new entanglements, the smothering densities his horrible imaginings force upon him. The actor's speech in these passages must accomplish two things - both render the entanglement and attempt to press on through it. He must negotiate the way *soliciting* comments back on *supernatural*, try to get out of it with *cannot be ill*, only to be pulled back further in *cannot be good*.

I have said Macbeth tries to snatch into the thickness, but he does this with varying intentions and results. Sometimes it's a fascinated sinking, as when he yields to the suggestion of murder in I.iii, sometimes it's a brief pulling out, as in the same scene when he says:

> If chance will have me King, why, chance may crown me.
>
> (I.iii.144)

Not much later than this in the play, Macbeth begins to deal with the thickness another way, by wielding it, projecting the thickness he finds in his thoughts into nature and calling on nature to sustain the atmosphere he has created:

> Stars, hide your fires. (I.iv.50)
>   Thou sure and firm-set earth,
> Hear not my steps which way they walk, for fear
> Thy very stones prate of my whereabout. (II.i.56-8)

145

Come sealing night. (III.ii.46)

As a character, Macbeth is distinguished by his imagination, which is quite literally an image-making capacity of frightening intensity. It is a moral imagination, in that the images it registers most vividly have to do with the moral status of Macbeth's acts and desires. But Shakespeare gives these images a powerful histrionic setting by having Macbeth use them, much like an actor rehearsing a role, to explore and indeed to discover his new emotions. *Macbeth* shows us not only a man betraying and murdering his king, but learning to perform the act, as an actor might. That is, he uncovers in himself what a modern actor might call his motivation. But this term, though natural enough, is misleading. For what the actor playing a murderer and traitor must discover is not some nuance of intention – not why Macbeth wants to kill Duncan – but a convincing capacity for the act. He must discover what it is *like* to be able to commit such a crime, to have desires and proclivities and mental activity large enough to propel him into the act. And this is exactly what Macbeth, in the early scenes, discovers in himself.

Macbeth observes carefully, and with surprise, the psychic readjustments by which he becomes a criminal. His first soliloquy allows the actor to develop the capacity for Macbeth's grand passion as part of his performance. And, of course, it involves us in this development and makes it part of the central material of the play. In this speech, Macbeth maps and explores his new mental topography:

> Why do I yield to that suggestion
> Whose horrid image doth unfix my hair,
> And make my seated heart knock at my ribs,
> Against the use of nature? Present fears
> Are less than horrible imaginings. (I.iii.134–8)

He begins with an image and a reaction to it. He fights against, questions, and gradually becomes absorbed in a picture of himself doing murder, a picture which is both his and not his, ambiguously placed by his vocabulary neither quite inside him nor outside him – it is a 'suggestion' (or, more obscurely, the image of a suggestion), to which he 'yields'. The image in his mind frightens him, and the actor is given specific terms in which to explore his fear: heart beating

violently, scalp tingling, and that jumpy, up-and-down-move-
ment of breath and thought which L.C. Knights has aptly
described as a 'sickening see-saw'.

The process by which Macbeth explores the capacity for
evil that has appeared, as if out of nowhere, in his mind may
be traced in its full variety in the dagger speech. Macbeth
begins with a series of investigations and discoveries:

> Is this a dagger which I see before me,
> The handle toward my hand? Come let me clutch thee.
> I have thee not, and yet I see thee still.
> Art thou not, fatal vision, sensible
> To feeling, as to sight? or art thou but
> A dagger of the mind, a false creation?
>
> (II.i.33–8)

Like the image of murder which springs to his mind when he
hears that he is Thane of Cawdor, the dagger is something
Macbeth examines with close attention to physical detail.
And the process of exploration itself becomes a theme for
startled discovery:

> I see thee yet, in form as palpable
> As this which now I draw.
> Thou marshall'st me the way that I was going. (lines 40–2)

To confirm the reality of his 'false creation', Macbeth draws
his own dagger, and then, staring at the knife he holds,
realizes what his exploration has led to. The vision has placed
a weapon in his hand, drawn him a step further toward
murder.

Like the prophecies he has heard from the witches, the
dagger strikes him at once as both a cunning trap and an
extraordinary revelation – a kind of supernatural solicitation:

> Mine eyes are made the fools o' th' other senses,
> Or else worth all the rest. (lines 44–5)

Now begins the process of projecting this terrible instigation,
the dagger in his mind, outward into the world around him.
Again Macbeth ambiguously defines the source of the image
which obsesses him. He locates his murderous 'creation' not
in his mind but in a deceptively objectified future – the

'business' he must soon perform has created the vision:

> It is the bloody business which informs
> Thus to mine eyes.   (lines 48-9)

The phrase almost acknowledges - but also helps to obscure - the mental origin of the dagger.

Next comes the decisive movement outside Macbeth's mind:

>   Now o'er the one-half world
> Nature seems dead, and wicked dreams abuse
> The curtain'd sleep: now witchcraft celebrates
> Pale Hecate's offerings; and wither'd murder,
> Alarum'd by his sentinel, the wolf,
> Whose howl's his watch, thus with his stealthy pace,
> With Tarquin's ravishing strides, toward his design
> Moves like a ghost.
>   (II.i.49-56)

What is striking here is that, as Macbeth thrusts the thickness in his thought out into nature, he converts it into yet another image, which allows him to develop his murderous propensities further. He transforms his passion into action by imitating the very image of murder he has projected. The bloody business now informs all nature, and through it moves the figure of Murder, whom Macbeth proceeds to imitate. The reference to Murder's 'pace' and 'stride' leads naturally to Macbeth's own steps:

>   Thou sure and firm-set earth,
> Hear not my steps which way they walk, for fear
> Thy very stones prate of my whereabout,
> And take the present horror from the time,
> Which now suits with it.
>   (lines 56-60)

The psychological and mimetic process by which the actor can become a murderer has been very thoroughly laid out.

At this point, the histrionic complexity of the speech can be felt in a single word:

> Whiles I threat, he lives.   (line 60)

What process of articulation in the previous lines has allowed Macbeth to describe them as a *threat*? Surely it is a movement like the one just described, the projection of his murderous design outward into the world. He sees his speech as a step toward murder, a threat. And though he can now dismiss what he has just said as merely verbal ('Words to the heat of deeds too cold breath gives'), the speech has quite literally got him moving. Moreover, it has done so by transforming him into the image of murder he has projected. Macbeth has become the very atmosphere of horror which he describes. It is typical of him that he now sees the mental process he has just gone through as no more than 'words', that he wishes to accelerate away from imagination toward pure deed. Macbeth, of course, regularly tries to silence or 'outrun' his moral imagination by hurrying into action, but it should be noted that in this habit of action he simply parallels his habits of thought and speech. Both verbally and politically, Macbeth's way of dealing with the evil he discovers in himself is to recreate the universe in its image. The Scotland he creates, like the thick night he invokes or the meaningless universe he describes in Act V, is a product of the dagger in his mind. From the time the witches appear to him, Macbeth lives in a false creation, governed by a 'fatal vision' that is his own.

As we have seen, Macbeth's movement of mind often takes off from an image or idea that will not go away, that insists on persisting. His thoughts thicken around it – the horrid image of the suggestion of murder, the air-drawn dagger, the fact that Banquo lives, the memory of Banquo's ghost. He keeps coming back to it, and his language allows the actor to feel the persistent image thickening his thought, sometimes accompanied by the effort of his thought to rise out of the thickness ('It will have blood, they say') – until he makes the move that gets him for the moment beyond the ob-struction in his head, but leaves him as it were coated, stained, and smeared by it.

Two other incidental features of the part help throw this habitual action into relief. First, Macbeth in public speech often negotiates groups of parallel words more firmly than in private, establishing their relation as one of wit, which depends on and enforces moral clarity:

Who can be wise, amaz'd, temperate and furious,

149

Loyal and neutral, in a moment? No man.

(II.iii.107–8)

The murkier soliloquies suggest that the action here is an effortful keeping apart of polar opposites. They collapse and contaminate each other when Macbeth is alone. Thus the characteristic combination of movements in the more private passages: quick, forward, out of the murk; slow, mesmerized, sinking deeper into it.

The second point has to do with what happens when Macbeth gets angry. All Shakespeare's tragic heroes, with the exception of Brutus, are given passages of explosive rage. It is interesting that Macbeth's efforts in this line are very different from the rest, as well as being relatively infrequent and not so memorable. For when Macbeth rages we feel he is rising, very temporarily, from the more absorbing arena of his own thoughts. While he rages, we note again the habit he has, or that his mind has, of keeping a single image obsessively before him:

—— The devil damn thee black, thou cream-fac'd loon!
Where got'st thou that goose look?
—— There is ten thousand –
—— Geese, villain? . . .
Go prick thy face, and over-red thy fear,
Thou lily-liver'd boy. What soldiers, patch?
. . . What soldiers, whey-face?

(V.iii.11–17)

Even here, it is the obsessive image, the pallor of the messenger, which focuses his attention. More typically, he is quick to drop back into the inner arena:

Accursed be that tongue that tells me so,
For it hath cow'd my better part of man.

(V.viii.17–18)

Rage is a diversion; it is the horror in his own mind that absorbs him and spurs him into action.

All Macbeth's movements in, through, and against the thickening texture he apprehends represent his effort to adjust to the evil that has erupted inside his head. What he keeps doing, in one form or another, is poking around to find

150

where the evil comes from, or, rather, wondering at and attempting to come to terms with its equivocal presence in himself. We may understand Shakespeare's concern here more fully if we note a curious motif that keeps cropping up in the various portions of Holinshed's *Chronicles of Scotland* which Shakespeare drew on for *Macbeth*. This is the motif of the ambiguous origin of promptings to murder. There is, for example, the story of King Natholocus, who in a time of civil strife, sends a trusted friend to a witch to learn what fortune holds in store for him. The witch declares that Natholocus soon will be murdered, by the hands of the very friend who is asking the question. This leaves the friend in some perplexity. He reflects that if he tells the king the truth, Natholocus may put him to death just to be on the safe side, while if he conceals the truth, he may be put to death for that. And so he solves his problem - by killing Natholocus. In another place we learn that certain noblemen who conspired with witches against King Duff, 'Had been persuaded to be partakers with the other rebels, more through fraudulent counsell of diverse wicked persons, than of their owne accord.' And we are later told that Donwald orders the murder of King Duff, 'Through the instigation of his wife . . . though he abhorred the act greatlie in heart.'

What these passages have in common is the ambiguous instigation of evil, the feeling that the source of evil action is both inside and outside the mind that undertakes it. This, of course, is Macbeth's experience with the witches, the dagger, the voices in the night, the bell which 'invites' him to kill Duncan and which he himself has ordered rung. The experience of the play puts us inside Macbeth's head as he finds himself wholly committed to deeds whose moral abhorrence he registers with the intensest sensitivity.

I have certainly not meant to account for all Macbeth's actions in these pages, nor to describe his character entire. But I hope I have succeeded in suggesting that his play forces us not only to imagine evil but to imagine what it is like to *commit* evil. The character of Macbeth is constructed so that he keeps imagining the horror of what he is doing even while he keeps on doing it. And the actor who plays Macbeth constructs his grand passion by a series of attacks on the thick and thickening atmosphere which seems, from the very beginning of the play, to fall upon him like a thundercloud, but seems equally to be rising from his own imagination. The movement of the play in performance should be a flight from horror into horror, always a little faster than we expect, a flight like Macbeth's own flight from and toward the horror in his mind. Macbeth can never escape the weight of that instigation in his head, and his language, properly performed, performed as Shakespeare has designed it to be performed, allows us to share his experience of an evil which he discovers unaccountably present, a sudden deposit, a condensation at once natural and unnatural, inside him. For this ultimately is what holds Macbeth rapt through the whole play: the fact that the evil he grapples with is *his*.

Part 4

Special studies

8
History, politics and *Macbeth*

Michael Hawkins

To a historian, such as the author of this chapter, discussion of Shakespeare's works in a historical context is unavoidable if difficult: he cannot, professionally, regard any individual as 'outside' history by virtue of his or her intellectual originality or artistic greatness. In so far as the historian is unable to assimilate such greatness to his historical pattern, he fails in his task. Equally, he must not discuss the historical 'background' to Shakespeare, if by that is meant an account of contemporary ideas and practices: no one has history as a background in this sense; everyone is part of it. Nevertheless, on reading even a sample of the literary criticism of Shakespeare's tragedies, the historian soon becomes aware of at least two schools which, though opposed, both question implicitly or explicitly the significance of historical understanding. To characterise them briefly and too crudely, they give primacy either to character and plot or to poetry: both, as originally presented, for example, by A.C. Bradley and G. Wilson Knight, have a certain timelessness and ahistorical quality.

The historian notes, however, that the elaboration of both positions has tended to introduce a historical dimension. Bradley has long been criticised for failing to appreciate the differences between Elizabethan ways of thought, particularly psychological theory, and our own, and for not appreciating the continuity of medieval ideas. The other position, attacked for approaching each play or poem as a *tabula rasa*, 'cut[ting] off from ... consideration ... all matters which are not immediately intrinsic to it',[1] in practice involves (or should involve) asking what meaning particular symbols, images and

155

allegories had for Shakespeare's generation and being careful not to read modern attitudes into them. As a particular example may be noted the discussion of Duncan's 'golden' blood.[2] On a larger scale the historian cannot accept L.C. Knights's view, which agrees with Wilson Knight's, that *Macbeth* is a 'statement of evil',[3] without asking what was peculiarly evil to the Jacobeans about the murder of Duncan as portrayed in the play. Even Holinshed's *Chronicle*, not a notably subtle work, makes it clear that murder within the extended royal family was viewed somewhat differently in eleventh-century Scotland. Nowadays we hardly regard the assassination of political leaders in underdeveloped countries, even if we could envisage ones as saintly as Duncan is apparently portrayed, as a totally evil act. It is not sufficient to reify abstractions like 'evil' as, for example, Lucy Campbell and Irving Ribner do.[4] Our moral sense *may* be blurred by the twentieth-century horrors we have 'supp'd', but that too is part of historical change. Vocabulary has a normative content which varies over time[5] and provides both opportunities and limitations for the literary imagination.

Of course the historical approach itself has had powerful critics. C.H. Herford defended Bradley for rejecting 'the current doctrine . . . that Shakespeare, like lesser men, can be interpreted only through the historical conditions in which he wrote.' Kenneth Muir writes that, even if Campbell 'convinced us that Shakespeare's understanding of human behaviour was circumscribed by the theories of the age, the light thrown on his plays would be disappointingly narrow.'[6] The historian notes here the improper imputation of words like 'circumscribed' and 'narrow'. Shakespeare was not 'circumscribed': he had the same facility to use and develop ideas as anyone (which does not imply the development of theory in a formal academic sense) and is, in that sense, part of a historical development.

Certainly, historical study is not simply a matter of outlining the norms and conventions which predominate at a particular period: such loss of historical individuality is, as Ribner says, a perversion of historical scholarship. The historian will also recognise the force of Robert Ornstein's view that literary ideas and forms do not necessarily change with general opinion.

Equally, it hardly needs adding that to stress the inevitability of a historical dimension does not mean accepting the 'naturalistic' fallacy: Shakespeare's characters are not 'real' people, though there is a creative tension between conventionalism and naturalism.[7]

Many critics have gone to the other extreme and saddled Shakespeare with a fully-fledged political and religious philosophy or even eschatology, so that his plays become *exempla* of the lessons that history teaches. Exponents of this approach have generally expended much effort in placing Shakespeare's ideas in their historical context and it is certainly significant to consider how Shakespeare amended his sources to give a play a particular structure. But the conclusions drawn have often been disappointingly generalised. To show that Shakespeare illustrates the dangerous consequences of 'vaulting ambition', the hardening effects of sin, the value of order, a cyclical view of history or the working of divine providence does not, in itself, go much beyond commonplace. Most political philosophies have stressed the value of order above disorder and many have related it to a society based on degree, while, in that right triumphs, tragedy may easily be held to reveal the working of providence. Historical study is littered with attempts to impose a global pattern. Ornstein reminds us in *The Moral Vision of Jacobean Tragedy* (p. 17) that the intellectual pieties of the Renaissance were not its creative ideas and John Wilders in *The Lost Garden* (1978, p. 8) goes so far as to argue that every political problem was unique in Shakespeare's view. The more a dramatist makes specific application of these rather orotund generalities the more he is likely to limit the depth of his writing. It would be more significant in sixteenth-century terms (and certainly would focus debate) if Shakespeare were to maintain that order was best achieved through hereditary monarchy based on primogeniture rather than republicanism on the model of the Italian city states, or that the divine providence at work was based on Thomist rather than Augustinian principles. But while such positions may be argued in particular works (though never I believe without qualification), they are not presented as general principles. The cost in dramatic flexibility and range would be enormous and Shakespeare did not pay it. Though the historian will recognise that there is a limit to the range of legitimate interpretation, he will note that attempts to force Shakespeare into a procrustean bed of advocacy of a particular 'philosophy' reduce the eclecticism, ambiguity and irony on which drama thrives. Without going so far as T.S. Eliot's 'rag-bag philosophy', it may be stated that Shakespeare was not a philosopher or a philosophical poet. Still less was he a political-philosophical poet.

He was, however, clearly aware of the current vocabulary of political debate and the contribution of history to that debate: both informed the writing of *Macbeth*. Certain caveats are necessary: first, the material he used cannot be limited to printed works. To an active playwright enmeshed in the patronage network, day-to-day political practice could be as significant as structured treatises in raising issues and forming opinions. This does not mean another attempt to show *Macbeth* was a topical 'royal' play: it does mean a recognition of the interaction between the theory and practice of politics and also of the limitations of theory when compared with practical experience.[8] On the other hand, too precise a correlation between the supposed health or otherwise of the Elizabethan and Jacobean polity and the development of tragedy should be viewed more sceptically than it often is.[9] A contemporary malaise, even if established, is doubtfully related to tragedy which may, as we have seen, be regarded as ultimately optimistic and dependent on an ethical view of the world. Equally doubtful is the relationship claimed between tragedy and the supposed undermining of the place of man under the attack of the relativistic views of Copernicus, Montaigne and Machiavelli as is argued in Theodore Spencer's *Shakespeare and the Nature of Man*. In fact, Renaissance science may as well be argued to have enhanced as diminished man's place in the world by emphasising his potential for control over nature. In political theory Machiavelli was particularly ambiguous in this respect. It seems very difficult to generalise about the relationship between political practice, political ideas and drama except at a somewhat vapid level. Even Ornstein tells us (*op. cit.*, pp. 26-7, 31) that the 'Machiavel' flourished because the Jacobeans were caught between a 'dying feudal order and modern society struggling to be born'. Marx's (and Marxists') crudities have a lot to answer for.

Theory cannot be avoided altogether. Any statement has theoretical implications, whether realised and articulated or not, but it is not necessary (and may be positively a hindrance) to try to distinguish the intellectual roots of various positions. To label ideas as medieval or Renaissance (or even counter-Renaissance), scholastic or humanist (or even Christian or pagan humanist) may or may not be useful for historians of political theory:[10] as far as Shakespeare is concerned the ideas themselves are what matter. Such distinctions, whatever their analytic use, did not accord with the reality of contemporary politics, in that most views were an amalgam of them; and still less did they accord with the eclectic needs of drama.

What can be done is to raise the questions which concerned contemporaries and see how Shakespeare dealt with them. What was perhaps the basic issue in the discussion of politics – whether to take part in political life at all[11] – is raised in a somewhat different form from some of the other plays. There a pastoral idyll or a venerable ecclesiastic detached from political intrigue represents the *vita contemplativa* and in some ways stands above, or at least outside, the life of courts. *Macbeth* is a picture of activism. 'I'll do, I'll do, and I'll do', says the First Witch (I.iii.10). 'Chance may crown' Macbeth without his stir (I.iii.143–4), but he rejects that line and accepts Lady Macbeth's insistence that opportunity must be taken (I.vii.51–4); *cf.*II.i.60–2). All the major characters are participants, fully committed to the *vita activa*. The brevity of the play and the rapidity of the action strengthen this impression. The obsession with time has often been noted, focusing on the contrast between Macbeth's murdering time and Macduff's statement at the end that time is free. Macbeth's action 'outrun[s] the pauser, reason', while Banquo's murder occurs so rapidly that it has been termed a 'kinetic release'. Macbeth and his wife are imprisoned by time, 'What's done cannot be undone', and he ends as a man of action even if life is meaningless. *Macbeth* may be a Senecan play, but not in terms of Stoic endurance. The emphasis on action is quite compatible with Anne Righter's stress on analogies between the world and the stage and on the double meaning of the word 'act'. Nor is this frenetic activism tainted by its association with the wicked: Malcolm may in real life have learnt the value of a stoical approach to politics during his long years in exile at Edward the Confessor's court, but he is denied this in the play, being committed to the rapid overthrow of a weakening regime. One possible alternative view – Campbell's argument that

159

Shakespearean tragedy was primarily concerned with passion rather than action – may be rejected as making an unreal distinction. In the circumstances of Jacobean theatre, as opposed to medieval morality or miracle plays or Tudor interludes, the working of the passions was demonstrated through action.

The real alternative presented is not withdrawal from politics but the desperate search for a mind at rest, the necessary counterpart to the 'hurly-burly' of political action. The loss of sleep by Macbeth and his wife is their most terrible continuing affliction, while the tranquillity portrayed at the courts of Duncan and, especially, Edward shows that a successful political role is compatible with peace of mind.

To bolster all this activity, no doubt is left that it is significant in its effects on society (and indeed nature and the cosmos) as a whole. The relationship between microcosm and macrocosm need not be discussed again here, except to note that much scholarly work on the subject remains ambiguous about whether there was conceived to be a causal or merely an analogous relationship between change in one part of the cosmic, natural and human orders and its counterparts elsewhere. In a formal sense the relationship, whatever it was, may be presented as evidence in *Macbeth* that politics was thought to matter, that it was not conceived as a 'closed' activity and in particular that the initiating role of the Prince was crucial. The last is a theme to which we shall return, but here should be stressed that amendment of Holinshed which makes the *whole* of Macbeth's reign one of terror in Scotland, a disruption of nature and the 'chain of being', and equates his overthrow with the restoration of order and concord to the whole of society.

So politics was significant and should be participated in. But what sort of politics was being discussed? There were perhaps four types of political relationship available in that society. They may be placed, schematically, at levels of different sophistication and may be said to derive from different types of social structure and from different periods. As a new form arose it diminished the significance of, but by no means destroyed, previous ones: much political tension resulted from the efforts of those with an interest in the survival of

earlier forms to withstand the pressure of more developed
ones. The most primitive form may be designated as pre-
feudal: politics based on blood and kinship relationships.
Secondly, the feudal form: relationships still based on
personal obligation but no longer necessarily confined to
familial ties. Contractual relations with outsiders are formed,
producing a hierarchy of ties. Thirdly, the position of the
king is enhanced. In a feudal system that position was ambiguous: the king was the peak of the feudal hierarchy but
bound by feudal ties both to protect and consult his leading
vassals. In post-feudal Europe kings attempted to elevate
themselves from a feudal role of *primus inter pares* among
the elite and to reduce their contractual obligations. In
return that elite felt itself threatened. No longer was power
to be diffused among myriad local autonomous units. The
early modern world placed monarchy at the centre of the
stage: Righter has pointed out (*Shakespeare and the Idea of
the Play*, p. 33) that from at least the time of Skelton's
Magnyficence and Lindsay's *Three Estates* the dramatic
emphasis shifts from the spiritual well-being of Everyman to
the problems of government and recent works have properly
concentrated on the significance of 'king-killing'. Fourthly,
there was the growth of institutional politics, fed by several
sources. The elevation of the king highlighted the probable
gap between the fallibility of the actual king and the in-
fallibility of his office. This facilitated the slow growth of
the doctrine of the king's two bodies.[12] Kingship became
institutionalised, that is, the king could act impersonally,
he could not die and he could do no wrong. (One must
not forget the feudal roots of this last doctrine: the feudal
principle that a lord could not be sued in his own court
unavoidably led to the king, as head of the judicial system,
being free from judicial process though he might redress
error on petition through grace.) As fiscal, judicial and
military monopolies became more established in the Crown,
so too did the growth of bureaucratic forms to administer
them. The process was strengthened by the decline in the
sixteenth century of papal authority compared with that of
secular rulers (a process not confined to Protestant countries)
and, what is less often stressed, the growing reliance on the
government to regulate social and economic life. These new
pressures coexisted with a long-standing need to guard against
claimants to the throne and to quell disruptive private feuds,

the existence of which being itself used as further justification for strong government.

Inevitably this bureaucratisation had the ironic consequence of limiting the personal royal authority it was designed to buttress. We find kings at war with their bureaucracies, less publicly but as seriously as earlier feudal elites had been with them. It was not only royal power which encouraged the institutionalisation of politics: groups anxious to question or contain the growth either of the personal power of the king or of his administration used institutional forms – varieties of assemblies of estates – as platforms for their views, even if the main functions of such estates were the gathering of information and opinion by the Crown and consent to various fiscal demands.

One level of politics – the modern development of institutional politics called mass democracy – was not available to Shakespeare. As Northrop Frye says, Shakespeare was not so much anti-democratic as pre-democratic.[13] It was the tension between the varying forms of existing political relationships which caught the attention of Tudor England and provided Shakespeare with the topics he explored. Explored, not decided: the varying forms of political life had different values which, to right-thinking Englishmen like Shakespeare, could not be seen in black-and-white terms. A man was expected to feel for and defend the interests of his family, but also had obligations to his locality, master or employer, and patron, extensive networks of regional allegiance and clientage having subsumed earlier strictly feudal ties. Further, his obligations to the king were both personal and, if he was a man of influence, institutional, extending to participation in both local government and representative assemblies. He might support an active royal policy for the defence of the realm and true religion, the alleviation of poverty (not least to avoid riot) and the regulation of industry and commerce in the national interest: he might also question the cost and central interference demanded by such a policy. All was tension. *Schema* such as those of the 'Elizabethan world picture' were propounded – although some critics properly question their use in drama – but they were no more than grandiose attempts to show that all was in harmony, to pretend that in fact political problems did not exist. They were propounded by those, from the king downwards, with an interest in the *status quo*, helped by a degree of, albeit inefficient, censorship. Such views could be sustained only as long as they avoided specifics, talking about the king as the sun but not dealing with the question of his power to tax at will. In practice political compromise was inevitable and affected political thought. The divine origin of government was hardly an issue: of course, legitimate government had a divine sanction, but that said nothing in itself about the powers of government. James I might write, according to some views, in terms which have been called absolutist: his behaviour in practice was defensible constitutionally. Ornstein has an inflated view of the novelty of James I's political thinking: that he felt he had 'absolute power over the lives and property of subjects' (*op. cit.*, p. 29). Of course he was the 'literal possessor' of the realm, but that was medieval feudal theory, all land being held by the King: it did not prevent the law courts from working, the Crown's property rights being regulated *vis-à-vis* other subjects' and questions about prerogative taxation being discussed frequently. In fact, even *The Trew Law of Free Monarchies* was hardly objectionable in content. It was subtitled *The Reciprock and Mutuell Duetie betwixt a Free King and his Naturall Subjects* and stressed that the main function of government was, as in the middle ages, decisions on property matters. Ornstein (pp. 36, 265) correctly stresses the uncritical accumulation of rights, laws, prerogatives and prohibitions which complicated politics, though his characterisation of Lear's role as judge as 'bearer of the sacred word of heaven' is grandiose compared with the realities of the administration of royal justice.[14]

Macbeth concentrates on the first three of the levels outlined above. The only significant collective institutional act, which takes place offstage, is the choice of Macbeth as king. The camouflaged approach of the army to Dunsinane, a collective act, does not, for all its dramatic function, apparently materially affect the outcome of the final war, which seems to be settled in personal combats. This lack of institutional ways of resolving issues gives prominence to the variety of personal links, illustrated by Macbeth's three-fold tie with Duncan – as kinsman, host and subject. Due weight is given to the fact that Duncan is murdered by a blood relative. The murder of Macduff's family gives him a case for a vendetta, the classic solution of a blood feud. By implication Malcolm and Donalbain are similarly revenged by the former's participation in the campaign against Macbeth. We have here a slightly different gloss from that normally given to Macbeth's 'blood will have blood' (III.iv.122) and his and his wife's fruitless efforts to cleanse their hands of blood. Bloodshed is foul: there is no contradiction here with the notion of the sacredness of blood as the 'residence of life and of racial and family identity'. Only one case of non-revenge occurs: Fleance, though told by his father to seek revenge, offers to take no part in the conspiracy against Macbeth. Banquo's revenge is of a less direct but more enduring kind. Generally the decision to seek revenge, in a polity which offered no institutional justice, gives further impetus to the activism of the play: the oppressed do not seek solace in resignation.

It is, however, important to note that, while the power of blood revenge is shown, its legitimacy is not settled. Private revenge is not legitimised in its own right but by the wider justification of killing a usurping tyrant. Whether or not the murderers accept Macbeth's proffered justification for Banquo's murder – that he has wronged them – it is interesting that he makes it and does not simply pay them to kill (and that he uses the same appeal to their 'manliness' as was used to him by Lady Macbeth). But the issue is not resolved: the murderers are still being commanded by the king. The lesser cause is subsumed in the greater and this is therefore not a 'revenge tragedy' in the normal sense. However, Macbeth hardly fits Campbell's argument that private revenge would bring God's vengeance against anyone engaged in it, even if the avenger himself was an instrument of God's vengeance.

We are, however, not left in doubt about two other aspects of family relations: the dangers of wifely domination and uxoriousness and the hollowness of childlessness. Macbeth not only murders his kinsman, he allows his household to be subverted by, in Holinshed's words, a 'very ambitious' woman (even if the ambition in the play may be not personal but directed towards Macbeth himself) and he fails to perpetuate his line. Of course the role of the dominant woman – an offence to decorum like Lady Macbeth's claim that she wishes to be unsexed – cannot be sustained: from the moment of her failure to murder Duncan herself (on kinship grounds), Lady Macbeth gradually plays a less significant role and is progressively excluded from her husband's counsels. Macbeth's uxoriousness has often been commented on, even to the extent of stressing doubts about his masculinity. Richard Flatter claims the pair commit murder to secure each other's happiness. By contrast the avenger Macduff is not 'born of woman' and is noted for his independence from his wife's feelings.[15]

In an age in which all kinds of authority and possessions, including kingship, property, public office and honours, could be inherited and in which efforts were made to strengthen the principle despite the bureaucratisation of public life, Macbeth's childlessness and his sense of being 'rebuked' (III.i.53–69) by Banquo's line, which holds the future, are a key issue, which only strengthens doubts about Macbeth's masculinity and may explain the butchery of Macduff's family. Macbeth's childlessness, compared with his rival's fruitfulness, becomes obsessive. It may be said that one political issue is resolved at the end because Macbeth has no son to perpetuate the blood feud.

This pre-feudal core of the tragedy is entirely appropriate to eleventh-century Scotland, a society on which feudal ties had not yet been imposed. However, more complex relations are also illustrated. Formal feudal bonds are not explicitly made, but the existence of a thanely class, supposedly possessed of the chivalric virtues of personal courage, loyalty and honour, among whom the political action occurs, enables feudal imagery to be employed. But, as family bonds may be overcome by ambition and the proper ties of blood and family subordination perverted into the bloody imagery and unsexed womanhood of *Macbeth*, so too are feudal values shown as potentially deeply flawed. There is an ambiguity, anyway, in a society organised for war, since the object of fighting is to win and thus stop fighting: Macbeth, in one sense, presents the problem of the newly unemployed soldier which the *Calendar of State Papers Domestic* shows was so familiar to the Elizabethans. Feudal ties were themselves ambiguous: an expression both of loyalty to death and of common self-interest. Feudal society stressed formal statements of unity: oaths, initiation ceremonies, ritualised hospitality, which were attempts to bind members of the military elite to agreed standards of behaviour. Needless to say such ceremonies would not have been stressed had these standards been naturally accepted. Banquo may protest he is 'with a most indissoluble tie / For ever knit' (III.i.17–18) to Macbeth, but we may be sure that, as at their previous meeting (II.i), he carries a sword. The greater the need to curb men of violence, the greater the emphasis on oaths of loyalty, perjury being defined as a sin. This was bolstered in feudal society because only a few were men of honour, capable of taking oaths. We may find echoes of such ideas in the general notion that tragedy was appropriate only to those of high social status. In *Macbeth* it seems to be assumed without question that the grooms could not commit regicide solely on their own initiative (II.iii.126 *et seq.*). But this ascription of both the most prized virtues and the highest crime to the elite did not solve the problems. In *3 Henry VI* (III.i.81) the argument was adduced that oaths could be broken if they had been taken to a king who no longer held power: in *Macbeth* Banquo's protestation does not detract from his role as a man of honour.

We will return below to this theme of the ambiguous virtues in *Macbeth*. It is, however, the Banquet which is the most significant affirmation of feudal unity in the play. As has often been said, its failure marks the beginning of Macbeth's loss of power. Certainly the Banquet should be seen as a 'symbol of solidarity' and contrasted with the anti-feast of the Cauldron scene. It was an opportunity to cement the 'golden opinions' which Macbeth treasured and which were essential in a closed, personal society. But it is not only a symbol of fellowship: in feudal society it was also an affirmation and recognition of superiority and a demonstration of power. In a society in which control of food supplies was the most significant attribute of the powerful, the ability to bestow lavish hospitality was a public manifestation of that power. Banquets are normally given, as in *Macbeth*, by superiors to inferiors with heavy emphasis on formal degree. Even when there was a superior honoured guest (a king) whose position was recognised, most guests were inferior to the host. The refusal to accept hospitality is an insult to that superiority. Macbeth orders Banquo not to fail the feast: the manner in which Banquo does is a studied insult. Macbeth's discomposure is a demonstration of his failing authority far more significant than the supposed admission of guilt into which he is led.

If the Banquet has an ambiguous role as a demonstration

of both unity and authority, so too does this ambiguity extend to many of the virtues of the feudal elite. Does Macbeth's mode of fighting, as reported in I.ii, set him apart from 'civilised' society, as Campbell, for example, claimed? Was this an 'excess of fortitude' and recklessness, the courage of a beast, not a man, as in the final fight with Macduff? We may doubt it: on Campbell's own analysis, Macbeth is not yet a 'slave to passion' and his action is commended by Duncan as that of a 'valiant cousin, worthy gentleman' (I.ii.24). The wounds he inflicts are 'on the front' like those that simple feudal soul, Siward, is glad his son received. Medieval and Tudor society was not squeamish about the bloody nature of feudal fighting (no less bloody in Shakespeare's age of artillery, musket and pike) and did not see its protagonists as set apart from society. But the ambiguity remains: Wilbur Sanders has pointed out, in criticising the Christian providential view of the play in his article, 'The Strong Pessimism of *Macbeth*' in the *Critical Review* (1966), the power of Macbeth's 'demonic energy' in contributing to an awesome sense of the vitality of evil, and questions will be asked below about the triumph of 'good' at the end. We may agree about the 'demonic energy', but if we are to discuss 'evil' it must be related to the mores of that society, the acceptance and integration of the dark side of the military code. An even starker example of the ambiguity in that code is the unquestioned acceptance of the practice, which certainly follows that of later medieval Europe, of fighting essentially for money: it is pinpointed in I.ii.61-4, when Sweno's men are refused burial until he has paid ransom. These practices are wholeheartedly accepted by the 'saintly' Duncan: this is not meant to imply his saintliness is a myth, but that the concept had to embrace the realities of life in an age of feudal battle. The final decapitation of Macbeth is the last example of such realities, as well as being a proper punishment for traitors of high birth.

Generally doubt surrounds the code of honour and the nature of 'manliness'. Some questions about Macbeth's have been referred to: here we must highlight Lady Macbeth's taunting him with cowardice, the main weakness in a soldier of honour. It has been argued that this shows her limited view and that truer manliness is revealed by Macduff, whose final epithet on Macbeth is 'butcher', clearly not a man of honour. We have, however, to accept that Macbeth's crimes are compulsive – guilt, remorse or repentance do not enter – and give full weight to the 'appalling sense of duty' with which Bradley acutely says he murders. It is too facile to portray the story as simply that of a great soldier becoming a cowardly assassin. Macbeth's 'beast-like' end has often been stressed, but so too has his 'hyperbolic courage' and 'kind of nobility'. In fact if Shakespeare had wished to make Macbeth's death literally bestial, he could have followed his source: the real Macbeth dies after flight like a hunted animal. We must note the Elizabethan ambiguity about even the notion of despair, a deadly sin: it has been noted that the courage of a desperate man could be admired. 'What man dare, I dare' (III.iv.99). Macbeth's distinction between the various types of man in III.i.90 *et seq.* is intended to insist on the 'manliness' of 'tak[ing] your enemy off'. What Macbeth offers is not a caricature of fearless manhood: it is one dangerous manifestation of it, and also a demonstration that manliness may be inseparable from fear.

Equally, it is doubtful if Macduff represents a simple polarity on this issue. In the most extreme form he has been presented as a medieval 'harrower of hell', but he is also the 'equivocator' who enters 'Hell's gate'. He is actually a much more ordinary human figure. He faces an appalling dilemma when he flees from his family and fails in his 'manly' duty to protect his wife and child. This failure may be justified in terms of his responsibilities to a wider cause (I do not agree with Campbell that Ross's defence of him is 'vague' – it seems a firm statement of principle), but it is a failure nevertheless. Malcolm is reasonably suspicious of him and he himself says he is a sinner (IV.iii.224–7).

Macduff was making practical decisions which sometimes have horrific costs in the real political world. His practicability can be seen in his willingness to accept a less than perfect king in Malcolm during the testing scene, though his questioning of Malcolm's fitness to be king is of doubtful orthodoxy in Tudor thought.

Similarly the comparison between Macbeth and Banquo is by no means as absolute as has often been depicted – usually, it is held, in order to compliment James I. We are not given a final answer to the problem of how Banquo would have acted had he not been murdered, how the 'hope' with which he ends his last soliloquy (III.i.10) might have been fulfilled. It has been claimed that Macbeth knew Banquo best and that his description of the latter in III.i.48 *et seq.*, reveals his knowledge of his nobility of character, but the words 'He hath a wisdom that doth guide his valour / To act in safety' are ambiguous, implying a quite proper political caution. Of course Banquo is not shown giving way to temptation (he has no opportunity anyway after this), but the fox's outlook is illustrated by his early response to Macbeth's overtures (I.iii.155; II.i.26-9) and his acceptance after the coronation of Macbeth's title and his protestations of loyalty (III.i.15-18), despite his inside knowledge of the Weird Sisters' prophecies. Earlier he, like the guilty Macbeths and unlike Duncan, has been unable to sleep (II.i.6-9). Robert Speaight divides the characters in *Macbeth* into three groups with Macduff, Banquo and Malcolm representing 'average sinful man' between the evil of the Macbeths and the innocence of Duncan and Edward.[16] While these absolute categories are not wholly useful, Banquo is certainly no better than that: indeed he is more equivocal in his reactions than Macduff.

Macbeth does not deal with the greater complexities in the expected conduct of the upper classes which had developed by the end of the sixteenth century: the roles of religion and education in moderating the behaviour of the military elite are not discussed at any length and Macbeth is not a 'man' in the sense of Brutus and Horatio. Nevertheless, there is as serious a critique of the code of honour as that offered by Falstaff, a critique which is not only sceptical but which recognises how good and bad effects may follow from the same premises and indeed how difficult it is to categorise such effects. It is not simply a gap between innate nobility and conduct. Innate nobility in a military elite might well embrace ambition. As Kristian Smidt points out when discussing *Doctor Faustus* and *Macbeth* in *English Studies* (1969), the Elizabethans were told ambition should be shunned, but it was close to the admired virtues of love of greatness, magnanimity and desire for fame.[17] In Macbeth's case this is strengthened by his membership of the royal house. Macbeth's own word 'vaulting' as a description of his ambition has ambiguous overtones, implying both aspiration and excess. A further ambiguity arises over the end of these ambitious endeavours: real power or the winning of 'golden opinions' (I.vii.32-5), which are clearly to be seen not as mere reputation but as an essential part of the solidarity of the elite. The irony in the end, of course, is that Macbeth loses both.

The theme of the ambiguity of the virtues may be widened. A. Harbage's discussion of 'Shakespeare's Ideal Man' (published in *Adams Memorial Studies*), after stressing that he is to be scholarly, soldierly and honest, notes that lying was accepted as compatible with honesty and that generally obligations were felt to other men, not to transcendental virtues. The former we have seen in Banquo, the latter was to be expected given the nature of feudal bonds. But even Harbage does not say what happens when these attributes conflict. It was easy to desire the mean - temperance itself was a virtue - and the control of the passions by reason. Certainly that element is present (*cf.* I.iii.84–5), but in Iago Shakespeare presented a man whose passions are totally controlled by his reason. Passions were often recognised as natural, even, as Ornstein says (*op. cit.*, pp. 40–4), in excess. Macbeth is quite right to ask (and he is convincing enough to be crowned king), 'Who can be wise, amaz'd, temp'rate, and furious, / Loyal and neutral, in a moment?' (II.iii. 107–8). The classical virtues, much discussed in the Middle Ages and Renaissance, were very variously defined in practice: even the notion of decorum - the virtues felt to be appropriate to particular types of men - did not help, for soldiers were expected to be ambitious.

Nowhere was ambiguity more evident than at our third level of politics, the conduct of personal monarchy. Both the connected themes of the rise of the initiating role of the Prince and the growing awareness of possible distinctions between his personal and institutional functions focused attention on the conduct of princely politics and gave an urgency to certain questions which hitherto had been dormant. Were the virtues morally absolute or should they be modified as political circumstances dictated? Was not such a cardinal virtue as prudence capable of being interpreted amorally? Pride was a deadly sin but Aristotelian magnificence was to be admired in a Prince (Ornstein, p. 15). How far could and should Christian piety be retained? Although it was by no means generally agreed, there was a growing uneasy awareness that political or public morality might have to be different from private. It was not just that it was unfortunate, as Maynard Mack, Jr, says in *Killing the King* (p. 11), that in practice the 'fallible body natural was not properly subordinate to the infallible body politic', but that for effective politics it ought not to be: the judgment of an individual, sinful man was necessary to the state, not simply the existence of an abstract *persona* however infallible. Such lines of thought have been, and still are, associated with Machiavelli, but were perhaps as much, like Machiavelli's work itself, the product of the particular pressures and needs of courtly politics in the early modern period.

The interplay of the three levels of political activity focused attention on other issues: monarchy was the key, but the political elite remained small and we have seen that personal honour and ties of blood retained importance. Despite references to the 'State' and the general frame of the commonweal, personal, even blood, loyalty was still a very live issue. In fact in some ways as power and decision-making became concentrated in the monarch and his council of advisers, so the close, sometimes claustrophobic atmosphere of Renaissance court intrigues delayed the evolution of a politics owing more to institutions and office. Courts became more obviously the centres of authority and therefore of all ambition: as the focus of greatest achievement, they were also the places of greatest corruption. As Cardan wrote, 'The pallaces of princes are ever open to great evils.' Political debate came to emphasise not only the role of the Prince but also the quality of his advisers: the suspicion that the latter used their influence for private, not public, ends became a key issue. The management of court factions and patronage became even more significant in the era of personal monarchy. In general Jacobean tragedy concentrates on the 'secret, political nature of life at courts', while Shakespeare shows himself well aware of the dangers of favouritism and sycophancy, and of the need to prevent aristocratic degeneration. The weakening of Elizabeth I's control of factions in the later decades of her reign is a particular example of a problem which had long existed.[18]

The rise of royal power, discussion of its nature and the continued existence of other claims to loyalty produced a volatile politics which kept at the forefront other connected issues: the validity of the social hierarchy, the legitimacy of rule and the justification for resistance. It is now recognised that Shakespeare's attitude to the 'Elizabethan world picture'

171

was more questioning than used to be assumed. It has been said that Ulysses' own character makes him an ambiguous mouthpiece for the most famous exposition of the notion, but whatever else the speech says it emphasises both the need for the practical application of the arts of government while being remarkably unspecific about what should be done. It could be added that an actor and playwright might have his own doubts about a social doctrine which might seem to question the propriety of talent being rewarded. In any case, social mobility, especially in politics, offered too rich dramatic opportunities to be ignored. The pieties of an unchanging social hierarchy could be used as a reference point, but it was change – the rise and fall of great men – which held the attention. Increasingly, in the sixteenth and seventeenth centuries, political theory became concerned with the right of resistance: under what circumstances and by whom was it legitimate to take up arms against existing political authority? When, in short, could the 'Elizabethan world picture' properly be changed?

A monarch's rule might be illegitimate in two ways: through improper acquisition of power or through misuse of power. The first was clearly an issue in *Macbeth*, though generally, given the establishment, with some hiccoughs, of dynastic stability based on primogeniture, it was less of one in most Western European states in the sixteenth century than was the second. With the concentration of religious and secular authority in the same hands after the Reformation, the conduct of government focused more and more on the ruler's willingness to uphold the principles of his or her particular brand of Christianity. But, since sixteenth-century Christianity had strong secular implications, the justification for tyrannicide, though couched in religious terms, could include conduct held to be prejudicial to the commonweal in general. Doing justice, protecting widows and orphans and even defending property could be, and usually were, given a religious gloss. No exponent of the Divine Right of Kings failed to stress the awesome responsibilities of kingship while denying the right of resistance, even to a tyrannical monarch. Resistance to the king had a long theoretical history, being in practice much based on the circumstances in which a feudal oath of loyalty could be broken and a vassal put a dispute with his liege lord to the arbitrament of war, but sixteenth-century developments in the role of monarchy produced first the fully-fledged doctrine of Divine Right and its associated doctrine of non-resistance and the subsequent attempt to broaden the basis on which armed resistance might be taken up. But this right of resistance, even when claimed, was limited to the political elite: this was denied only by some small groups of religious radicals. Both feudal tradition and social prudence dictated that, if rebellion was to be legitimised, its leaders should not be the fickle populace: the 'Elizabethan world picture' might be modified, but only within strict limits.

It has been claimed that Shakespeare's greatest political concern was with the qualities making for ideal kingship and that the list in IV.iii.92-4 shows that he used James I's standard list of qualities. But James I, as a quite acute practising politician giving useful advice to his heir, was, like Shakespeare, fully conscious of political realities. There is a neat Machiavellian overtone to his recommendation that one of the cardinal virtues, temperance, should be used in applying another, justice. Generally in *Basilikon Doron* James I was well aware of how far princely behaviour had to be based on grounds of expediency rather than morality. The character of Henry V shows that Shakespeare too recognised a gap between public and private morality: it is too simple to see the issue, as Tillyard does, as one of a choice between public chivalric virtues and private sloth and vanity. Conversely Henry VI was a good man but a poor king.

Many of these issues are raised in *Macbeth* with significant twists. We may, if we wish, make a clear distinction between the good and the bad: the idealised patriarchal kingship of Duncan may be compared with Macbeth's tyranny. Macbeth, in murdering him, has been said to kill a father-figure and cut off the source of his own nourishment (in political terms, read patronage). Thus the first and third levels of political relations are linked: the murder is termed sacrilege and Duncan's virtues are trumpeted by Macbeth himself. But D.B. Barron has properly pointed out (*The American Imago*, 1960, p. 144) that Duncan is no threat to Macbeth's self-esteem: this is no classic killing of a dominant father-figure. Many of the attributes ascribed to Duncan have a questionable double edge in a king. Is his gentleness what was required? I. Robinson has spoken (*Critical Review*, 1968, pp. 101-2) of Duncan's court as no model, but disorderly compared with the orderly proceedings of the 'committee of witches': early

on the Witches' is the real world, not Duncan's. More specifically Duncan is shown as unable to make accurate judgments
about either Cawdor or Macbeth (I.iv.11-14). Duncan's
virtues are those of a private man: his innocence that of the
martlet.

Certainly, as Helen Gardner has said (*English Studies*,
1948, pp. 53-4), Macbeth's crime is without the excuses
offered by Holinshed, but that needs to be glossed. Duncan's
government could have been made incompetent and weak
without qualification: it is more subtle for Shakespeare to
show the significance of monarchy while still leaving doubts
about Duncan's judgment. Monarchy is an 'imperial theme'
(I.iii.129), giving 'solely sovereign sway and masterdom'
(I.v.67). Duncan condemns a traitor to death without trial
(though there is said to have been a confession: I.iii.115) and
reallocates his title (I.ii.66-7). Cawdor implores the king's
pardon (I.iv.5-7) and Duncan's bestowal of patronage on
Macbeth, Banquo and the assembled nobility (I.iv.28-32,
39-42, 54-6) reciprocates the obeisance of Macbeth and his
wife (I.iv.22-7; I.vi.14-20, 25-8). On the other hand, although
Duncan and Edward may be both men in a state of innocence,
Duncan's kingdom is subject to a succession of foreign in-
vasions and domestic insurrections while Edward can launch
a successful attack on a foreign country. Edward, not Duncan,
can cure scrofula. William Rosen adds, 'Shakespeare purposely
elevates Macbeth's stature above that of Duncan and Banquo.
Too often this is not stressed . . . in studies which set off
patterns of order against those of disorder, or in analyses of
imagery only.'[19] In thinking about possible political hints
in *Macbeth* we should not ignore the fact that apparently
minor political errors are swiftly punished. Not only does
Duncan misjudge his leading thanes, but the consequences
of Malcolm and Donalbain's reaction to their father's murder
are harsh: exile and reliance on foreign help to regain the
throne (*cf*. II.iii.98, 118 *et seq*.; II.iv.23-7). Medieval kingship
is shown to require the exercise of both power and judgment:
it may not be an unreal question for Macbeth to ask whether
Duncan is going to heaven or to hell (II.i.64). As Sanders
points out (*op. cit.*, p. 43), Shakespeare 'realised what a
disaster it would be for the earth if the meek did inherit it.'
Given the nature of political life as it is illustrated, the early
contrast between Duncan and Macbeth is marked. Macbeth is
the effective dominant figure even in his absence: it has been

said that Duncan almost exaggerates his worth and unconsciously promotes treason: he is a 'peerless kinsman', a phrase which in feudal society needs to be taken literally as denoting someone without equals and set above the rest of the aristocracy. There is due to him 'more than all can pay' (I.iv.21), itself a confession of royal inadequacy. The fact that Macbeth has to pay himself makes his crime, as has been neatly put, 'strongly if not justly motivated'. We may perhaps ask, as Mack has done of Richard II, Gaunt and Bolingbroke, 'who has more substance as king, Duncan or Macbeth?'[20]

Duncan's final misjudgment is his nomination of his son Malcolm as his successor (I.iv.36–9). Again a more overt statement of Macbeth's claims could have been made by referring to the Scottish law of tanistry, under which the succession varied, at the choice of the baronage, between the main lines of the royal house, depending on suitability and political power. Elizabeth Nielsen has made the strongest case for Macbeth's actions under this head, stressing that Duncan was attempting to alter the succession rules: if tanistry had applied Macbeth would have had the strongest claim to succeed him. But, apart from other criticisms, this thesis is irrelevant to the play since, as Roy Walker pointed out long ago, Shakespeare refers neither to the law of tanistry nor to Duncan's own unlawful tenure of the throne.[21] There is a constitutional issue, but it is as clouded as most of the other political topics in the play: certainly this is no simple paean to hereditary monarchy by primogeniture, as Henry Paul maintains in his claim that *Macbeth* was written specifically for a Royal Command Performance to please James I. Several constitutional positions are postulated in the play. First, Duncan attempts to impose not a hereditary succession by primogeniture, but a *nominated* one: these are not identical, even if the eldest son is nominated, since the whole point of nomination is that he need not be (that the issue was still alive in sixteenth century England may be seen from Henry VIII's will). Second, the baronage, we assume, set aside this nomination, presumably mainly (? wholly) on the grounds that the nominee is thought guilty of murdering the nominator. Macbeth is chosen, which is the nearest the play comes to tanistry. Third, Malcolm and his supporters base their claim on hereditary right, his nomination by his father not having been accepted. But while the constitutional issue is unavoidably present, it is not stressed. Macbeth is not shown to have a legal grievance, but a claim of power. In the play Duncan makes errors of judgment, not of law. Tanistry is not omitted because it would offend the susceptibilities of James I (on that argument it would have been as appropriate to have included it explicitly so as to show its evil effects), but because its working (the choice of Macbeth as king) could be demonstrated without explicit focusing on legalistic claims. Malcolm's legal claim is sharply contrasted with the work done for the monarchy by Macbeth and the other military leaders. As in *Lear*, Shakespeare is more concerned with the conduct of existing kings – in both Lear and Duncan's cases with their provision for the succession as an aspect of their competence – than with abstract rights, though the management of the latter is an aspect of monarchy.

Any discussion of *Macbeth* as a play written for royal performance must focus far more sharply than Paul does on the issue of king-killing. It was, of course, in the interests of incumbent kings, like James I, to fulminate against usurpers and Macbeth may be seen simply as a criminal opposed by a lawful and hereditary king. But the play does not postulate only that (especially if one is then going on to argue, as does Paul, that *King* Macbeth is killed off-stage so as not to offend James by having a king killed before his eyes). The doctrine of non-resistance was double-edged. It was clear and absolute in the case of a legitimate king: Macdonwald is called a 'slave' (I.ii.20), in contemporary usage a chattel without full human personality. A usurper successfully established in power was a more difficult case. The killing of a usurper may be lawful: but the problem is to define usurpation. Whether or not Macbeth is a legitimate holder of the office of king is again left ambiguous. As far as we are told, Macbeth is chosen king by the proper procedure and is generally accepted apart from Macduff's act of feudal defiance. It will not do simply to say that he has misled the thanes and is improperly chosen: apart from Banquo's inside knowledge, it could be claimed that divine will has worked through the choice and the crowning of Macbeth. The difficulty is revealed in Muriel Bradbrook's sentence, 'As rightful heir, Malcolm alone has the power to depose an anointed king, usurper though he be' (*Shakespeare Survey* (1951), p. 38). Apart from the problem of the status of those fighting in Malcolm's army (or that of the English king, of Siward and of Macduff who actually kills Macbeth), this blurs the problem of the anointing. One strand of orthodox opinion (including James I) held that the worst tyrant's oppression should be willingly accepted since it was sent by God to test the Christian humility of the subject.

This last point introduces another complication: Shakespeare's amendment of his sources to make the whole of Macbeth's reign tyrannical (instead of merely its last few years) makes it questionable whether he falls because he is a usurper or because of the nature of his reign. If anything the balance of allegiance seems more influenced by the latter. Of course once he has fallen his claim on the doctrine of non-resistance equally lapses and he can be castigated as a usurper: he becomes a 'butcher'.

If Macbeth's status as a ruler is in doubt, there is no such ambiguity about his achievement. In *Hamlet*, Shakespeare shows an elected king, Claudius, equally guilty of murder, ruling rather competently; but Macbeth is a failure. Two points may be noted: first the difference between acquiring power and holding it, and second Machiavelli's stress, in discussing the holding of power, on the easier task of those who have acquired it by clearly legitimate means. A 'little water' will not cleanse the deed without a great deal more effort and care. This is perhaps the most useful way of presenting the argument put, by Macbeth himself ('foul deeds will rise') and many later commentators, that the guilty party cannot get away with it: that there is not only moral degeneration but political incapacity. What Macbeth in fact could not get away with was not Duncan's murder (which he does), but incompetent rule and, as will be discussed later, an attempt to gainsay the prophecies by murdering Banquo. Ornstein asks (p. 230) the rhetorical question, who has succeeded in reaping the benefit of peace and order which Machiavelli thought would come from violent deeds? The answer, apart perhaps from Claudius in *Hamlet*, is the real-life Macbeth to a large extent. Shakespeare knew he had survived well after the assassination of Duncan.

In practice the Prince's initiating role in politics was obviously limited by the need to react to, or at best anticipate, dangers. This is very well illustrated in *Macbeth*. Macbeth lets loose events to begin with, but gradually the initiative switches to the rising opposition and, in Campbell's terms, fear replaces ambition as Macbeth's dominant passion. The standard propaganda of the opposition about Macbeth's rule includes, like most such, accusations of vices which Macbeth hardly had time, let alone inclination, to commit (such as 'luxury and avarice'),[22] but what Macbeth is actually seen doing is eliminating possible threats to his position. Historically it was probably not open to Shakespeare to make anything of Holinshed's report of Macbeth's years of good rule: not only was Macbeth a representative of a rival line to the one in power in England, but equally representative of a rival tradition of Celtic independence from the Anglicising influences on Scotland of the allies and supporters of Edward the Confessor and successive English kings. Nevertheless it means Macbeth in the play is a poor Machiavellian: he makes efforts to dissimulate in showing a proper public face at the time of Duncan's murder but this is unavoidable and anyway collapses at the Banquet. As king perhaps his only Machiavellian act is offering 'politic' reasons for not murdering Banquo himself (III.i.117-24).[23] He is unable to make the transition from a good 'second in command' to that of chief politician; from the frenetic activism of his military role to the preservation of peace and order. This transition had been required from European monarchs: Macbeth, arousing opposition when he most needed to quieten it, cannot make it. He ends with the most complete political failure: execution following civil war and invasion.

We have seen that there may be good reasons, in terms of public policy and the dramatic argument, for Shakespeare to suppress the real Macbeth's years of competent exercise of power, but from other points of view the historian (and perhaps the literary critic?) may regret the change. This is not in the interests of historical veracity (we have no way of knowing whether, and in what senses, Macbeth was a 'good' king), but because the change removes from Shakespeare's picture interesting complexities. A usurping Macbeth, maintaining himself in power by the exercise of judicious, even moral, kingship, would have enabled Shakespeare to explore further the possible ambiguities, evident in other plays, in the whole notion of the improper rise to power of those not born to it. The social hierarchy, if by no means upset, would at least have been wrinkled. Also such a change would have avoided the danger of simplifying the difficulties contemporaries faced of trying to prove that God's justice is executed in this world. This was always easier to assert than to prove satisfactorily. It is true, as Ornstein points out (p. 275), that simply to show the restoration of a moral order does not wholly remove the difficulties since it may not offset the evil done: in particular, Duncan, Banquo and Macduff's family are recompensed only indirectly. But a Macbeth who reigned well certainly would have produced a sharper awareness of the problems than has been evident in much critical writing.

The divorce between the institutional and personal roles of the king and the gap between the expectation that he could control affairs and the reality that he was merely reacting to them were the background to much imagery, in *Macbeth* and other Shakespearean plays, about the distance between illusion and reality. Often this extends in *Macbeth* beyond the political realm but it focuses on the latter. It has produced much discussion of the 'borrowed clothes' metaphor, and is inverted by Malcolm in IV.iii. The king as stage-manager, Machiavellian master of stratagems, coexists with his role as manipulator of nothingness, seeing a meaningless world: again Macbeth, however he may have begun, ends by losing control and being more deceived than deceiving.

In short Shakespeare, like other Jacobean playwrights, recognised the political jungle: this was necessary on both realistic and dramatic grounds. The relationship between political intrigue, political morality and political success was complex: he refused to make simplistic judgments that political success was achieved by the exclusion of either morality or intrigue. It was not a matter of comparing an older, idealised form of kingship (represented by old Hamlet, Gaunt and Duncan) with a newer, efficient amoral one (cf. Mack *op. cit., passim*), but of assessing the strengths, difficulties and anomalies in both models. Each should contain elements of the other, the claims of legitimacy having to be balanced against those of expediency and political acumen. As Frye wrote (*op. cit.*, pp. 14, 18), kingship has to be effortful.

The end of *Macbeth* may appear to resolve the difficulties: a somewhat easy harmony is achieved with Malcolm handing out the spoils, but the basis of his success needs to be

179

recognised. The 'new regicide' under the 'label of revenge' (Mack, *op. cit.*, pp. 74-5) is done by an active military leader who has learnt to be a cleverer politician than either of his two predecessors as king. If Malcolm is another claimant for Shakespeare's ideal king, let us appreciate the ambiguity of the portrait: he has shown successful dissimulation in the testing of Macduff; and harmony is, as usual, achieved at the cost of further innocent deaths. It is a function of successful monarchy that people should die for it: the bleeding sergeant saved Malcolm earlier; now young Siward and other loyal Scots die. We should remember that in Jacobean drama the disinherited, like Malcolm, are often fallen men, loss of property being morally degrading in that society, and note the ambiguity in Tillyard's assessment that Malcolm is 'the ideal ruler who has subordinated all his personal pleasures, and with them all personal charm, to his political obligations.'

Surprisingly many critics, while recognising the theme of equivocation, have been unwilling to extend it to the political and moral spheres and have been content with establishing polarities between absolutes. As a fifteenth-century morality had it, 'A Soul is both foul and fair' and so is political man. Gardner writes (*op. cit.*, p. 47) that Macbeth is in rebellion against the 'essential facts of things': in fact he, like everyone in the play, has a partial vision. (Even the eventual victor, Malcolm, makes a serious initial mistake.)

All operate in partial darkness in a very volatile political world. Generally in the Middle Ages and the Renaissance the volatility of politics gave much cause for concern: much attention was devoted to the question of the degree to which political life might be controlled, or at least reasonable in-surance obtained for the future, generally by politicians and particularly by princes. Despair at the vagaries of fortune, not necessarily offset, in the clearest minds, by any vision of a providential pattern of historical development, coexisted with a grandiose view of man's capabilities. Perhaps Machiavelli presented this ambivalence most sharply: it is uncertain whether the greatness or the insignificance of man is being celebrated. The lack of any analysis of political or social structures and the concentration of decision-making in a few hands with rapid changes of fortune had perpetuated through the Middle Ages the classical notion of the power and inscrutability of fortune and man's inability to control it. The Middle Ages gave the notion a Christian frame by emphasising the role of the Divine Will in the affairs of man. But since, given original sin, Divine Providence might take the form, in this world, of punishing the righteous or exalting the wicked, this did not give a more secure foundation for political action. The later medieval emphasis on the absolute freedom of God's Will hardly increased man's certainty: it was presumptuous of man to assume he knew the workings of a mysterious God. There was no psychological determinism to permit judgment about individual motives: contemporary psychology might be based on physiology, but the Elizabethans believed the individual could conceal, offset or heighten his dominant characteristics (see the earlier discussion of dissimulation). There was indeed 'no art / To find the mind's construction in the face' (I. iv.11-12).

Nevertheless, as in the physical sciences the elevation of divine freedom undermined the Thomist notion of a rational theology, facilitating the separation of faith and reason and permitting the development of the latter, so too in politics the Renaissance saw a paradoxical re-emphasis on man's ability to work at least with fortune, if not against it, and the appearance of an embryonic science of politics.[24] To achieve political success exceptional ability was required and much time was spent in the fifteenth and sixteenth centuries discussing the various virtues that might be needed. From these repetitive discussions *Macbeth* picks up four issues. First, as we have seen, the stress was on being active. 'Fortune favours the brave' was a recurrent theme: not only was an active life preferred to withdrawal from it, but in it an initiating and decisive role was commended as most likely to bring success among political uncertainties. Second, whatever the particular status of the Witches, it is surely true that Macbeth remains a free agent, not a pawn of Fate: this is necessary politically, morally and dramatically. Third, from a political point of view, Macbeth has one great advantage over his contemporaries (and indeed over his opponents in Acts IV and V): he actually knows the future on demand. He is neither lied to nor, despite frequent assertions, is any deception practised on him by the Witches. Furthermore the prophecies do not seem to be equivocations in the sense under contemporary discussion: the enunciated statements are not contradicted but supplemented and given a compatible, if alternative, meaning by the Witches' reservations.

Macbeth is told or shown the literal truth but still gets his policies wrong. Fourth, Macbeth is successful while he works with the prophecies, unsuccessful when he tries to thwart them. He may call on Fate to champion him (III.i.70–1), but it will not. His error is not, as Father Bernard (*Shakespeare Quarterly*, 1962, p. 60) said, in paying 'too careful attention' to the 'juggling fiends', but too little. He first appears 'disdaining Fortune' in his early fight (I.ii.17); and this takes on an ironic meaning, since such disdain will in the end destroy him. A further irony may be noted in Macbeth's attempt to convince the Murderers that Banquo has held them under fortune. If there is a lesson it may be that the twists of politics continue to defeat even those granted a little insight. Fortune is still a 'rebel's whore' and the Witches castigated as 'imperfect speakers'.

Let us add one final twist: those who left a performance of *Macbeth* interested enough to pursue the study of Scottish history would soon discover that Malcolm's son is murdered by the Donalbain who disappeared to Ireland in Act II. The despised 'kerns and gallowglasses' of the Celtic reaction thus got some revenge on the Anglo-Scottish political establishment, but not even Shakespeare would have dared to show that in the decade of the Plantation of Ulster.

NOTES

1 H. Weisinger, 'The Study of Shakespearian Tragedy since Bradley', *Shakespeare Quarterly*, 6 (1955), p. 387, quoting Cleanth Brooks.

2 W.A. Murray, 'Why was Duncan's Blood Golden?', *Shakespeare Survey*, 19 (1966), pp. 34–44.

3 L.C. Knights, *Explorations* (London, 1946, edition cited 1964), p. 29; G. Wilson Knight, *The Wheel of Fire* (London, 1930)) chap. 7.

4 L.B. Campbell, *Shakespeare's Tragic Heroes* (London, 1930, edition cited 1978), p. 3; I. Ribner, '*Macbeth*, the Pattern of Idea and Action', *SQ*, 10 (1959), p. 147. However, Campbell adds, 'we must find how men looked at this problem of evil in the day when these tragedies were first played.'

5 Q. Skinner, *The Foundations of Modern Political Thought* (2 vols, Cambridge, 1978), vol. 1, pp. xiii–xiv.

6 C.H. Herford, *A Sketch of Recent Shakespearean Criticism* (London, 1925), quoted in Campbell, *op. cit.*, p. 242; K. Muir, *Shakespeare's Tragic Sequence* (London, 1972), p. 14.

7 I. Ribner, 'Political Doctrine in *Macbeth*', *SQ*, 4 (1953), p. 203;

R. Ornstein, *The Moral Vision of Jacobean Tragedy* (edition cited, Madison, 1965), p. 20; A. Harbage, 'Shakespeare's Ideal Man', (eds) J.G. McManaway *et al.*, *Joseph Quincy Adams, Memorial Studies* (Washington, 1948), pp. 67–8; S.L. Bethell, *Shakespeare and the Popular Dramatic Tradition* (London, 1944), *passim*.

8 H.N. Paul, *The Royal Play of 'Macbeth'* (New York, 1950) will be discussed below and in an appendix; Ornstein, *op. cit.*, p. 15.

9 Even such an intelligent work as A. Righter, *Shakespeare and the Idea of the Play* (edition cited, London, 1967), p. 154, refers to a 'commonplace . . . that with the turn of the century there came a pronounced darkening in the temper of the age.' The Essex plot does duty for a great deal in this connection! Muir, *op. cit.*, p. 18, points out that there is no evidence tragedy is written in times of disillusion and uncertainty, but is on much weaker ground in dismissing the connection because the great tragedies were written after 1603 when apparently the worst of the crisis was over. A malaise in society does not cure itself that quickly. Anyway the Gunpowder Plot can always be resurrected to provide the 'atmosphere of treason and distrust' which informs *Macbeth* (Bethell, *op. cit.*, p. 46).

V.Y. Kantak, 'An Approach to Shakespearian Tragedy: the 'Actor' Image in *Macbeth*', *SS*, 16 (1963), p. 42, presents the opposite and equally untenable view: he refers to the 'intense vitality of the Elizabethans . . . their confident and adventurous participation in a world of expanding horizons.' The pessimistic view could be presented as more significant by stressing the chronic food shortages and underemployment, the monopolistic outlook on economic questions, the colonial failures and doubtfully successful piratical and naval ventures, the adverse balance of payments and struggling basic industries. In fact all such generalisations about a society of even a few million people have little validity.

10 C. Hoy, 'Jacobean Tragedy and the Mannerist Style', *SS*, 26 (1973), pp. 49–67, attempts interestingly to present the connections between the crisis of the Renaissance (i.e. the 'Counter-Renaissance') and Shakespearean tragedy through the medium of mannerism. Apart from the fact that many of the ideas (e.g. the gap between appearance and reality) have roots much earlier than the Counter-Renaissance, this is marred by its links with Hauser's Marxist analysis: the latter stresses the development of commodity production and the sale of labour as the roots of 'alienation'. These were certainly not new, and doubtfully more widespread, in the sixteenth century.

11 See the discussion of this theme in Skinner, *op. cit.*, *passim*.

12 This is discussed in E. Kantorowicz, *The King's Two Bodies* (Princeton, 1957) and applied to Shakespearean tragedy in M. Mack, Jr, *Killing the King* (New Haven, 1973) and (ed.) J.G. Price, *The Triple Bond* (London, 1975), p. 116. The doctrine particularly concerned

the executive arm of government and should be applied to the role of Parliament only with caution (Mack, p. 7).

13 N. Frye, *Fools of Time; Studies in Shakespearean Tragedy* (London, 1967), pp. 18-19. Democracy in the modern sense is of course not the same as the popular government of a city state, the value and viability of which were a contemporary issue discussed in other Shakespearean plays.

14 Cf. my article, 'The Government and its Aims' (ed.) C. Russell, *The Origins of the English Civil War* (London, 1973), pp. 35-65.

15 R. Flatter, 'The Question of Free Will, and other Observations on *Macbeth*', *English Miscellany*, 10 (1959), pp. 100, 104. B. Goode, 'How Little the Lady knew her Lord: a note on *Macbeth*', *American Imago*, 20 (1963), pp. 349-56 claims Lady Macbeth is manipulated by her husband.

16 R. Speaight, 'Nature and Grace in *Macbeth*', *Essays by Divers Hands*, 27 (1955), pp. 96, 100-1 and 106.

17 I. Robinson, 'The Witches and Macbeth', *Critical Review*, ii (1968), pp. 103-4, argues that Macbeth does not have ambition but conceives a passionate desire to be king and a bloodthirsty tyrant. The evidence for the latter and the distinction between ambition and desiring to be king seem obscure, but his more general point that Macbeth fulfils his nature in so acting is acceptable.

18 J.E. Neale, 'The Elizabethan Political Scene', *Essays in Elizabethan History* (London, 1958), pp. 59-84.

19 W. Rosen, *Shakespeare and the Craft of Tragedy* (Cambridge, Mass., 1960), p. 64.

20 Mack, *op. cit.*, p. 50.

21 For the controversy see E. Nielsen, '*Macbeth*: the Nemesis of the Post-Shakespearian Actor', *SQ* 16 (1965), pp. 193-9; M.J.C. Echeruo, 'Tanistry, the "Due of Birth" and Macbeth's Sin', *ibid.*, 23 (1972), pp. 444-50 and Nielsen's reply, *ibid.*, 24 (1973), pp. 226-7; R. Walker, *The Time is Free: A Study of 'Macbeth'* (London, 1949), pp. 39-40; see also R.J. Adam, 'The Real Macbeth: King of Scots, 1040-1054', *History Today*, 7 (1957), pp. 381-2. Nielsen's claim that 'all England' would be conscious of Scottish history after James I's accession may also be viewed sceptically.

22 J.H. Jack, 'Macbeth, King James, and the Bible', *A Journal of English Literary History*, 22 (1955), pp. 185-6, points out that these vices may be taken as symbolic of evil, but that merely compounds the problem by adding further dramatic ambiguity.

23 W. Clemen, *Shakespeare's Dramatic Art, Collected Essays* (London, 1972), p. 83, n. 2, quoting Hunter, says Macbeth cleverly extracts from Banquo all the details he needs to carry out the murder. This does not seem very clever in the text: he simply asks him. Also Macbeth's 'chilling coldness' is difficult to detect (J.B. Harcourt, 'I Pray You, Remember the Porter', *SQ* 12 (1961), pp. 397-8). Perhaps Macbeth's spy system should be mentioned, but

this seems less effective than the real-life one of Queen Elizabeth I under Walsingham: it does not catch Macduff.
24 Skinner, *op. cit.*, i, p. 106.

APPENDIX TO CHAPTER 8

Paul's *Royal Play of 'Macbeth'* and related points

I have made explicit or implicit criticisms of Paul's argument that *Macbeth* is a 'royal command' play. It is a significant topic because I believe acceptance of Paul's argument would undermine my belief in the ambiguity of the political 'lessons' and characterisation of *Macbeth*. I refer to the discussions of Duncan, Macduff, Banquo and Malcolm, of James I's views of kingship compared with IV.iii, and of the legitimacy of resistance and regicide. Paul claims (p. 150) Shakespeare was 'careful to keep these progenitors of the king [Duncan, Malcolm, Banquo, Fleance and old Siward] free from any thing which might seem unworthy of his royal family': I do not believe Shakespeare so limited himself. It may be added that James I would not have regarded it as a sufficient justification that Macduff was free to kill the incumbent king because he had not taken a personal oath of allegiance (pp. 195–6): how many millions of James's subjects at home or Catholics abroad, who were potential assassins, were in such a position? Nor would he have been satisfied that Kings Duncan and Macbeth were killed offstage (p. 407).

I have stressed that James's views on kingship were stronger and more subtle than either the somewhat elementary reference to the virtues in IV.iii (therefore I also disagree with *SQ*, 2, pp. 281–5) or the portrayal of Duncan's kingship, Shakespeare's 'most ideal king' to Paul (p. 197; and cf. pp. 132, 136–7, 140–1, 149, 359–60, 364–5 and 391–2; see also *Adams Memorial Studies*, pp. 257 and 266–7). Paul often praises Duncan's effectiveness as king (pp. 197–8, 221, 338 and 348–9) but on p. 185 he says Macbeth recognises his weakness. I do not accept the 'lofty ethical tone' of *Basilikon Doron* which is said (p. 132) to find its 'complete exemplification' in *Macbeth*.

Another major plank in Paul's argument is his frequent stressing of Shakespeare's dependence on James I's *Daemonologie* for the use of the psychological and the supernatural

185

in *Macbeth*. However, he also says that Shakespeare left the door open for different interpretations and indeed invited the king to take a more rational view. Since James's view was, on Paul's claim, elastic and changing, an exact comparison and assessment of indebtedness are difficult. Paul also claims that, while the Witches are based on a Scots pattern, they include English elements to make them more effective: this is an odd argument given his analysis of the audience as primarily Scots. They certainly appear as English hags, not 'well-conditioned' Scots witches. It is better to stress the eclecticism of the sources of the Witches, and perhaps the 'superiority' of Shakespeare's treatment to that of 'all his contemporaries, including King James' (see comments by W.A. Murray and W.M. Marchant in *SS* 19 (1966), pp. 42–3 and 80–1).

The 'imperial theme' is not simply to be equated with hereditary dynastic succession (p. 183n, *Adams Memorial Studies*, pp. 253–5). *Imperium* had the much more significant connotation of freedom from superior authority, whether temporal or ecclesiastical. Oddly Paul quotes (*Adams Memorial orial Studies*, p. 257) the Holy Roman Empire as a model: this was in fact a monarchy based not on hereditary primogeniture, but nomination and election.

Some specific points about Paul's thesis:

(i) It is doubtful if it would be primarily a Scottish audience at a command performance for King James and King Christian of Denmark: the Scots were not that prevalent.

(ii) p. 418. We are asked to believe that a work so full of complex word-play and cross references would have been suitable as a command performance before a king (Christian) who could not speak English.

(iii) pp. 37, 160–1, 331 and 344. It does not require the visit of a Danish king to account for the substitution of Norwegians for Danes in the play: the existence of a Danish queen of England would have been sufficient.

(iv) p. 40. The argument that the phrase 'dead butcher and his fiend-like Queen' (V.viii.69) is acceptable only because it was intended for the two kings is doubtful: it seems precisely what the victors would be likely to say anyway.

(v) p. 156. It is very odd to quote Seyton's loyalty to Macbeth as a way of complimenting James I, and even odder that insomnia should be dwelt on (p. 187) because James suffered from it.

(vi) *Adams Memorial Studies*, pp. 258 and 265–6. The stressing of the Scots king's lineal descent from father to son needs to be reconciled much more strongly with the fact that James VI's predecessor in Scotland was a woman.

(vii) *Ibid.*, pp. 264–5. Paul seems to equate the appointment of Earls at the end as a means of stabilisation: reducing the aristocracy would be much more of a compliment to monarchy in the sixteenth and early seventeenth centuries.

(viii) Paul, pp. 333, 336. The view that the early Macbeth is simply heroic needs qualifying in the light of the doubts about his reported conduct in I.ii.

(ix) The relationship of the play to the king's interests differs: over the question of touching for the king's evil Shakespeare is said (pp. 367–87) to be trying to induce in the king a more 'superstitious' attitude (or at least others are said to be trying): over witchcraft the reverse is said to be true (*cf. SQ*, 24, p. 22 and *The Triple Bond*, pp. 233–4).

(x) The attitude to Scotland needs qualifying. Paul states rather vaguely (pp. 157–8) that James I was 'interested' in the process of Anglicisation of Scotland. It is necessary to confront directly the portrayal of Scotland as a diseased society needing purgation, while England and her king are the physicians: this is an odd compliment to a Scots king (*cf. SS*, 9, pp. 126 and 131). (Similarly Echeruo, *SQ*, 23, p. 449, makes an odd point in saying that a play meant to compliment James I would not have insisted on a creditable view of Scottish values.) It is true that one issue raised is one on which English and lowland Scots (including James I) could unite: their dislike of the Highlanders, Islanders and Irish (*cf. Adams, op. cit.*, pp. 382–7).

Generally it may be said that, apart perhaps from a Scottish dimension in the demonology, Shakespeare derives his ideas from a wider range of thought than that provided by James's own writings which anyway were often derivative. Paul asserts (p. 388) that the play does not suffer from adaptation to the king's interests: it is my belief that had it been so adapted it would have suffered. This applies *a fortiori* to Jack's adaptation (*JELH*, 1955, pp. 173–93) of Paul's argument which stresses a common concern of Shakespeare and the king with Christian imagery and pattern: again it must be asked what was the king's specific contribution to these commonplace themes.

A complication is introduced by Amneus' argument ('Macbeth's "Greater Honor",' *Shakespeare Studies*, 6 (1970), pp. 223-30) that Shakespeare actually made Duncan nominate Macbeth, not Malcolm, as his successor in the public performance and only substituted the present version as a royal compliment. It is unclear how this deals with I.iv. 48 *et seq.*, which, as has been seen, may be read as a recognition that Malcolm has to be killed (made unnecessary by his flight). Amneus uses Banquo's speech (II.i.26-9) as evidence, but this may be read simply as a recognition of a possible hypothetical situation: Macbeth could become a candidate for the Crown, or even king, and thus a recipient of Banquo's loyalty, without harming Duncan or his family. The reference to a 'greater honour' (I.iii.104) is compatible with Duncan's recognition that he cannot properly reward Macbeth: his sudden nomination of Malcolm is further evidence of his ineptitude. On p. 227 Amneus does not recognise that *public* assassination and seizure of the throne were clearly possible in that society. The whole argument rests much on Forman's account, but he is as likely to have been in error in writing Macbeth for Malcolm as Northumberland for Cumberland. Why anyway should Malcolm and Donalbain flee? In general this change would have to be further integrated with the rest of the play.

9

Macbeth
and witchcraft

Peter Stallybrass

For students of *Macbeth*, witchcraft[1] has always presented a problem. At the one extreme, we have scholars like T.A. Spalding and W.C. Curry who have unearthed some of the historical *minutiae* of medieval and Renaissance concepts of witchcraft;[2] at the other extreme, we have critics who accept the play's witchcraft only as a form of psychological symbolism. Since the publications of Keith Thomas's *Religion and the Decline of Magic* (1971) and Alan Macfarlane's *Witchcraft in Tudor and Stuart England* (1970),[3] the latter position has seemed less tenable. But this does not mean that we should return to the (admittedly useful) positivistic data-gathering of Spalding and Curry to understand the function of witchcraft in *Macbeth*. I see little point, for instance, in attempting to *classify* the Weird Sisters as witches or warlocks or norns (distinctions which were rarely observed by Tudor and Stuart witchcraft treatises or reports of trials). Such classifications tend to emphasize the exoticism of witch-craft beliefs without beginning to explain how such beliefs could ever have been held.

It is, indeed, worth emphasizing the 'normality' of witch-craft beliefs. Although witchcraft accusations reached epi-demic proportions in sixteenth- and seventeenth-century Europe, witchcraft beliefs are endemic in many societies. Their frequency, however, should not be taken as evidence for the truth of witchcraft (there is no proof, for instance, that 'witches' eat their own children, cause sickness, plague or famine, or have sexual relations with devils) but as evidence of the social utility of such beliefs in a variety of societies. An adequate explanation of witchcraft, then, needs to have a double focus: on the one hand, it must describe the actual beliefs and explain how they fit within a particular cosmology; on the other hand, it must take into account the *function* of such beliefs ('a myth provides a charter for action').[4]

Witchcraft beliefs are one way of asserting distinctions; they 'sharpen definitions,'[5] as Mary Douglas puts it, including definitions of political and familial roles. They can be used, for instance, to account for the 'unnatural' ambition of a rival or for the 'unnatural' power of a woman. In doing so, such beliefs imply and legitimate their opposite, the 'natural'. In short, witchcraft beliefs are less a reflection of a real 'evil' than a social construction from which we learn more about the accuser than the accused, more about the social institutions which tolerate/encourage/act on those accusations than about the activities of those people (in England, mainly women, mainly poor) who were prosecuted as witches. What Mary Douglas says of dirt could be said of witchcraft: it 'is never a unique, isolated event' but rather 'the by-product of a systematic ordering and classification . . . in so far as ordering involves rejecting inappropriate elements.'[6] Witchcraft accusations are a way of reaffirming a particular order against outsiders, or of attacking an internal rival, or of attacking 'deviance'. Witchcraft in *Macbeth*, I will maintain, is not simply a reflection of a pre-given order of things: rather, it is a particular working upon, and legitimation of, the hegemony of patriarchy.

WITCHCRAFT AND MONARCHY

The English government had, at least since 1300, been concerned with 'witches' – 'with sorcerers, because they might attempt to kill the king, with prophets (including astrologers) because they might forecast the hour of his death.' The Duke of Buckingham, accused of treason in 1521, had been encouraged by a prophecy that he would be king, although he had been warned that the prophet, a Carthusian monk, 'might be deceived by the devil'. In 1558, Sir Anthony Fortescue was arrested for sorcery, having cast a horoscope which stated that the Queen 'should not live passing the next spring', and in 1580, Nicholas Johnson was accused of 'making her Majesty's picture in wax'.[7] This last case was one of the factors in the passing of a new Act in 1580-1 which attacked the 'divers persons wickedly disposed' who had 'not only wished her Majesty's death, but also by divers means practised and sought to know how long her Highness should live, and who should reign after her decease, and what changes and alterations should thereby happen.'[8] The Act went on to attack all those who, 'by any prophecying, witchcraft, conjurations or other like unlawfull means whatsoever', attempted to harm the monarch or to meddle in her affairs. In England, then, there was already a clear connection between prophecy, witchcraft, and monarchy before James ascended the throne.

In Scotland, James was making his own connections. There is little evidence that he had an interest in witchcraft before 1590, but the sensational trials of that year changed his attitude. More than 300 witches were alleged to have met and confessions were extorted, with the aid of torture, which pointed to a conspiracy directed by the Earl of Bothwell against the king himself. James took an active part in the trial, and Agnes Samson's report of 'the very words which passed between the King's Majesty and his Queen at Oslo in Norway the first night of their marriage' made him give 'more credit to the rest'.[9]

But if the trial triggered James's interest in witchcraft, we may suggest two possible determinants of the actual form his interest took. The first is, paradoxical though it may seem, his very desire to be in the intellectual vanguard. We need to remember that the witch craze was not the last fling of residual medieval 'superstition', but, at least in part, the potent construction of some of the foremost intellectuals of the time, including Bodin. It may well be, as Christine Larner has suggested,[10] that it was James's attempt to keep up with intellectual developments on the Continent after his contact with scholars in Denmark in 1589 which first aroused his interest in witchcraft.

But if his interest was stimulated by Continental ideas, his new belief consolidated his pre-existing interest in the theory and practice of godly rule. If the King was God's representative on earth, then who could be a more likely victim of the devil's arts than he? In his early work on the Book of Revelations, James had associated the devil with Antichrist, in his guise of the Pope, but it was not difficult to imagine that the devil employed more than one agency. To suggest, then, that the monarchy was under demonic attack was to glorify the institution of monarchy, since that implied that it was one of the bastions protecting this world from the triumph of Satan. As Stuart Clark says, 'demonism was, logically speaking, one of the presuppositions of the metaphysics of order on which James's political ideas ultimately rested.'[11] Clark also shows how this kind of *antithetical* thinking is the logical corollary of *analogical* thinking. If kingship is legitimated by analogy to God's rule over the earth, and the father's rule over the family and the head's rule over the body, witchcraft establishes the opposite analogies, whereby the Devil attempts to rule over the earth, and the woman over the family, and the body over the head.[12]

Henry Paul, in his important study of *Macbeth*,[13] argues in great detail for the indebtedness of the play to James's views on the nature of witchcraft and kingship. The play was performed before James and his father-in-law, the King of Denmark, at Hampton Court in 1606, and Paul argues that the play was shaped in important ways by royal patronage. But it is not demonstrable, in my view, that James's views (as set forth in his *Daemonologie*, for instance) were *sources* for the play, although they undoubtedly set ideological limits to it. In 1604, a play called *Gowrie*, performed by the King's Men, had been banned [14] The play was presumably based on the Earl of Gowrie's attempt to murder James in 1600. Gowrie had been killed in the attempt, and on him had been found a bag 'full of magicall characters, and words of inchantment, wherein, it seemed that he had put his confidence.'[15] Whatever the reason for banning the play, the King's Men would have been unlikely to risk a second offensive play on the sensitive topics of the attack upon kings and the uses of the black arts.

But if James's ideas were not a source, they provide an analogue, sharing and partially determining the ideological terrain of *Macbeth*. Like James's works, *Macbeth* is constructed around the fear of a world without sovereignty. Similarly, Robert Bolton, preaching in 1621, attempted to legitimate sovereignty by constructing the imaginary horrors of a world without it:[16]

Take Sovereignty from the face of the earth, and you turne it into a Cockpit. Men would become cut-throats and cannibals one unto another. Murder, adulteries, incests,

rapes, robberies, perjuries, witchcrafts, blasphemies, all
kinds of villainies, outrages, and savage cruelty, would
overflow all Countries. We should have a very hell upon
earth, and the face of it covered with blood, as it was once
with water.

'MACBETH' AND HOLINSHED

If it was the ascension of James to the English throne which
suggested a play about Scottish history, and about James's
own ancestry in particular, it is worth noting how Shakespeare utilized Holinshed, his main source for the play. To
begin with, he simplified the outlines of the story to create
a structure of clear antitheses. Holinshed's Duncan is a weak
king, 'negligent . . . in punishing offenders,'[17] and unable to
control the kingdom, whereas Shakespeare's Duncan is, as
even Macbeth admits, 'clear in his great office' (I.vii.18).
Holinshed's Macbeth has a legal right to the throne, since
'by the old lawes of the realme, the ordnance was, that if
he that should succeed were not of able age to take the
charge upon himselfe, he that was next of bloud unto him
should be admitted' (Holinshed, p. 172), whereas Shakespeare
makes little of Macbeth's claim. Moreover, Shakespeare omits
any reference to the 'ten yeares in equall justice' during
which Holinshed's Macbeth ruled after 'the feeble and
slouthfull administration of Duncane' (Holinshed, p. 173).
Finally, Holinshed's Banquo is a party to Macbeth's plot to
murder Duncan, whereas Shakespeare's Banquo is not.
What is striking about all these changes is that they trans-
form dialectic into antithesis. Whereas Shakespeare's second
historical tetralogy undoubtedly raises dialectical questions
about sovereignty, *Macbeth* takes material eminently suitable
for dialectical development (the weak ruler being overthrown
by a ruler who establishes 'equall justice') and shapes it into
a structural antithesis. One reason for the shaping of the
sources in this way was, no doubt, royal patronage. This
meant, for instance, that Banquo, James's ancestor, had to
be shown in a favourable light, and it may be that James's
views on godly rule and on 'the trew difference betwixt a
lawfull, good King and an usurping Tyrant' were taken into
account. Certainly, *Macbeth* differentiates as clearly as
James's *Basilikon Doron* between the good king whose

'greatest suretie' is his people's good will and the tyrant who builds 'his suretie upon his peoples miserie'.[18]

Holinshed's account, though, suggested another factor by which the tyrant might be distinguished from the godly ruler: his relation to witchcraft. For Holinshed describes how Macbeth 'had learned of certaine wizzards' and had gained (false) confidence from a witch who told him 'that he should never be slaine with man born of anie woman' (Holinshed, p. 175). But even over the issue of witchcraft, Holinshed is not entirely clear, because the crucial prophecies which embolden his Macbeth are made by 'three women in strange and wild apparell, resembling creatures of elder world', and these women are later described as 'either the weird sisters, that is (as ye would say) the goddesses of destinie, or else some nymphs or feiries, indued with knowledge of prophesie by their necromenticall science' (Holinshed, pp. 171-2). It was probably these three women whom Dr Gwin transformed into the *Tres Sibyllae* who hailed James as King of Scotland and England in a performance presented to the king at Oxford on 27 August 1605.[19]

But for the Witches in *Macbeth* to have been presented as godly sibylls would have weakened the antithetical structure of the play. Only by making his Sisters forces of darkness could Shakespeare suggest demonic opposition to godly rule. And here Shakespeare had to supplement Holinshed's account of Macbeth. For although the political effects of usurpation are suggested by Holinshed's account of how, after Macbeth murdered Banquo, 'everie man began to doubt his owne life' (Holinshed, p. 174), there is little sense of the natural holocaust which Bolton saw as the logical outcome of the overthrow of sovereignty. For an image of a king's murder and the consequent turning of a country into 'a very hell upon earth', Shakespeare had to turn back to Holinshed's account of Donwald's murder of King Duff, a murder which is itself the consequence of the King's execution of Donwald's kinsmen for conspiring with witches against him. Many of the horrifying events which follow Duff's death (the darkening of the sun, lightning and tempests, cannibalism amongst animals) reappear, more or less transformed, in *Macbeth*, reaffirming through antithesis the order which has been overthrown – the order of monarchy, of patriarchy, of the head, of 'reason'.

THE WITCHES

'For Rebellion is as the sin of witchcraft' (I Samuel XV. 23). And the first two scenes of *Macbeth* present both witches and rebellion. But what kind of witches are they? In the first scene, we can note several aspects of them: they are connected with disorder in nature (not only thunder and lightning but also 'fog and filthy air'); they are associated with familiars (Graymalkin and Paddock), the common companions of English witches but rarely mentioned in Scottish or Continental prosecutions; they can 'hover'; they reverse moral values ('Fair is foul, and foul is fair' (I.i.10); they presumably foresee the future, since the third witch knows that the battle will be over by sunset. The third scene, though, shows more clearly what seems to be an ambiguity in the presentation of the Witches. On the one hand, they have features typical of the English village 'witch', being old women, 'wither'd' and with 'choppy fingers' and 'skinny lips'. (Reginald Scot described English 'witches' as 'commonly old, lame, bleare-eied, pale, fowle, and full of wrinkles'.) [20] Moreover, the second witch kills swine and the first witch pursues a petty vendetta, typical offences in English witch prosecutions. But, on the other hand, they are mysterious and 'look not like th' inhabitants o' th' earth' (I.iii.41), and they prophesy the future.

What is the function of this ambiguity? At one level, no doubt, it enabled Shakespeare to draw upon the common belief in an 'evil' at work in the English countryside whilst never reducing the play's witches to village widows. But it was also structurally convenient because it established a double perspective on evil, allowing for the simultaneous sense of reduction in Macbeth as he becomes increasingly dependent on the 'midnight hags' (IV.i.47) and of his aspiration as, after 'Disdaining Fortune' (I.ii.17) in the battle, he attempts to grab hold of Providence itself. The double perspective operates throughout the play. On the one hand, Macbeth is reduced to the image of 'a dwarfish thief' (V.ii. 22) before being literally reduced to the head which Macduff carries onto the stage. At this level, evil is conceptualized as eating up itself until nothing is left. But the conceptualization leaves no role for militant 'good' (and therefore would not require the 'great revenge' (IV.iii.214) of Malcolm and Macduff), and so the world of self-consuming evil is combined with a dualistic world in which both the Witches and Macbeth threaten to bring the world back to its first chaos or, as Bolton puts it, to create 'a very hell upon earth', the hell of a world without sovereignty.

LADY MACBETH, THE WITCHES, AND FAMILY STRUCTURE

The Witches open the play, but they appear in only the first and third scenes of the first Act. In the fifth and seventh scenes, the 'temptress' is Lady Macbeth. In other words, scenes in which female figures champion evil alternate with public scenes (Duncan and news of the battle in scene 2; the honouring of Macbeth, Banquo, and Malcolm in scene 4; Duncan's reception at Macbeth's castle in scene 6). And the public scenes, with the exception of the last, are exclusively male. If this foregrounds the female figures, Lady Macbeth is also equated with the Witches in more specific ways. As Mark Rose says, 'the third scene opens with the Witches alone, after which Macbeth enters and they hail him by his various titles. The fifth scene opens with Lady Macbeth alone, practising witchcraft . . . .And when Macbeth enters she, too, hails him by his titles.'[21] Moreover, Lady Macbeth and the Witches are equated by their equivocal relation to an implied norm of femininity. Of the Witches, Banquo says:

> You should be women,
> And yet your beards forbid me to interpret
> That you are so. (I.iii.45–7)

And Lady Macbeth invokes the 'murd'ring ministers' (I.v.45) to unsex her.

The enticement of Macbeth both by the Witches and by his wife is briefly suggested in Holinshed's account of Macbeth, and in Holinshed's earlier account of Donwald's wife Shakespeare found a much expanded role given to a murderer's wife. But in neither account is any connection made between witchcraft and the murderer's wife. Again, we see the antithetical mode being strengthened in *Macbeth* by the development of analogies between 'perverted femininity', witchcraft, and a world turned upside down. The analogy was not, of course, new, and it is notoriously enshrined in *Malleus*

Maleficarum where *Femina* is derived from *Fe* and *Minus* 'since [woman] is ever weaker to hold and preserve the faith.'[22]

But it is important to note the shift of emphasis when Lady Macbeth 'replaces' the witches. By this movement from the already damned to the secular world, the implications of the rejection of 'womanhood' are made explicit. Whereas the witches are difficult to categorize at all within the implied norm, in I.v, Lady Macbeth is shown in the very attempt of overthrowing a norm inscribed in her own body. 'Remorse', 'compunctious visitings of Nature', and the 'milk' of 'woman's breasts' (I.v.41-5) are established as the 'feminine' virtues even as Lady Macbeth negates them. Indeed, because of the inscription of those virtues in Lady Macbeth, her relation to witchcraft is not as clear at the psychological as it is at the structural level. Although Lady Macbeth might say, like Joan la Pucelle, 'I exceed my sex' (*1 Henry VI*, I.ii.90), her relation to witchcraft is never as explicit as Joan's. For Joan is not merely *accused* of being a 'witch' and 'damned sorceress' (III.ii.38); her conjurings lead to the actual appearance of fiends upon the stage.

Nevertheless, Lady Macbeth's invocation of the 'murd'ring ministers' (I.v.45) as her children has particular resonance within the context of witchcraft, even if her ministers never appear. For her proclaimed role as mother/lover of the spirits implicitly subverts patriarchal authority in a manner typically connected with witchcraft. If the first Witch plans to come between a sailor and his wife in I.iii,[23] Lady Macbeth herself breaks the bond with her husband by suggesting both his metaphysical and physical impotence (he is not 'a man' (I.vii.49)) because he is unworthy of the respect due to a patriarch, because he is 'a coward' (I.vii.43), and, possibly, because, as we learn later, his is 'a barren sceptre' (III.i.61). It is particularly ironic, then, that Macbeth says 'Bring forth men-children only' (I.vii.72). For the structural antitheses which the first act develops establish the relation between women, witchcraft, the undermining of patriarchal authority and sterility.

But how can the family be conceptualized if women are, literally, faithless? One way is to show that not all womanhood falls under the curse of witchcraft, and this is surely an important reason for the introduction of Lady Macduff in IV.ii, a scene which has no base in Holinshed. Indeed, it is the destruction of this 'ideal' family which leads to Macduff's revenge and the final dénouement. But Lady Macduff is introduced late in the play, and we have already been presented with another way out of the dilemma: a family without women – Duncan and his sons, Malcolm and Donalbain, Banquo and his son Fleance (at the end of the play, Siward and his son Young Siward). On the one hand, there are the (virtuous) families of men; on the other hand, there are the antifamilies of women. And here, the notorious question, 'How many children had Lady Macbeth?' is not entirely irrelevant. For although Lady Macbeth says, 'I have given suck' (I.vii.54), her children are never seen on the stage, unlike the children of Duncan, Banquo, Macduff, and Siward. Are we not asked to accept a logical contradiction for the sake of a symbolic unity: Lady Macbeth is *both* an unnatural mother *and* sterile? This links her to the unholy family of the Witches, with their familiars and their brew which includes 'Finger of birth-strangled babe' and the blood of a sow which has eaten its own litter (IV.i.30 and 64–5). Like the Witches, Lady Macbeth and her husband constitute an 'unholy' family, a family whose only children are the 'murd'ring ministers'.

THE DEVELOPMENT OF LADY MACBETH AND THE WITCHES

I have been writing mainly of the ways in which the Witches and Lady Macbeth function in the first Act. But their functions are not constant throughout the play. Lady Macbeth is beginning to be developed into her own antithesis even before the murder takes place. 'Nature' is reasserted through her in its most compelling guise – the Law of the Father which, in this society, founds and is founded by the Law of the King. Thus, Lady Macbeth says that she would have murdered Duncan herself 'Had he not resembled / My father as he slept' (II.ii.12–13). And in the last act, she is transformed from the pitiless instigator to murder to the guilt-ridden sleep-walker whose thoughts return to 'the old man' who had 'so much blood in him' (V.i.38). Curry interprets her sleep-walking as 'demoniacal somnambulism'.[24] But surely this is to miss the dramatic point, which is the reassertion of 'the compunctious visitations of Nature' if only in sleep. Lady Macbeth's last words, indeed, are not of her own guilt but of the solicitous wife's care for her husband: 'give me your hand.... To bed, to bed, to bed' (V.i.64–6). But the transformation of Lady Macbeth is used to affirm developmentally the antithetical structure. It operates as a specific closure of discourse within the binary opposition of virago (witch)/wife.

If Lady Macbeth's changing function is marked by psychological change, the Witches' changing function is marked by the changing function of their prophecies. Much has been made of the fact that the Witches speak equivocally, that they are, as Macbeth says, 'imperfect speakers' (I.iii.70). But the apparitions of the fourth act are progressively *less* equivocal, moving from the 'armed head' to the 'bloody child' to the 'child crowned' to the 'show of eight kings, the last with a glass in his hand' which shows Banquo's descendants stretched out 'to th' crack of doom' (IV.i.117). The Witches here, far from being 'imperfect speakers', conjure up a vision whose truth is established by the presence of Banquo's descendant, James I. In this prophecy of the 'good', dramatic fate (as yet incomplete) joins hands with completed political fate.

As with Lady Macbeth, then, so with the Witches: they are constructed so as to manifest their own antithesis. Cursed witches prophesy the triumph of godly rule. At one level, no doubt, this implies that even evil works providentially. As James himself had declared in the preface to *Daemonologie*:[25]

> For where the devilles intention in them is ever to perish,
> either the soule or the body, or both of them, that he is
> so permitted to deale with: God by the contrarie, drawes
> ever out of that evill glorie to himselfe.

But at another level, the association of the Witches with the workings of Providence is part of the process by which attention is focused upon Macbeth alone. In I.i, the Witches are invoked by their familiars; in I.v, Lady Macbeth invokes the spirits. But, in the third act, it is Macbeth, who had to be 'invoked' to do the deed, who invokes the night to 'Scarf up the tender eye of pitiful Day' (III.ii.47). But Macbeth's conjunctions made even

> though the treasure
> Of nature's germens tumble all together,
> Even till destruction sicken
>
> (IV.i.58–60)

lead to a future in which he, with his 'fruitless crown' (III.i.
60), has no place. At the end, his only 'familiar' is 'Direness,
familiar to my slaughterous thoughts' (V.v.14).

THE DEVELOPMENT OF THE PLAY

The first act of the play is framed by images of witchcraft,
rebellion and murder. At the end of the second act, an old
man describes a world turned upside down, in which owls
kill falcons, horses revolt against men and cannibalize each
other, and night strangles day. In I.i, I.iii, III.v, and IV.i,
thunder sounds.[26] And in III.v and IV.i Hecate, who, according to Jonson, 'was believed to govern in witchcraft',[27]
appears. Indeed, IV.i, the last scene with the Witches, can be
seen as the emblematic centre of the play, containing as it
does both the vision of kings and the fullest display of the
workings of the 'secret, black, and midnight hags' (IV.i.48).
It is not my purpose to enter into the dispute about the
authorship of the Hecate passages. Whether Shakespeare
wrote them or not, they are perfectly in keeping with the
structure of the play. Indeed, the dance of Hecate and the
six Witches gives a concrete dramatization of the 'deed
without a name' (IV.i.49) which reverses the whole order
of 'Nature'. We need to imagine something like the Witches'
dance in Jonson's *The Masque of Queens* (1609), which was[28]

> full of preposterous change, and gesticulation, but most
> applying to their property, who at their meetings, do all
> things contrary to the custom of men, dancing back to
> back and hip to hip, their hands joined, and making their
> circles backward, to the left hand, with strange fantastic
> motions of their heads and bodies.

In the rituals of Shakespeare's Witches, as of Jonson's, a
Jacobean audience could contemplate the systematic undoing
of the hierarchical ceremonies of speech, of cooking, of
dancing.

It is also in Act IV, though, that the 'prayers' for a 'swift blessing' (III.vi.47) which will restore those ceremonies begin to be answered by the discovery of medicines for 'the sickly weal' (V.ii.27). At the same time, the impotence of literal medicines is made explicit by two minor characters: the English doctor who admits the impotence of his art to cure scrofula, the Scottish doctor who admits the impotence of his art to cure 'infected minds' ('More needs she the divine than the physician' (V.i.72)). The introduction of these characters should warn against any attempt to give too naturalistic an explanation of the play, since their function is largely to assert the dependence of physical health upon political and metaphysical order. Indeed, the only function of the English doctor is to dramatize the difference between his own weak art and the medicine of King Edward's 'sanctity' (IV.iii.144). (The King's power to heal scrofula, a belief which originated with Edward I, was a useful piece of royal propaganda and, although James I was himself sceptical, he ultimately agreed to take part in the healing ceremony; its propaganda value may be suggested by the fact that Charles II touched 90,798 persons in nineteen years.[29]) Of course, King Edward offers Malcolm the practical aid of troops as well as the metaphysical aid of the 'sundry blessings' which hang about his throne (IV.iii.158). But the 'med'cines' of Malcolm's and Macduff's 'great revenge' (IV.iii.214) are guaranteed and legitimated by a godly magic which surpasses 'the great essay of art' (IV.iii.143).

Witchcraft, prophecy and magic function in *Macbeth* as ways of developing a particular conceptualization of social and political order. Witchcraft is associated with female rule and the overthrowing of patriarchal authority which in turn leads to the 'womanish' (both cowardly and instigated by women) killing of Duncan, the 'holy' father who establishes both family and state. This in turn leads to the reversals in the cosmic order which the Old Man and Ross describe, and to the reversals in the patriarchal order, culminating in the killing of Lady Macduff and her son. The conclusion of the play reestablishes both the offended (and offending?[30]) father, a father, paradoxically, 'not born of woman' (V.iii.4) (does this imply that he is unnatural or untainted?[31]), and the offended son/king. And the Witches can simply disappear, their evil supplanted by the prophetic vision of Banquo's line and by the 'heavenly gift of prophecy' and 'miraculous work' (IV.iii.157 and 147) of a legitimate king.

CONCLUSION

This aspect of *Macbeth* as a work of cultural 'ordering' could, of course, only make claims to 'truth' within a cosmology which accommodated witchcraft beliefs. That cosmology was largely defined by the Bible. There are, indeed, interesting parallels between *Macbeth* and the story of Saul and the Witch of Endor in the Book of Samuel (I Samuel XXVIII), a text which was dealt with by nearly every Renaissance treatise on witchcraft. Jane Jack has explored this parallel in an important article, where she writes:[32]

> Like Saul, Macbeth hears from the witches the confirmation of what he most fears. The crisis of the story is the victory of the witches: the resolution of the story is the judgement passed on Macbeth at the end – the same judgement that is passed on Saul: 'So Saul dyed for his transgression, that he committed against the word of the Lord, which he kept not, and in that he sought and asked consel of a familiar spirit' (glossed in Geneva version as a 'witche and sorceress').

Jack goes on to assert the essentially religious tenor of *Macbeth*, a view which most critics of the play seem to hold. Murray, for example, maintains:[33]

> [*Macbeth*] is, if ever a poem were so, a *traditional Catholic Christian poem*, the vitality of which is rooted in an uncompromising medieval faith, and in a prescientific view of the nature of reality. Consequently it preserves in a tremendously powerful and well unified set of images one of the greatest forces in Western European culture, a force which, however alien it may seem to many of us today, we can afford neither to forget, nor to neglect, for it contains, and can still convey, much of the wisdom of human experience.

The 'Christian' interpretation is, I believe, right in so far as it recognizes that *Macbeth* can only be understood in relation to a particular cosmology. But Murray, like Jack, attempts to separate religion from politics in a way which was totally foreign to sixteenth- and seventeenth-century thinking. For instance, the Fifth Commandment ('Honour thy father and thy mother' – but Sir Robert Filmer lopped off . . . 'and thy mother'[34]) received new emphasis during this period so as to give religious underpinnings to the patriarchal state.[35] Indeed, analogical thinking could be used not only to draw close parallels between the law of Moses and the law of the State but also to collapse traditional distinctions. Thus, in *The Six Bookes of the Commonweale* (1586), Bodin rejected Aristotle's distinction between political and domestic hierarchy, claiming that the family 'is the true seminarie and beginning of every Commonweale.'[36] Nor is it surprising that Bodin also wrote an influential attack upon witchcraft, *Démonomanie des Sorciers* (1580). If state and family were founded together, witchcraft founded the antistate together with the antifamily. James I also made the connection between state and family ('By the Law of Nature the King becomes a naturall Father to all his Lieges at his Coronation'[37]) and he too saw witchcraft as the antithesis of both. If the family was theorized as the site of conflict between hierarchy and witchcraft, that was, no doubt, because of its symbolic importance in early modern Europe when, as Natalie Davis writes,[38]

> the nature of political rule and the newer problem of sovereignty were very much at issue. In the little world of the family, with its conspicuous tension between intimacy and power, the larger matters of political and social order could find ready symbolization.

Witchcraft, sovereignty, the family – those concepts map out the ideological terrain of *Macbeth*, a terrain which should be understood as a field of conflict, not a 'given'.

I would argue, then, that Murray is wrong in attempting to collapse the present moment of analysis back into the 'eternity' of a past 'wisdom'. What, after all, are those 'well unified set of images', which give us 'the wisdom of human experience', *about*? 'Unreasoning womanhood', 'eternal motherhood', mind as 'a male quality only', Murray tells us.[39] He points, I believe, to important elements in the play, but he then requires that we *empathize* with its symbolic orderings without reference of those orderings as embodying particular manoeuvres of *power*.

Those manoeuvres as they relate to 'unreasoning woman-hood' are spelled out clearly enough in Krämer and Sprenger's *Malleus Maleficarum* (1486), the most influential of all the Renaissance witchcraft treatises. In it, a section is dedicated to answering the question 'Why Superstition is chiefly found in Women.' The roots of witchcraft are there discovered to be in the very nature of women, a nature which includes her desire, following Eve, to betray mankind. 'She is more carnal than a man'; 'as she is a liar by nature, so in her speech she stings while she delights us'; 'her heart is a net, and her hands are bands. He that pleaseth God shall escape from her; but he that is a sinner shall be caught by her'; 'can he be called a free man whose wife governs him . . . ? I should call him not only a slave, but the vilest of slaves, even if he comes of the noblest family'; 'nearly all the kingdoms of the world have been overthrown by woman.' (All of these statements have analogues in *Macbeth*.) In the *Malleus*, misogyny leads to the conclusion that 'it is no matter for wonder that there are more women than men found infected with the heresy of witchcraft.'[40] Krämer and Sprenger's advocacy of a programme of ruthless repression is a logical consequence of their fear of a supernatural power in the hands of the power-less. For who would the powerless direct their power against if not the powerful?

If Krämer's and Sprenger's beliefs were grounded in medieval Christian traditions, similar beliefs can be found in modern African societies which have been analysed by anthropologists attempting to understand the social functions of such beliefs. Esther Goody, for example, observes that amongst the Gonja in Ghana only women are punished for witchcraft, and she accounts for this by showing the relation between witchcraft and the prohibition against aggression amongst women, since they have been consigned to an exclusively nurturing role: [41]

> There are two regular characteristics of the female domestic role. First, in the role of mother, a woman is a focus of emotional ties . . . . Then, as wife, woman is defined as subordinate to her husband. Aggression, if permitted, would threaten both these characteristics . . . . And if a woman strikes her husband with a stirring stick . . . he will become impotent; aggression in a woman's

role renders a man powerless – it cannot be permitted.

A woman's refusal to be subordinated, then, is often accounted for by witchcraft. Similarly, Max Gluckman notes that[42]

> In Nupe the evil witches who kill are women .... Nadel seeks to answer why. He finds a striking conflict between the roles which, ideally, women ought to play and that many women in fact do. Ideally, a Nupe woman should be a good wife, subservient to her husband, bearing him many children, and staying at home to care for them and their father. In reality, a great deal of trade is in the hands of women.

Women seem to be particularly vulnerable to witchcraft accusations in patrilineal, patrilocal societies, where women are cut off from their own kin and expected to merge their interests with those of their husbands' kin.

Two versions of how women operate in this kind of situation are constructed in *Macbeth*. Lady Macduff submerges her interests in her husband's, and when he flees she is totally defenceless; Lady Macbeth actively pursues her husband's interests, but only those interests which separate him from his kin. In the latter case, this leads to Macbeth's murder of his cousin, to the isolation of the husband with his 'dear wife' (III.ii.36), cut off from 'honour, love, obedience, troops of friends' (V.iii.25), and finally, to the total isolation of Macbeth in the field of battle. But the play, concentrating increasingly on Macbeth himself as it develops, does not analyse the position of women; rather, it mobilizes the patriarchal fear of unsubordinated woman,[43] the unstable element to which Krämer and Sprenger attributed the overthrow of 'nearly all the kingdoms of the world', to which the Gonja and the Nupe attribute witchcraft.

I am not proposing to conflate the imaginary society of *Macbeth* with Gonja or Nupe society. But I am arguing for the *general* relevance of anthropological and sociological models of the relation between witchcraft beliefs and structures of political and social dominance. We need such models, I believe, if we are to analyse, rather than repeat, the terms of the play itself. What I have attempted to show here is the use of witchcraft as a form of ideological closure within *Macbeth*, a returning of the disputed ground of politics to the undisputed ground of 'Nature'.

But the play is not, of course, *about* witchcraft, nor does the threat of the Biblical 'Thou shalt not suffer a witch to live' (Exodus, XXII.18) hang over *Macbeth* as it hangs over *The Witch of Edmonton* (1621), for instance. And it cannot be said that the witches in *Macbeth* provide the only explanatory element in the play. If their prophecies provide one motive for the killing of a king, the radical instability of the concept of 'manliness' is sufficient to precipitate the deed. But it would be misleading to interpret this overdetermination as a *conflict* between supernatural and natural modes of explanation, since, within the cultural context, there was no necessity to choose between those modes. (For example, Mother Sawyer in *The Witch of Edmonton* is at first abused as a witch merely because, as she complains, 'I am poor, deform'd and ignorant' (II.i.3); but the fact that she is presented sympathetically as a scapegoat – the natural explanation – is not seen as contradicting the fact that she becomes a witch – the supernatural explanation – and therefore presumably 'deserves' her death.) Nevertheless the coexistence of those modes suggests that the structural closures which I have been examining do not preclude a problematic relation between 'highly' and 'holily' (I.v.17-18).

NOTES

1 C. L'Estrange Ewen, in *Witchcraft and Demonianism* (1933), p. 76, defines 'true witchcraft' as 'the joint accomplishments of spirit demons and their human converts'. But Keith Thomas notes that 'the term "witchcraft" was used loosely in Tudor and Stuart England, and was at one time or another applied to virtually every kind of magical activity or ritual operation that worked through occult methods' ('The Relevance of Anthropology to the Study of English Witchcraft', in *Witchcraft Confessions and Accusations*, ed. Mary Douglas (1970), p. 48).

2 T.A. Spalding, *Elizabethan Demonology* (1880) and W.C. Curry, *Shakespeare's Philosophical Patterns* (Louisiana, 1937).

3 For a valuable critique of their work, see E.P. Thompson, 'Anthropology and the Discipline of Historical Context', *Midland History*, I (1972), pp. 41-55.

4 Malinowski, quoted by Philip Mayer, 'Witches' in *Witchcraft and Sorcery*, ed. Max Marwick (1970), p. 48.

5 Mary Douglas, Introduction to *Witchcraft Confessions and Accusations* (1970), p. xxx.

6 Mary Douglas, *Purity and Danger: An analysis of concepts of pollution and taboo* (1978), p. 35.

7 G.L. Kittredge, *Witchcraft in Old and New England* (Cambridge, Mass., 1929), pp. 226, 229 and 260-1.

8 'An Act against seditious words and rumours uttered against the Queen's most excellent Majesty' (23 Eliz., c. 2), quoted in *Witchcraft*, ed. Barbara Rosen, *Stratford-upon-Avon Library 6* (1969), p. 56.

9 *Newes from Scotland* (n.d.), sig. B2.

10 'James VI and I and Witchcraft', in *The Reign of James VI and I* (1973), pp. 74-90.

11 Clark, *The Damned Art* (ed.) S. Anglo (1977), pp. 156-7.

12 Ibid., pp. 175-7.

13 *The Royal Play of Macbeth* (New York, 1950).

14 E.K. Chambers, *The Elizabethan Stage* (Oxford, 1923), I, p. 328. Chambers quotes a court gossip as saying, 'I hear that some great councellors are much displeased with [*Gowrie*].'

15 *Gowrie's Conspiracie* (1600), in *The Harleian Miscellany* (London, 1809), III, p. 86. See also Steven Mullaney, 'Lying England', *ELH*, 47 (1980), pp. 32-47.

16 Quoted in William Lamont, *Godly Rule: Politics and Religion, 1603-60* (1969), p. 49.

17 Holinshed, *Chronicles of Scotland*, quoted in *Macbeth*, ed. Kenneth Muir, *The Arden Shakespeare* (London, 1972), p. 167. All quotations from Holinshed are taken from the Arden *Macbeth*.

18 *Basilikon Doron*, in *The Political Works of James I*, ed. Charles H. McIlwain, Harvard Political Classics (Cambridge, Mass., 1918), pp. 18-19.

19 Paul, *op. cit.*, p. 163.

20 Reginald Scot, *The Discoverie of Witchcraft*, ed. Montague Summers (London, 1930), p. 1.

21 Mark Rose, *Shakespearean Design* (Cambridge, Mass., 1972), p. 88.

22 Heinrich Krämer and Jacob Sprenger, *Malleus Maleficarum*, in *Witchcraft in Europe 1100-1700: A Documentary History*, ed. A.C. Kors and E. Peters (Philadelphia, 1972), p. 121. James I answers the question of why there are twenty female witches to one male witch by affirming that 'as that sexe is frailer than man is, so is it easier to be intrapped in these grosse snares of the Divell' (*Daemonologie* [London, 1603], pp. 43-4).

23 The connection between the witches and sexuality is made by Dennis Biggins, 'Sexuality, Witchcraft and Violence in *Macbeth*', *Shakespeare Studies*, ed. J. Leeds Barroll III, VIII, pp. 255-77.

24 Curry, *Shakespeare's Philosophical Patterns*, p. 89.

25 *Daemonologie*, sig. A4.

26 See *Daemonologie*, p. 46: '[Witches] can rayse stormes and tempests in the ayre, eyther upon Sea or land.' For actual accusations, see L'Estrange Ewen, *Witchcraft and Demonianism*, p. 89: 'in

1582, suspicion fell upon Joan Robinson as being responsible for a great wind which blew down a house, and Michael Trevisard (1601) caused the wind and weather to destroy the Mayor's new fold.' But there is an obvious discrepancy between the limited destruction of these latter 'witches' and the vision of a world turned upside down in *Macbeth*.

27 Ben Jonson, *Selected Masques*, ed. S. Orgel (New Haven, 1970), p. 360.

28 Ibid., p. 92.

29 Thomas, *Religion and the Decline of Magic*, p. 193.

30 Lady Macduff accuses her husband of lacking 'the natural touch' (IV.ii.9).

31 See Lucan, *Pharsalia*, VI, 554 ff.: 'She [the witch] pierces the pregnant womb and delivers the child by an unnatural birth.' Jonson quotes this passage in his commentary to *The Masque of Queens* (Ben Jonson, *Selected Masques*, p. 357).

32 Jane H. Jack, 'Macbeth, King James and the Bible', *ELH*, 22 (1955), pp. 182-3.

33 W.A. Murray, 'Why was Duncan's Blood Golden?', *Shakespeare Survey*, 19 (1966), p. 43.

34 Sir Robert Filmer, *Patriarcha and Other Political Works*, ed. Peter Laslett, Blackwell's Political Texts (Oxford, 1969), pp. 188, 269, 289.

35 See Gordon J. Schochet, *Patriarchalism in Political Thought: The Authoritarian Family and Political Speculation and Attitudes Especially in Seventeenth Century England* (New York, 1975), pp. 37-98. For patriarchalism in the later part of the Seventeenth century, see also James Daly, *Sir Robert Filmer and English Political Thought* (Toronto, 1979). It is worth noting that even More's *Utopia* is founded on the patriarchal family: see J.H. Hexter, *The Vision of Politics on the Eve of the Reformation* (New York, 1973), pp. 40-5.

36 Jean Bodin, *The Six Bookes of a Commonweale*, trans. Richard Knolles (1606), reprinted, ed. Kenneth D. McRae, Harvard Political Classics (Cambridge, Mass., 1962), I.ii, p. 8. On the popularity of the *Six Bookes* in England, see Quentin Skinner, *The Foundations of Modern Political Thought* (Cambridge, 1978), II, p. 300.

37 James I, *The Trew Law of Free Monarchies*, in *The Political Works*, p. 55.

38 Natalie Z. Davis, 'Women on Top: Symbolic Sexual Inversion and Political Disorder in Early Modern Europe', in *The Reversible World: Symbolic Inversion in Art and Society*, ed. Barbara B. Babcock (Ithaca, 1978), p. 150.

39 Murray, *op. cit.*, p. 39.

40 *Malleus Maleficarum*, pp. 120, 126, 127, 124, 124, 127.

41 Esther Goody, 'Legitimate and Illegitimate Aggression in a West African State', in *Witchcraft Confessions and Accusations*, ed.

Mary Douglas, p. 241.

42 Max Gluckman, 'Moral crises: magical and secular solutions', in *The Allocation of Responsibility*, ed. Max Gluckman (Manchester, 1972), p. 19.

43 A fear which, in Davenant's version of *Macbeth*, Lady Macbeth herself is made to share:

> You were a man
> And by the Charter of your sex you should
> have govern'd me.   (IV.iv.62–4)

Christopher Spencer, *Davenant's Macbeth* (New Haven, 1961), p. 132.

10

Hurt minds

Derek Russell Davis

Let us regard the fictive characters in *Macbeth*, not merely as poetic ideas, not merely as protagonists in a drama, but as if they had been living persons. The play then becomes a study, in the form of a narrative, of what happens to two persons who have committed murder. Literature contains many other accounts of what happens to murderers, e.g. Genesis, to Cain after he has killed Abel; the Greek plays, to Orestes after he has killed his mother; and *Hamlet*, to Claudius after he has killed his brother.

This approach is the one usually adopted in psychopatho-logical studies of plays.[1] Freud,[2] on the other hand, found it 'impossible to guess' how in a short space of time 'the hesi-tating, ambitious man' can turn into 'an unbridled tyrant, and his steely-hearted instigator into a sick woman gnawed by remorse.' For this reason he seized on the idea that they were a conjoined pair complementary to one another – 'two disunited parts of a single psychical individuality', invented by the playwright to represent different aspects of the con-flicts engaging his attention.[3]

They are also portrayed in the play as whole persons who, although partners, act more or less independently, and this is how we shall regard them. We shall examine what they say and do in relation to the context, circumstances, causes and connections given in the text. These are the data, which are to be given here the coherence of a case-report.

SYSTEMS THEORY

The psychopathological theory guiding this discussion pays particular attention to the part a person plays in relationships within a 'system', i.e. an organisation of two or more persons interacting with one another and regulating one another's behaviour.[4] A husband and wife form such a system. This is open in the sense that it is also part of other systems, such as a nuclear or extended family, which in turn is part of the larger system of the community. Macbeth and Lady Macbeth do not seem to belong to a family, but they do belong to a larger system based on the royal court, a feature of which is its hierarchical organisation, with the king and thanes serving particular functions.

A system gives a degree of stability to its members because it reacts to external events homeostatically, i.e. in such a way as to preserve their relationships. But homeostasis fails, and the system is disrupted, if something happens of special force or significance. This is a crisis, or turning point, which is followed by a period of instability. The members explore the implications and consequences. Sometimes they become reconciled, the system then being reorganised. Sometimes they become estranged.

The system at the royal court is disrupted when Duncan is murdered. The investment of Macbeth as king in his place does not restore stability, and the system disintegrates, with dispersal of its members. At the end of the play, after Macbeth's death, Malcolm, named as king, states the terms on which a new order is to be established.

THE FIRST CRISIS

The ending of the campaign in victory brings Macbeth to a crisis. He has achieved high position as a trusted general and valiant warrior, but the future offers no clear role for him, and he has to work out, in the new circumstances, the terms on which to relate to Duncan, Malcolm and others at the court. His relationships with them hitherto, even with Banquo, seem to have been slender.

He has come to something like the demobilisation crises with which psychiatrists became familiar at the end of the Second World War. Men demobilised from the armed forces had to make the transition to civilian life. Most did so without difficulty. A few, especially among those who had achieved senior rank, persisted in a faulty appraisal of themselves and their circumstances and sought in civilian life a position giving them as much authority, or more, as they had enjoyed in the services. A similar tendency is sometimes observed in men in senior positions who, when their firms close down and they become redundant, apply, inappropriately, for a new position of greater seniority.

After the hurly-burly Macbeth is susceptible to what the witches say to him, especially 'Thou shalt be King hereafter!' (I.iii.50), which he accepts uncritically. Banquo, in contrast, who is to make the transition to civilian life without apparent difficulty, questions sceptically the reality of what they see and hear. Are they 'fantastical' (l.53) or 'bubbles' (l.79) of the earth? Have Macbeth and he 'eaten on the insane root' (l.84)? He is aware of the danger that 'the instruments of darkness' are liable to 'betray's in deepest consequence' (ll.124–6). They are clever in their timing when they tell us truths. The revelations of dreams, which come from the unconscious, show a similar timeliness.

Macbeth does 'start and seem to fear' (l.51). The probable reason is that he already aspires to the kingship, and has considered what Lady Macbeth calls 'the nearest way'. Although in his nature 'too full o'th' milk of human kindness' and lacking 'the illness' that 'should attend ambition (I.v.14–17), there is little doubt that he has contemplated killing Duncan and is ready to 'yield to that suggestion' (I.iii.134), which, however horrid its image, is attractive because it would remove the uncertainties in his future role. When Duncan names Malcolm as his successor, Macbeth sees immediately that he must 'o'erleap' that step (I.iv.48–50). 'Black and deep desires' reflect a further yielding.

The witches are peculiarly effective in destroying the order in Macbeth's relationship with Banquo, who has been his partner in battle, not only because the one is credulous and the other sceptical. Macbeth becomes 'rapt' (I.iii.143), i.e. immersed in thoughts he does not and cannot share. The stage-direction in modern editions, 'They walk apart' (l.127), marks a turning point in their relationship. They do not again speak their 'free hearts each to other'. Although he tells Banquo of his intention of doing so, 'the interim having weighted it' (II.153–4), he puts him off when he is reminded

(II.i.20f.) because he has to dissemble, the murder of Duncan being imminent. He does not heed the warnings in Banquo's scepticism.

The effect of his estrangement from Banquo is immediate. A person normally modifies or corrects his appraisal of himself and his circumstances in the light of the comments of those in whom he confides. They provide checks for him on what is fact and what fantasy. No longer confiding in Banquo, Macbeth becomes prey to 'horrible imaginings', which are not corrected, and enters into a world of fantasy in which actions do not have their normal consequences and 'nothing is but what is not'. Fantasy becomes part of his reality, and the power to act is 'smothered in surmise' (I.iii. 137-42).

We are told little about the quality of the marriage to which he is returning. A sketchy picture of how he is seen by others emerges during the opening scenes, and Lady Macbeth tells us how she sees him (I.v.13-27), but, except for casual references to her qualities as a hostess, we are told nothing about her. This lack of information hampers any psychopathological interpretation of her behaviour. Freud, too, found it impossible to come to any decision about 'her deeper motivation'.

The Witches' promise of greatness conveyed to her in his letter causes her to review the assumptions on which their marriage is based, and she decides to 'pour . . . spirits' in his ear and to 'chastise' with her tongue all that impedes him (I.v.24-7). Learning of Duncan's visit that night, she resolves to deny her womanly feelings, to dedicate herself to the direst cruelty and to stop up the access and passage to remorse. She thus recognises that a great effort is needed on her part to compensate for the human kindness and lack of resolution she discerns in him. She does not lack the 'compunctious visitings of nature', although she intends to override them. What she is to do will be possible only if it is hidden by thick night and the dunnest smoke of hell so that she does not see the wound her keen knife makes. The situation demands ruthlessness.

We do not know what previous experiences determine that she reacts with such cruelty and resolution, and can only guess that she suffered serious disturbances in her relationships during childhood. We may note the lack of any role except as wife. She has had a pregnancy – she has given suck

(I.vii.54) – but she does not appear to have children to care for.

He is a husband but not a father. 'He has no children', Macduff tells us (IV.iii.216). In the view of Freud, *Macbeth* is 'concerned with the subject of childlessness'. Certainly, his childlessness adds to his isolation and lack of companionship. Only because he was himself childless could he murder the children of others, it has been said. What they are to gain from the murder of Duncan is for themselves alone, as the terms of the Witches' predictions make clear, whereas Banquo shall 'get kings' though he 'be none' (I.iii.67). When there are children to benefit, hope can be deferred, and ambition is then more easily controlled.

Not having fathered children makes him more sensitive to her taunts when he vacillates in his decision to murder Duncan, and she is the more able to arouse in him the fears that his love for her is worthless and of being 'a coward in [his] own esteem' and not doing 'all' that becomes a man. Playing on his doubts about his manliness, she gives him the motive 'to be the same in thine own act and valour as thou art in desire' (I.vii.35-45).

His doubts are expressed too in his admiration for her 'undaunted mettle' which 'should compose nothing but males' (I.vii.73-4). That he is so sensitive to her taunts suggests that his bravery in battle 'disdaining fortune' (I.ii. 17) is an over-compensation for his doubts. Insecurity in this respect would hamper him in his relationships with peers, and has also to be considered in speculating about his relationship with her. The murder of Duncan would help her to break out of a situation in which, because of his weakness and insecurity, she has felt unfulfilled.

They confide little in one another. He explores on his own the implications and consequences of the assassination of Duncan. It would give him security if it 'could trammel up the consequences', but he is apprehensive: 'but we still have judgement here.' He remembers Duncan's virtues and his duty to him, and recognises that he has 'no spur . . . but only vaulting ambition'. He sees the danger that 'bloody instructions . . . return to plague the inventor' (I.vii.1-28). But her taunts overcome his hesitations.

To contrast his apprehensiveness with her single-mindedness is too facile. She will herself dispatch the 'night's great business' (I.v.65), but can only do so by denying her feelings.

In the event she cannot carry out her 'fell purpose' (l.43). She had done it, 'had he not resembled my father as he slept' (II.ii.12–13). It is not only he who has to screw courage to 'the sticking place' (I.vii.60). Her apparent strength proves brittle.

While he awaits the signal from her, reality and fantasy become blurred. Is the dagger he sees 'in form as palpable as this which now I draw' 'a false creation, proceeding from the heat-oppressed brain?' It 'marshall'st me the way that I was going.' He enters into a 'half-world' in which 'nature seems dead' and he is subject to 'wicked dreams'. Moving 'like a ghost' and as if watching himself in a dream in which 'the sure and firm-set earth hear not my steps' (II.i.33–64), he goes to murder Duncan. He does so while in a dream-like state and partly disconnected – dissociated – from reality.

THE PSYCHOPATHOLOGY OF MURDERERS

In contemporary Britain murder is overwhelmingly a domestic crime in which men kill their wives, mistresses and children, and women kill their children.[5] Four out of five murderers know the victim well. In half the cases the victim is a member of the family, and in half, a child. In one in three cases a sharp instrument is used. One in two murderers is intoxicated by alcohol or drugs, and thus partly dissociated from reality. One in five is mentally ill at the time of the act or becomes unfit to plead. One in four kills himself before coming to trial. Many more are men than women, but the proportion of women among those killing themselves is relatively high.

The proportion of murderers, as of other kinds of violent offender, in the less advantaged social classes is high, this fact probably reflecting the circumstances of their lives rather than their characters. The differences between ethnic groups and between sub-cultures suggest that circumstances are important. Homicide is common in so-called primitive cultures. That opportunity is important is illustrated by a recent report[6] that with the increasing ownership of firearms in the USA has been associated a sharp increase in the frequency of homicide of a family member with the use of a firearm.

Combinations of influences, circumstances and opportunity lead a person with particular flaws in character and with particular experiences to commit murder. The differences between Scotland at the time of *Macbeth* and contemporary Britain being very large, it is not surprising that counterparts to the circumstances and motives of Macbeth and Lady Macbeth are hardly to be found among modern case-reports,[7] nevertheless these do throw some light on the psychological processes. Systematic information about the state of mind at the time of the murder is sparse for several reasons, however, since only a small proportion of murderers, these making up biased samples, are subjected to expert examination, usually not until several weeks or months have passed. Recall tends to be impaired and the examination is usually concerned with such forensic questions as fitness to plead and diminished responsibility.

Both Macbeth and Lady Macbeth would be judged in a modern court to have been of sound memory and discretion when they killed Duncan with malice aforethought. They knew the nature and quality of the act and that it was wrong. Evidence that Macbeth had been in a dream-like state would not persuade the court otherwise. Neither suffered from any abnormality of mind arising from inherent cause or induced by disease or injury which would convince the court that their responsibility was diminished.

Murder, in common with other criminal acts, may be regarded as an attempt at 'intrapsychic adaptation,[8] i.e. at relieving stresses within the person. A person in distress may try to change his circumstances. Someone recently bereaved moves house, for instance. A deeply unhappy person hits out at the world. What he does may seem to be a clumsy, inept or even incongruous way of dealing with the stresses. To infer what these have been from what is done may be unsatisfactory, therefore, and the killing of Duncan may have had only a remote bearing on the needs of Lady Macbeth. And for Macbeth himself it was not in furtherance of a decision made after a cool appraisal of the realities. On the contrary, his exploration of the probable consequences had led him to decide to 'proceed no further' (I.vii.31). One at least of his motives is to remove, however ineptly, a threat to his conception of himself as a man of valour and to reinstate himself in his own esteem and in the esteem of Lady Macbeth.

The psychological restraints on killing are strong, and the conditions in which an ordinary man can kill, restricted. One condition is intense emotion, such as fear or anger. This is the condition in which Macbeth is able to kill in battle:

'as cannons overcharg'd with double cracks' (I.ii.37). Killing, even when it is sanctioned as it is in warfare, may only be possible when the killer is able to protect himself in some way from realising that his target is a living human being. Modern technology helps in this respect because, when there is a complex device in-between, action and result are disconnected at least partly. Psychological defences protect a pilot able to see his living targets. He may report afterwards that the experience has the quality of a dream in which he has been a horrified spectator rather than the doer. If it is recalled, as it may be in repetitive 'battle dreams', it tends to be fragmented, although there may be disturbing visions of the victims. A murderer usually says that he felt detached or that it was unreal or happening in a dream. Some loss of the sense of reality is the rule.

It has some significance that Duncan was asleep when Macbeth killed him. 'I have done the deed' (II.ii.14), he says, without reference to Duncan or its nature. That the grooms are asleep has significance for her: 'The sleeping and the dead are but as pictures' (ll.53-4).

Another condition is despair. One of the murderers of Banquo thus speaks of 'the vile blows and buffets of the world' that have so 'incensed' him that he is 'reckless' what he does 'to spite the world'. The other, 'so weary with disasters, tugged with fortune', would set his life 'on any chance to mend it or be rid on't' (III.i.108-13). What they say anticipates the condition which will enable Macbeth after Banquo's murder to kill many more.

Shakespeare knew something of the restraints. Hamlet spares the king when he surprises him at prayer. Critics have attributed to weakness of character his delay in carrying out the duty imposed on him to revenge his father,[9] but the delay occurs after each has seen through the other's veil of dissembling. He sees the king for the first time, not as a creature of his fantasies, but as a real person. Psychoanalysts, e.g. Ernest Jones, argue that the reasons for the delay lie in hidden motives arising out of oedipal conflicts. Similar motives affect Lady Macbeth ('Had he not resembled my father'). However, oedipal conflicts are only one aspect of the restraints. Overcoming them when he kills Duncan, Macbeth acts like a son who puts himself in his father's place.[10]

217

THE IMMEDIATE EFFECTS

Immediately after the murder Macbeth becomes highly sensitive to noise: 'How is't with me, when every noise appals me?' (II.ii.58). This is a significant symptom which reflects, not only a high level of arousal and a general alertness, but also some disorganisation in behaviour. This is indicated by his ineptness in bringing the daggers from the place (l.48). When so much competes for attention, concentration is impaired, and action is paralysed. He loses his nerve –'Your constancy / Hath left you unattended' (ll.68–9), she says, and he becomes 'infirm of purpose' (l.52). She retains her grasp of the situation.

Sleeplessness, another aspect of the general alertness, results when a person breaks down, as Macbeth does, after an experience he cannot come to terms with psychologically. Macbeth is to be denied the sleep which is 'the balm of hurt minds' (l.38). When it does come, it is disturbed by dreams in which frightening details of the experience are recalled.

Attention, normally selective, is distracted in these circumstances, being withdrawn from some things – 'look on't again, I dare not' (l.52) – and being paid to other things, which may appear inessential. Macbeth thus becomes preoccupied with the bloodiness of his hands, which cannot be washed clean by 'all great Neptune's ocean' (l.60). She, unmoved by the blood except as evidence of their guilt, replies to his anxious preoccupation in practical terms – 'Go get some water' (l.46) – which do not take into account that his preoccupation is not so much with the fact as with the significance of the blood, which represents the irreversible spilling of the essence of the victim's life.

This significance, made more explicit in later scenes and in other plays by Shakespeare,[11] is derived from biblical warnings[12] about the shedding of blood as a vivid image for killing. Macbeth also expresses more directly his sense of being damned and his blood-guilt: 'I had most need of blessing, and "Amen" / Stuck in my throat' (ll.32–3); later he speaks of 'mine eternal jewel / Given to the common enemy of man' (III.i.67–8). References to blood are less prominent in what modern murderers have to say. Smaller and sharper, modern weapons can kill with little or no noticeable bleeding. Blood, known now to be replaceable, no longer evokes such awe. However, they express their sense of being damned in other, usually more direct, terms.

Her behaviour does not become disorganised, as his does, because she proves able to defend herself, at least for a time, by denial, which saves her from recognising the significance of what they have done: 'A foolish thought to say a sorry sight' (II.ii.21): 'I shame / To wear a heart so white' (ll.64–5). Her concern to hide their guilt from others supports this defence. Yet what she says contains warnings that it might break down: 'These deeds must not be thought / After these ways; so, it will make us mad' (ll.33–4). Feelings are not so easily disposed of, and she swoons when she hears him spell out what has happened to Duncan: 'his silver skin lac'd with his golden blood' (II.iii.109–11). She sees too the horror and suspicion evoked in others.

It is hardly necessary to suppose that her swoon is intended to divert attention from him, as some of Shakespeare's sources and some modern critics suggest,[13] or that it reflects womanly exhaustion. More likely, it reflects the precariousness of denial as a defence. When this defence fails, intense feelings are released, from which swooning gives a short-lived relief.

Because of his infirmity Macbeth does not serve her as a confidant. Because she lacks a confiding relationship, which would allow her to express and work through her feelings, her denial continues.

The murder of Duncan does not relieve Macbeth's sense of insecurity. On the contrary, it intensifies it. Also, a new more severe crisis ensues. Trues between him and others at the royal court is destroyed. 'Fears and scruples shake' Banquo and others (l.128). 'Where we are / There's daggers in men's smiles' (ll.138–9),[14] it is said. Many leave Scotland, but Banquo stays. Assumption of the kingship brings Macbeth no relief from insecurity.

A STRANGE INFIRMITY

Although he knows that Macbeth has played 'most foully' (III.i.3), Banquo is at pains to reassure him that he is obedient to his command (ll.15–18). Nevertheless, Macbeth's fears of him grow and 'stick deep' (l.49). 'We have scorched the snake', he tells her, 'not killed it' (III.ii.13). His crown is 'fruitless', his sceptre 'barren', whereas Banquo has been hailed as 'father to a line of kings' (III.i.59–61), but these are hardly sufficient to account for the intensity of his feelings that Banquo is a threat to him.

Fear and mistrust like Macbeth's, out of proportion to any occasion for them, are usually interpreted as a transformation of a sense of guilt. Shakespeare gives another example. Claudius, whose fear and mistrust are derived from a sense of guilt, takes steps to have Hamlet killed in order to 'put fetters upon this fear' (III.iii.25).

Macbeth's fear and mistrust are part of a more pervasive disorder. His world is falling apart – 'the frame of things disjoint'. Hope of restoring security recedes: 'We will eat our meal in fear', and be afflicted by 'terrible dreams' (III.ii. 16–18). Like other murderers do, he envies his victim: 'Better be with the dead' who 'sleeps well' (ll.19–23).

This disorder and especially his feelings of being threatened, his failure to test their validity, and his readiness to act on them warrant a diagnosis of a paranoid illness.[15] His incompetence during the banquet scene, his hallucinating of Banquo, and then his uncontrolled recall of fearful images confirm this diagnosis.

To make such a diagnosis contributes little to the understanding of the psychological mechanisms, but it does tell the clinician what the course of the illness is likely to be. There is a serious risk, not only of suicide, but also of violence towards others. In the greatest danger are those from whom the patient has recently been estranged; the closer the previous relationship, the greater the danger. Because of a passive desire to be killed, the patient may create the conditions in which this is the result. To be killed is attractive because it both meets the sense of guilt and confirms ideas of persecution.

After Banquo has been killed, and Fleance has escaped, Macbeth is 'bound in / To saucy doubts and fears' (III.iv. 24–5). His failure to restore order in the system of relationships at court is made clear in the banquet scene. Each person has a place which, knowing his own degree, he takes, but preoccupied by his fears Macbeth does not play his part as host. His place at the head of the table is taken by the ghost of Banquo.

The hallucinating of Banquo reflects the growing disorder in his thoughts and feelings. That he hallucinates is not in doubt. The ghost is 'the very painting' of his fear (III.iv.61).

He accepts him at first as real, but then dismisses him as 'horrible shadow! / Unreal mock'ry' (ll.106–7).

The hallucination of a person recently lost is common. One in two of the recently widowed, for instance, experience some form of illusion of the dead husband.[16] This is usually a solace, although it is sometimes painful if it follows closely on the death. Banquo's ghost is more persistent and more disturbing than is usual in the setting of bereavement. For a murderer to experience such a full recall of his victim while awake, although credible, would be unusual,[17] and the ghost is perhaps better considered as a symptom of the more general disorder, of which another symptom is the fearful imagery that the dead, sent back from 'charnel houses' and 'graves', rise again and 'push us from our stools' (ll.71–82).

Ross recognises that Macbeth is 'not well', and Lady Macbeth, that he is losing control. It is difficult to know what to make of her assertion that he has often been thus 'from his youth' (l.54), unless her intention is to dissemble. His own admission that he has 'a strange infirmity' (l.86) shows the intensity of his suffering and his awareness that others see that his hold over himself is giving way. He struggles to regain control, and reasserts his manliness: 'What man dare, I dare' (l.99). He anticipates further bloodshed – 'blood will have blood' (l.122) – although killing resolves nothing. Also, he becomes suspicious of Macduff, who has stayed away from the banquet. There is no going back, and he resolves to take action against those who threaten him.

THE ESTRANGEMENT OF MACBETH AND LADY MACBETH

The uneasy intimacy with which they plan the murder of Duncan does not last. Communication between them is impeded because of the different effects the murder has on them. While he is painfully aware of the significance of what they have done, she seems to be unmoved by it. They confide little in one another although both are under strain. She expresses some disillusionment that they have gained nothing – 'Naught's had, all's spent' (III.ii.4) – and complains that he has been staying away from her: 'Why do you keep alone, / Of sorriest fancies your companions making?' (ll.8–9). He does tell her of his fears of Banquo, but he plans and carries out the murder without her, although he does convey to her that something is afoot.

The banquet scene is a turning point. He notices the contrast between them: 'You make me strange' (III.iv.112-16). She taunts him - 'What, quite unmann'd in folly?' 'Fie, for shame!' (ll.73-4) - takes control over the situation and sends the guests away when the banquet breaks up in disorder. She persuades him to go to bed, dismissing with the facile comment, 'You lack the season of all natures, sleep' (l.141) the intense feelings of foreboding and despair he expresses in what has been called perhaps the most terrible passage in the play.[18] The passage ends: 'I am in blood / stepp'd in so far that, should I wade no more, / Returning were as tedious as go o'er' (III.iv.136-8). Her response to this and his decision to act on his own brings their partnership largely to an end.

MACBETH'S FRENZY AND DESPAIR

The interpretation of his second meeting with the Witches is controversial. Perhaps the whole scene is a dream. The apparitions' messages are then the product of Macbeth's imagination. His suspicion of Macduff is revived, and the advice, 'Be bloody, bold, and resolute' (IV.i.79) confirms his decision that things 'must be acted ere they may be scann'd' (III.iv. 140). Also, he learns that Banquo's issue shall reign.

A new element is introduced. He is given a sense of invulnerability. Because 'none of woman born' shall harm him, he can 'laugh to scorn the pow'r of man' (IV.i.79-80). He 'shall never vanquished be, until / Great Birnam Wood to high Dunsinane Hill / Shall come against him' (ll.92-4). He accepts his invulnerability uncritically and relies on it. Later he is to say 'I bear a charmed life' (V.viii.12). His unquestioning belief in his invulnerability has something of the quality of the delusions of grandeur and omnipotence which are typical of paranoid illnesses.[19] These are over-compensations for delusions of persecution. It is not uncommon for a paranoid illness to worsen after a dream confirms existing delusions and adds to them. The timing of such a dream is of significance.

Tendencies emerging before the second meeting with the Witches are now strengthened. The vicious circle started off by the murder of Duncan continues. Steps taken to restore security and order in fact add to insecurity and disorder. Threats at first specific become more general, so that there seem to be hostile forces on all sides. Despite his sense of invulnerability he decides 'to crown my thoughts with acts, be it thought and done' (IV.i.149). Hasty measures tend to be excessive and to make matters worse: 'Dangers breed fears, and fears more dangers bring', the adage puts it. As the crisis escalates, and 'each new day a gash / Is added' to the country's wounds (IV.iii.40-1), he becomes frenzied. 'Some say he's mad; others, that lesser hate him, / Do call it valiant fury' (V.ii.13-14).

His enemies unite against him, and he becomes more and more isolated. 'Those he commands move only in command, / Nothing in love' (ll.19-20). Immediately after the murder he has said to Lennox, perhaps meaning to deceive, although expressing feelings: 'There's nothing serious in mortality - / All is but toys' (II.iii.89-92). This despair grows' 'I am sick at heart .... I have lived long enough ... and that which should accompany old age .... I must not look to have; but, in their stead, / Curses not loud but deep' (V.iii.19-28). After Lady Macbeth's death, disillusion is added to despair: Life is 'a tale / Told by an idiot' (V.v.26-7).

His fears fade as he becomes resigned. Ready for death he does not openly seek it. Unwilling to die on his own sword, he 'must fight the course' (V.vii.2). This is to return to an activity in which he has proved himself. The reason he gives for his reluctance to fight Macduff, an aspect of his resignation, that 'my soul is too much charg'd / With blood of thine already' (V.viii.5-6), is a reminder that he is vulnerable and being taunted by Macduff for his cowardice, he prepares to fight in order to avoid the humiliations of yielding.

LADY MACBETH'S THICK-COMING FANCIES

The 'thick-coming fancies / That keep her from her rest' (V.iii.38-9), as we see in the sleep-walking scene (V.i), recapitulate in a fragmented form the horrifying experiences she has been through: the murder of Duncan, her husband's fearfulness, the appearance to him of Banquo's ghost, and the knocking at the gate, to which at the time she had seemed indifferent. Her continual washing of her hands is in sharp contrast to her easy assertion after the murder of Duncan that 'a little water clears us of this deed' (II.ii.67). 'Here's the smell of the blood still', she says from a 'sorely charg'd heart' (V.i.48-50). Her guilt and remorse are expressed, not directly but only in these metaphors. The concern she voices is that they should not be called to account: 'What need we fear who knows it, when none can call our pow'r to account' (ll.37-8). Her 'infected' mind discharges its 'secrets' to her 'deaf' pillow (ll.70-1).

The recall of so many painful memories in these ways and while sleep-walking is a sign of a serious breakdown of psychological defences and the development of a psychosis,[20] which the doctor calls 'a great perturbation in nature' (l.9). Typical of some forms of psychosis is the combination of obsessive attention to a particular detail, in this case to the 'damned spot!' (l.33), preoccupation by fantasy and apparent watchfulness, in this case 'at once the benefit of sleep' and 'the effects of watching' (ll.9-10). The fantasy tends to be fearful. Immersion in it is increased in the dark, which reduces engagement in the real world – hence her command to have 'light by her continually' (ll.21-2).

The doctor takes trouble to observe and record the manifestations of her illness, and his diagnosis is sound. He is too modest when he comments: 'This disease is beyond my practice' (l.57). Moreover, he anticipates that she will soon act violently to harm herself: 'Look after her; / Remove from her the means of all annoyance / And still keep eyes upon her' (ll.73-5).[21] There are several indications that the risk of an impulsive suicide is serious: the psychosis and, especially, the agitation; the tendency to aggression which her cruelty expresses; her desire for death, expressed in the remark ''Tis safer to be that which we destroy' (III.ii.6); her presentiment of death – 'The Thane of Fife had a wife; where is she now?' (V.i.40); and her feeling that there is no road back – 'What's done cannot be undone' (ll.65-6). The doctor's view on treatment, although approved by Jaspers,[22] is too negative: 'the patient / Must minister to himself' (V.iii. 45-6).

Freud argues that her transformation in the sleep-walking scene from what he calls, I think mistakenly, 'callousness to penitence' is a reaction to her continuing childlessness after many further years of marriage. However, her gentlewoman gives as the onset of the acute illness: 'since his Majesty went into the field' (V.i.3). This suggests two factors: a further disengagement from his affairs and, more important, the loss of whatever support she has had from him. Lack of support from an intimate is known[23] to make women more liable to become depressed after severe life-events, probably also men, and both men and women to other kinds of mental illness. Denial is more necessary as a defence when not able to confide in someone and to 'give sorrow words' in accordance with the advice offered by Malcolm to the stricken Macduff, which is cited with approval by modern psychiatrists.[24] Otherwise, 'the grief that does not speak / Whispers the o'erfraught heart and bids it break' (IV.iii.209–10).

THE NATURE OF THE TRAGEDY

The outcome is tragedy. Both suffer and die. She 'by self and violent hands / Took off her life' (V.viii.70–1). For him, 'certain issue strokes must arbitrate' (V.iv.20), and the end comes through military intervention, 'the usurper's cursed head' (V.viii.55) being cut off by Macduff. Malcolm's summing up, 'this dead butcher and his fiend-like queen', too simple if they are to be understood as human beings, does not relieve the sadness felt by playgoers that they should have been caught up in a train of events so destructive of not only others but also themselves.

In the train of events in the play, the murders of Duncan, Banquo and Macduff's wife and children appear to be distinctive. Demobilisation, the first meeting with the Witches, the estrangement from Banquo, the naming of Malcolm and Duncan's visit were things happening to them, to which they responded, whereas, *prima facie*, they decided together to murder Duncan, and he to murder Banquo and others. However, our examination has shown that neither was a free agent. Judgment, choice and insight were vitiated by intense conflicts within each of them. She could not carry out her decision to murder Duncan. He decided not to do so, and then changed his mind in order to relieve his doubts about himself. She killed herself, not by free choice, but at the height of a mental illness. He refuses to yield to Macduff, not as a decision based on the merits of fighting him, but in order to avoid the humiliation of kneeling to Malcolm and being 'baited by the rabble's curse' (V.viii.29).

This account of the play puts the emphasis on their step-by-step estrangement as the reason why neither could decide freely. As they became more estranged, so their appraisals of themselves and the world around them became more distorted, so much so eventually as to amount to mental illness. The tragic paradox is that the actions Macbeth took to dispel his fears that 'to be thus is nothing' (III.i.47) disrupted any system of relationships that could have made him something, and thus confirmed his paranoid attitudes.

The form taken by the mental illness in each case precluded any intervention that could have brought reconciliation. Each got caught up in a vicious circle. The remark of the doctor, 'More needs she the divine than the physician' indicates one of the ways in which the estranged can be brought back into a system of relationships. Helping them to acknowledge and repent what they have done, and with the promise of atonement, a divine administers the sacraments of the church to mark the return into fellowship. However, several hindrances would have had to be got over before Lady Macbeth would have felt able to accept help of this kind. Another form of intervention is through a court of justice. After the offences have been defined and acknowledged, the court prescribes the conditions and terms for a return to full membership of the community, as did the court in Athens for Orestes, with the calling off of the pursuit by the Furies. But there was no court in Scotland with the power to call either of them to account.

Psychotherapeutic intervention might have created conditions in which each could have given, within a confiding relationship, some expression to fantasies, which in consequence could have been modified or corrected. This would have reduced the power of internal conflicts to prejudice decisions. In general, psychotherapeutic intervention has two objectives: to free the patient from internal conflicts so that he can decide freely; and to mediate his reconciliation with others.

Had they found an occasion to speak their 'free hearts each to other' (I.iii.154-5), Banquo might have been able to modify Macbeth's belief that he is to be king, give him a sounder appraisal of himself and others and retained his friendship. Once Duncan had been murdered, the processes of estrangement were so strong that they could not have been easily arrested. Yet there were occasions when psychotherapeutic intervention might have had some influence on the progress to disaster. One was at the end of the banquet scene when Macbeth became acutely aware of the horrifying prospects facing him. Another was when he consulted the doctor at the time of his wife's acute illness. His question about the cleansing of 'that perilous stuff which weighs upon the heart' (V.iii.40–6) seems to reflect some concern about himself. The doctor's reply, that 'the patient must minister to himself', was perhaps addressed to him. At any rate, that opportunity to bring him to treatment was lost, as it was then for her. Macbeth rejected any idea of treatment for himself – 'Throw physic to the dogs! I'll none of it' (l.47) – showing that in his view the disease lay elsewhere, and the doctor, no doubt correctly, saw no 'profit' (l.62) in pursuing the matter. As his despair grew, so did his insight. Although resigned to death, he might have been more amenable to treatment.

In the event there could be no psychotherapeutic intervention to slow or arrest the progress to disaster, and each died a lonely death without reconciliation.

NOTES

1 The justification for this approach is discussed by Ernest Jones, *Hamlet and Oedipus* (1949), pp. 19–22.

2 S. Freud, *Some Character-types met with in Psychoanalytic Work* (Std edn 1957, vol. 14, pp. 316–24 (pp. 322–3 especially).

3 This idea is discussed in relation to *Macbeth* by R. Rogers, *The Double in Literature* (Detroit, 1970), pp. 48–51.

4 The place of systems theory in psychopathology is discussed by P. Watzlawick, J.H. Beavin and D. Jackson, *Pragmatics of Human Communication* (1968) and J. Bowlby, *Attachment and Loss: Sadness and Depression*, vol. 3 (1980).

5 T. Morris and L. Blom-Cooper, *A Calendar of Murder* (1964).

6 N.B. Rushforth, A.M. Ford, C.S. Hirsch, N.M. Rushforth and L. Adelson, 'Violent Death in a Metropolitan County: changing patterns in homicide (1958-74), *New England Journal of Medicine* (1977), pp. 297, 531–8.

7 D.J. West, *Murder Followed by Suicide* (1965).

8 M. Cox, 'Dynamic psychotherapy with sex offenders', in *Sexual Deviation*, ed. I. Rosen, (Oxford, 1977): citing M. Tuovinen, *Crime as an Attempt at Intrapsychic Adaptation* (Oulu, Finland, 1973).

9 E.g. J.D. Wilson, *What Happens in Hamlet* (3rd edn, Cambridge, 1951).

10 O. Rank, *Das Inzest-Motiv in Dictung und Sage* (2nd edn, Leipzig, 1926), p. 209.
11 E.g. in *Hamlet* Claudius speaks of 'the primal eldest curse' and the washing away of blood (III.iii.37–47).
12 Genesis IV.xi: the curse of Cain; and IX.vi: God's warning to Noah and his sons.
13 See A.C. Bradley, *Shakespearian Tragedy* (Student edn, 1978), p. 417.
14 S. Bachmann, 'Daggers in men's smiles – the truest issue in *Macbeth*', *International Review of Psychoanalysis*, 5 (1978), 97–104.
15 The essence of a paranoid illness is the use as a defence of projection, e.g. the attributing to others of the hate the patient feels for himself. On the International Classification of Diseases, Macbeth's illness would be classified as a psychogenic paranoid psychosis.
16 C.M. Parkes, *Bereavement* (1972).
17 Richard III is asleep when the ghosts of his victims appear. Brutus sits reading at night when the ghost of Julius Caesar appears.
18 J.D. Wilson, ed., *Macbeth* (Cambridge, 1947), p. 141.
19 For a discussion of delusions of grandeur and omnipotence in relation to paranoid illnesses see: C. Scharfetter, *General Psychopathology*, trans. H. Marshall (Cambridge, 1980).
20 By a psychosis is meant an impairment in mental functions sufficient to interfere seriously with the ability to meet the ordinary demands of living and especially to perceive and respond appropriately to the real world. Lady Macbeth's illness would be classified as a reactive confusion.
21 In *Hamlet* Claudius gives the advice about Ophelia: 'Follow her close; give her good watch' (IV.v.72).
22 K. Jaspers, *General Psychopathology* (Manchester, 1963), p. 839.
23 G.W. Brown and T. Harris, *Social Origins of Depression* (1978).
24 Parkes, *op. cit.*

Part 5

A director's view
of the play

11

Directing *Macbeth*

Peter Hall

in an interview with
John Russell Brown

JRB In *Crucial Years* (1963) you said that the theatre is always a 'quest'. That quest has led you twice to *Macbeth*. Why do you think this play has drawn you?

PH It is the most thorough-going study of evil that I know in dramatic literature. Evil in every sense: cosmic sickness, personal sickness, personal neurosis, the consequence of sin, the repentance of sin, blood leading to more blood, and that, in a way, leading inevitably to regeneration. Disease or crime, or evil, induces death, which induces life: *Macbeth* presents this cycle of living and, in that sense, I find it the most metaphysical of Shakespeare's plays – an unblinking look at the nature of evil in the person and in the state, and in the cosmos.

JRB Do you say that the evil in *Macbeth*, through some kind of purgation, leads to good for the protagonists and for society in the play or in a timeless judgment?

PH I suspect for the audience, for the audience watching it. You certainly cannot say that Macbeth's death is good for Macbeth except that in the last Act he does, in my view, reach nobility, clarity and strength, a sense of the reality of the consequences of actions.

JRB And that feeling for the truth of his situation is in some sense a good?

PH Yes, I think so: all Shakespeare's heroes are on a quest for self-knowledge and self-understanding. The calm that Macbeth has in some moments of the last Act is very hard and clear sighted. It is not sentimental penitence, not light in any way: it is a very clear statement

about himself and the transitory nature of life. He goes
on a marvellous journey for us, as spectators, to watch.

The play charts the progress of Scotland – which is a
metaphor for the society of the audience who is
watching it – from disease, sickness, corruption, terror,
lies, hypocrisy, evil, back into health or – at least –
the possibility of health.

JRB   The contrast between Macbeth and Malcolm seems
significant here. Malcolm's speech at the end of the
play is very expected and very astute, whereas Macbeth finishes with a fight which demands from the
actor an assured surge of strength and power. Moreover,
from a political point of view, it is an unnecessary
action: Macbeth knows by this time, that he has lost
and is damned, and yet he cries:

> Before my body
> I throw my warlike shield. Lay on, Macduff;
> And damn'd be him that first cries 'Hold, enough!'
> (V.viii.32-4)

He is not just going to die; he will do so in the way he
chooses.

PH   He is the master of his death, and he is also testing, to
the end, the prophecy of the witches.

JRB   You think he is taking on the witches?

PH   Yes. If his adversary is Macduff and he was 'untimely
ripped', then he must fight this, even though he knows
there is no hope of success.

There is also a sense that by going to his death
fighting, Macbeth makes the image of the wheel
coming full circle: the great thing about Macbeth when
we first meet him is that he is a superb warrior,
'Bellona's bridegroom' (I.ii.55). He goes back, or forward, to where he actually is. His valour is one of his
greatest attributes. It is perhaps difficult for us to
make the historical jump – I suppose we think of this
now in respect of athletes, such as Mohammed Ali –
but a lot of Renaissance drama, certainly *Macbeth*, is
based on absolute admiration, in the fullest sense of
that word, for the physical prowess of the warrior
individual: a self-assertion which has the courage to
be proud and to stake one's all, to risk one's very

being. Amazingly Shakespearian drama still deals with feudal societies in which conflict between Scotland and England, or France and England, can be reduced to single-hand combat. Theatrically this is a wonderful thing to be able to do; but it is also a true expression of the idea of Renaissance man as an individual.

And, opposed to Macbeth the warrior, is the intelligent ruler, Malcolm, somewhat as Antony is opposed by Octavius. It is very interesting that the politically adroit, more modern man, Malcolm, does not engage in hand-to-hand fighting; that is left to Macduff. Of course, Macduff needs to do this in order to revenge and expiate the crimes against his family, his wife and his children, but there is no suggestion that Malcolm is a warrior, wants to be, or is expected to be.

One of the strands of the play is that two kinds of leadership are necessary: political leadership in peace, heroic leadership in war. Macbeth is very good at the latter and very bad at the former: he has no political adroitness at all.

JRB You do not feel that Macbeth is politically able when he questions (III.i) Banquo's intention of leaving the Court, where he should remain for the Coronation festivities?

PH Macbeth is *trying* to be politically astute. But I feel a sense of strain in it. That is a subjective reaction, an interpretation; but it is very difficult to play that scene as easily as, shall we say, Duncan would have played it, or Henry V would have played it. Henry V I regard as Shakespeare's consummate politician.

JRB Yes, all the political scenes in this play are odd, aren't they? Because the announcement of Malcolm as Prince of Cumberland and therefore heir to Duncan's throne is done with a sudden abruptness. Some scholars have suggested that the original text has been cut around here.

PH I don't believe that: I believe that Duncan is deliberately challenging his thanes by taking this political initiative abruptly. He is testing the autocratic power which he believes is his. It is quite a gamble, and he plays it with deliberate unpreparedness.

JRB Is it difficult to stage this scene clearly, when the thanes have nothing to do in response to Duncan's bombshell – not in words at any rate?

PH   Yes; but, in production, we must use an historical sense. Over all the plays there hangs a knowledge of the Court, and Court behaviour. It is quite difficult for us to remember how an Elizabethan, a Jacobean courtier had to behave. The king is not what he is by acting in a kingly way: that would be an abstract. He is shown to be king by the way everybody else reacts to *him*, hangs on his every word and does not react if the situation is dangerous. The king is also careful of his own skin all the time. A situation in which the leader is a total autocrat is very difficult for us to imagine. No leader in Western democratic society has quite the wilful degree of power that perfectly reasonable leaders in Shakespeare have. So Duncan is the focal point of this scene, and the thanes are all watchful of each other to see if anybody reacts, one way or the other. In that sort of danger, it is safest to say nothing. And Duncan half expects that, because he goes on to deflect attention by announcing where he is going to have supper. He just rides over the crisis and it is left to Macbeth to address the audience. We are obviously interested in Macbeth's reaction to this sudden wilfulness, the wilfulness of power that Duncan demonstrates. (If Richard II had done this it could have caused a rebellion.)

I think Duncan is very adroit: there is no suggestion at all that he is murderable because of wilful old age; he is in control. As far as the other thanes are concerned, no power-base is building up against him.

JRB   Sometimes Duncan is presented on stage as if he had one foot in the grave, possibly because he doesn't take part in the fighting.

PH   I don't believe that is right. The Duncan I receive from the text is adroit and very much in command, very gracious. I think he is a perfect, courteous king, and very clever: I don't think he's senile and, equally, I don't think he's any kind of super religious figure.

JRB   That gives more force to the fact that he is wrong about two very important people, about Cawdor and Macbeth.

PH   It is worth noting that no one else was right.

When Duncan arrives at the castle on that pleasant

evening, all the values of hospitality and of grace are stressed. There is no feeling at all that he is a murderable king; the country does not want him murdered. When Ross retells the king's message to Macbeth, he is able to speak with kingly authority, dignity and control which are very impressive. That is almost an extension of Duncan's own part, almost an imitation of Duncan, and it shows how the state ought to work.

JRB What effect does the Scottish setting have on these issues? Duncan's was an elective monarchy and depended on the personal loyalty of the thanes who had their own armies and their own strongholds.

PH I think that this would make an Elizabethan audience more politically alert. The Wars of the Roses were not that far away, and the horror of England torn apart by a series of tribal wars was still fairly fresh in men's minds, despite the Tudor success-story of making the country one. The Scottish setting helps to focus on these issues in the minds of Shakespeare's audience.

JRB There seems to be a telescoped history of society in *Macbeth*, which reaches back to those great magnates who were figures of power around a king and had to maintain his power with their strong arms. The personal authority of the king is challenged by Macbeth, and then Malcolm founds a new state by the exercise of a new kind of political intelligence.

PH I agree with that. The England scene (IV.iii) is about that – among other things. It displays the workings of Malcolm's mind and how he learns kingship by the example of Edward, the King of England, and by the pragmatic use of power in the conversation with Macduff. There is a reasonable hope that Malcolm is going to be a very clever, very good king.

JRB Yes; but in contrast to Edward the Confessor who is a holy, miraculous king.

PH At a Court performance of *Macbeth*, James I, the 'Fool of Christendom' on the throne of England, was actually watching this play: then, particularly, the effect of political intelligence was a live issue.

JRB We've been talking about Macbeth and Scotland, but the play would never be done if the theatre company did not believe that it had not only a Macbeth but also a Lady Macbeth.

PH The dramatization of the relationship between Lady Macbeth and Macbeth makes the fable work, makes the story happen. There are political ramifications, but the extraordinary basic tension is that between a great warrior, a great physical leader, and his wife. Macbeth is capable of hand-to-hand fighting and has enormous charisma so that success comes naturally but he is not in any sense an extrovert. His mask is that of an extrovert; but his actual self is introverted, with a deep imagination and sense of fantasy, with a rapid, feverish ability to proceed from consequence to consequence, like someone in a dream or a nightmare. His imagination, even when he is happy and at peace, is restless. He is very perceptive and he studies himself; in modern terms one would say he was introverted and mentally effeminate, although he is also the most masculine man you can imagine. Left to his own devices – I know the dangers of guessing what would have happened 'if', but in this case it may clarify Macbeth's nature – if he hadn't actually married a Lady Macbeth, then his life would have been something else.

JRB He might never have done that murder because he has a sense of virtue, of right and wrong. Without this part of his character, *Macbeth* would not be a tragedy; we would be looking at a Hitler.

PH Yes, proceeding from the moment of grasping power to the bunker: which I would find tragic, but verminous.

Macbeth is I think very reluctant to engage in crime, to bloody his hands, partly because he has a sense of what's right and what's wrong, partly because he knows himself, his own imagination. But Lady Macbeth has a very limited imagination and this is why some actresses find the part unsatisfactory: they try to make it more than it is. I think it is a great role because she is a woman with little fantasy, little imagination, who is thoroughly practical and thoroughly pragmatic. She is also very, very sexy: that is one of her holds on him, as it is one of his holds on her.

Her sense of fantasy and nightmare – the inner life, the introversion – is not released obviously until madness and the sleep-walking scene (V.i). She is capable of going through with the murder: that is why she answers Macbeth's 'Duncan comes here tonight'

236

(I.v.56) with the simple question: 'And when goes hence?' The early interchanges in this scene show that they must have talked often of his ambitions. You can see that they have thought 'How long will Duncan last?', 'When will he die?', 'Will we get it?' – all that. The dialogue here is a very powerful shorthand: they also speak with their eyes, hands, beings.

Without Lady Macbeth, I don't believe he would have done the murder. After he has been alone for a time, he sounds fully persuaded that 'We will proceed no further in this business' (I.vii.31). It is Lady Macbeth who brings him back on course. And, once he has done the murder and he is alone with the consequences of it, it is then that he makes himself increasingly alone; and it is this shutting out of his wife, among other things, which drives her mad.

JRB I'm surprised you say that Lady Macbeth has little imagination. Surely she has a strong imagination but of a different sort from her husband's:

> Come, you spirits
> That tend on mortal thoughts   (I.v.37ff.)

is full of extraordinary imagination.

PH Yes, I think I must rephrase that. She has imagination in a broad sense, but she also has the courage to look at it unblinkingly – and to cope with it.

JRB Surely that implies an imaginative life of really astounding power.

PH Yes; and perhaps it gives the foundation for the sleep-walking scene (V.i).

> Come, thick night,
> And pall thee in the dunnest smoke of hell,
> That my keen knife see not the wound it makes,
> Nor heaven peep through the blanket of the dark
> To cry 'Hold, hold'
>   (I.v.47–51)

is really a most fantastic emotion, because she is imagining another world at that moment; and she is also imagining a kind of a physical confrontation with an idea. She is conjuring up a possibility in full, to her

fullest bent, in order to cope with it. When the messenger comes in and says 'The King comes here tonight',
her response, 'Thou art mad to say so', shows that
she is so imaginatively caught up that she not only
foresees the murder, but also what might happen
thereafter.

They have different kinds of imagination. Macbeth's
is feverish, ambiguous, qualifying; as soon as he has
made one statement he qualifies it with another.
Whereas she seems to create total propositions. There
is a practicality, a clear-eyed quality about Lady Macbeth.

I think that one of the problems always is that
actresses either make Lady Macbeth too ordinary
without sufficient imagination or search for a kind of
imagination that is independent of Macbeth; they
compete with him.

JRB How does she make Macbeth change his mind after
he's broken from the supper, and says 'We will proceed
no further' (I.vii.31)?

PH She flatters him as being an extraordinary male, and
so any absence of maleness gives her the ability to
handle him. I think this is the mainspring of the
scene. That's why her imagery is to do with the courage
– almost the maleness – of her femaleness. Towards the
end of the scene she manages to talk about what *they*
may not do. She has mastered the moment, and so has
united them. I think she handles him with extraordinary
sensitivity.

Once that relationship is broken by Macbeth's
actions and new initiatives, she has no further ability
to handle him. It doesn't work any more. He is not
open to her. He's gone on to the further reaches of
guilt, and she's terribly alone. That's when the consequences of her actions come home to her.

Even though it was played originally by a boy or,
I suspect, a young man, she has got to be very, very
sexy; and she must have an enormous imaginative
reach, with the ability to control and concentrate that
reach. That's what's difficult. Her mind is strongest
and most imaginative when she is in action: she doesn't
like doing nothing.

JRB When she enters while he is doing the murder, do you

think that is an opportunity for showing real fear?

PH   I think there is a sort of physical pleasure: the adrenalin is running very high; all senses at full stretch. Very, very frightened; very, very excited; very, very alive: that's what adrenalin is for. Certainly she is not timid; and she is not backing off at all. It is almost a cele-bration of fear: 'Infirm of purpose' (II.ii.52) to her frightened husband is clearly a key phrase. Once she's at something, she goes through with it.

JRB   Why does she faint when Duncan's murder is dis-covered (II.iii,117)?

PH   This is a very complicated moment. I've tried it in a variety of ways in productions, and I think that's inevitable because the faint can be rationalized in any way you like. She might faint because she sees the consequence of the crime on Macbeth, the new ability with which he tells the lie. That's one possibility. Or she may see all that is unleashed in the dramatic action: all those 'spirits that tend on mortal thoughts'... She sees them now: there they are, right in the head of her husband. Or it may be that she actually faints under the general pressure of events, the whole thing; but that's rather a boring choice for an actress to make.

JRB   It would make a bold choice if related fully to the rest of her part – 'Give me the daggers' (II.ii.53).

PH   Yes; you could argue, in the Stanislavskian sense, that it's the contradiction that makes her the most courag-eous person in the play, and 'give me the daggers' a huge achievement.

Or it may be that she pretends to faint in order to distract from Macbeth's phoney excuses.

How this moment is played must depend on the production, the Lady Macbeth and how it is all work-ing. That is one of the acts of bringing a play alive. There are often key moments which you can rationalize and say must be that way or that way, but there is no absolute in these matters.

How the faint is taken has, of course, great con-sequences. It may be the first time that Macbeth sees her vulnerability – which is going to lead to madness and the sleep-walking scene. It may be yet another demonstration of her social adroitness, that she can faint in a womanly way at exactly the right moment to deflect attention.

JRB   Yes, and 'What in our house?' (II.iii.86) would then be the kind of hostess's remark which is very well judged, and by its very tone puts off suspicion.

 PH   I think that's what that line is: they are both of them consummate liars, as I think – if we're honest – all men are.

One of the basic strengths of Shakespearian drama is that the audience is shown what a character is actually motivated by, and they then see him wearing a mask. This play is full of masks. An actor often makes the mistake of reminding the audience that it's a mask, and then he makes fools of those around him. The classic case is Iago, whom the entire cast say is honest all the time! I've yet to see an honest Iago on the stage because they can never resist reminding the audience that they're a villain. Now Lady Macbeth and Macbeth have to behave in a most socially acceptable way before and after the murder scenes.

JRB   There are many people in that scene of the discovery of Duncan's murder who must work very hard, in a short space of time, to find the right posture for what is the removal of the centre of their world.

 PH   They don't know what to do! They don't know whether to give the lead to the new power, or who's going to have that power, or from what source it is coming. They don't know why Duncan was killed. It's the world turned upside down.

JRB   Banquo, in particular, is in a difficult position: he is going to need a new mask.

 PH   Very difficult. I think I would only say one thing. Whatever choice is made about the faint, this is a very significant, eloquent moment, deliberately created in the play. It's not something you just throw away. It's political; and it's physical between Lady Macbeth and Macbeth.

JRB   Macduff's response to the murder: 'O, horror, horror, horror' is extremely difficult to do technically; he has to go in and then come back so changed that only that can be said. This seems to me to be another indication that things happen in this scene which overflow the measure of ordinary drama.

240

PH   Yes; it dramatizes an unimaginable reversal in their lives, unimaginable chaos. Such moments of specified action in Shakespeare have to be looked at very carefully.

JRB Another specified action is the airborne dagger and 'Come let me clutch thee' (II.i.34). It's one thing to see an apparition of an airborne dagger, another to have an actor attempting to clutch it.

PH   Yes; this also is very difficult to do: it has to be absolutely real to Macbeth because he does see a dagger. The audience only see a dagger if he sees a dagger. That is a wonderful image.

JRB There's an element of self-dramatization in that scene: 'Thus.... With Tarquin's ravishing strides' (II.i.54-5). Is that also a stage direction for a specified action?

PH   I would doubt if an actor should actually do that, but I think that's how Macbeth sees himself. It's not by accident that he finally sees himself, and sees mankind, as a performer on the stage of the world. From the word go, he has had an acute sense of himself as an actor in life's drama. It's part of his introspection that he sees the figure he's cutting.

   I think we make a great mistake if we ever take Shakespeare away from the idea of the theatre as the globe, the actor as man, man as actor, and life as play. I think whole areas of the plays get unlocked by remembering that. It's to do, I think, with outdoor drama, the sense of being an actor in front of people out of doors. Theatricality, in the proper sense, is part of Shakespeare's drama and I could make a case that the incident of the airborne dagger is the actor Macbeth getting his props ready, seeing himself ready for the action he has to take as the actor Macbeth.

JRB Because it's easier to act it than to do it?

PH   But one of the ways of doing it, is to act it.

JRB   Whiles I threat, he lives;
   Words to the heat of deeds too cold breath gives.
   I go, and it is done: the bell invites me.
                                           (II.i.60-2)

PH   There is your cue. I think that's an important tone in the play.

JRB He speaks to Duncan after that in a rhetorical way

which goes back to early Elizabethan drama:

> Hear it not, Duncan, for it is a knell
> That summons thee to heaven, or to hell.

PH He's going out to kill his imagination.

JRB In so far as the play is about imagination and fantasy, and about evil and good, the supernatural characters and events are of great importance. How can the characters called 'witches', Banquo's ghost and the visible apparitions be staged?

PH I believe that the witches are real old women and I think that's where you have to start from. We know about James I's obsession with witchcraft and Elizabethan and Jacobean interest in all its manifestations. But we also know about the old woman, usually a widow, who lived alone with her cat, very poor and outside normal society. Perhaps she made medicines out of herbs for the local village, but gradually this outsider became an object of hate, and everything that went wrong was gradually shifted on to her. In the end this poor old woman ends up being burnt. The history of witchcraft demonstrates an appalling kind of racialism. I think that if you don't take the coven of witches as real old women you don't get one of the most important shifts of gear in the play. The further and contrasting presence of Hecate is crucial to this.

I don't take the view that the Hecate scenes are corrupt, or that Hecate should not be played. She gives metaphorical presence to God or, rather, anti-God. This is essential to the dramatic action, like the later Shakespearian masque world, the arrival of Jupiter or Diana. What happens is that the real old women release supernatural evil through the actions of Macbeth; they have put into his mind something which is already there, and this becomes totally visible in the play.

JRB The witches, in themselves, could be pathetic, laughable, muddled . . .

PH They could. Perhaps their prophecies are often wrong, but sometimes they're right, as the fortune-teller on the pier can be.

JRB So while recognizing the witches as real people, you

242

believe they get caught up into something which is supernatural?

PH I think this is the importance of the Hecate scene (III.v) and of having all the elaboration of the apparitions and the dance of six witches. I believe that one has to accept the authenticity of Folio text. If there was a Quarto of the play without Hecate and another one with, then there would be a choice. But we have only one text of *Macbeth*, in the Folio, and there's Hecate. It seems to me presumptuous to assume that Shakespeare didn't write something because we don't quite know how to do it.

I can amass, to me, formidable reasons why Act III scene v must be authentic. First of all the verse is odd and mesmeric; it seems to me deliberately primitive, drawing on folk tradition of riddles, spells, incantations, nursery rhymes. It's not very far away from the rhythms of the fairy writing in the *Dream*, especially for Puck:

> I am for th'air; this night I'll spend
> Unto a dismal and a fatal end.
> Great business must be wrought ere noon.
> Upon the corner of the moon
> There hangs a vap'rous drop profound;
> I'll catch it ere it come to ground.

The climax of the speech is:

> For you all know security
> Is mortal's chiefest enemy.

That seems to me an extraordinary piece of writing. I don't see why we shouldn't think Shakespeare wrote that. The whole scene has been questioned because of its style, but I would say that's no justification for writing it off. It's a deliberate and theatrically exciting contrast.

JRB Did you find that the more you worked on that speech, the more sure you were that the style and the rhythms were making their own necessary contribution?

PH Oh yes; and it's deliberately different, as the goddesses in *The Tempest* are different, as Jupiter in *Cymbeline* is different.

Unless you have Hecate there is a static nature to the development of the characters of the witches. Whereas when Hecate is played the supernatural releases in Macbeth what he already wants, what he knows already; and he releases cosmic evil in the world which is given metaphorical shape in the presence of Hecate who provides this coven of mad old women with a baccanalia they had never dreamt of.

JRB And also raises images of the succession of Banquo, which should speak for a secure dynasty over against the crumbling political reality of Scotland.

PH The line of kings is a nightmare to Macbeth, but not in any other sense. It means security.

The central point to grasp about the cauldron scene (IV.i) is that it's to do with the masque, baroque theatre and dumb-show. Our post-Restoration theatrical tradition – I suppose we're still suffering from the nineteenth century – leads us to see emblems on stage as decorative and inferior, not as good as words: the metaphor of stage effects and scenery is uncomplex. I don't take that view at all. One of the miracles of Renaissance theatre is the concept of the theatre as a metaphor of the world. That evil and hell is underneath, that man struts his life as a player on the stage, and that God and the gods exist above metaphorically. That's very eloquent in Baroque opera and very eloquent in late Shakespearian drama. I think of Hecate and the cauldron scene as I think of the most potent manifestations of the masque in Inigo Jones and Ben Jonson, and that is no small thing. Jacobean audiences were trained to look at an action, or an emblem or a person, and say to themselves 'What does that show *mean*?' Therefore the line of kings is not just a group of kings, it means peace, succession, continuity.

The cauldron scene should be staged as a masque, with Hecate flying , with the apparitions coming out of the cauldron. You have to ask constantly what does it all mean: what is the child, what is the branch, the baby, the kings? At this time the play is a 'show', but that does not mean it is trivial. If you can do it well, it will work on an audience today as well as it did then. Of course once you do that, you get into a different form of theatre which I think fascinated Shakespeare in the later plays. It's emblematic theatre. The show will be supported by music, verse-rhythms which are deliberately structured differently, and rhymes and rhyme patterns, and the use of machinery such as Jupiter's eagle and the 'quaint devices' of *The Tempest*.

JRB   How does this different kind of attention affect our view of Macbeth?

PH   At the conclusion of the cauldron scene, we think of Macbeth as of Hitler in his bunker, a man of absolute evil who, in a sense, is then deliberately kept away from us. But then, when we see him again, he's at his most human – which is a surprise. Once he's gone through the experience of the cauldron, half of him is a total instrument of evil, cauterized from feeling. The early Macbeth could never have done the things he does now.

I'm interested in how somebody can have been 'Bellona's bridegroom' carving his way through lines of enemies, slaughtering like a butcher, and yet could have had Macbeth's degree of imagination right from the word go. It's a wonderful paradox: like Coriolanus who speaks almost more text than any other Shakespearian hero and yet is a dramatization of a man who can't speak. The man who is least likely to be able to kill because of his powers of imagination is the one who when killing bathes himself in blood. He doesn't just kill; he kills with a kind of celebratory relish. Amazing. Maybe Shakespeare kept such a theme within bounds by choosing to make such a man as Macbeth the best at it. Blood is called for throughout the play: blood is death and blood is life, and blood must have blood. That's been well documented and well noted: *Macbeth* is the play of blood.

Different levels of reality are used deliberately in the play. There is the bloody dagger which Macbeth sees and we don't. Apparitions which we all see because they are metaphors of the fantastic, of fantasy made concrete. Then there is the banquet (III.iv) to which Macbeth – if you want to be realistic – *imagines* Banquo coming, but he imagines so concretely that he sees it and we see it, but nobody else on stage sees it. Some directors try to hide the moment when Banquo's

ghost comes on stage, but I think his entry is very
well marked in the rhythm of the text. I am sure he
just walks on. The excitement for the audience is that
they see him first, and *then* Macbeth sees him. But
nobody else does. Time seems to stop in this scene, so
that it goes on only as it is experienced in Macbeth's
mind: it's a close-up of him talking to us.

The banquet scene doesn't work naturalistically.
There are moments when the guests and Lady Macbeth
have to do nothing except remember that the audience
is not looking at them; the audience is listening to
Macbeth and time is suspended.

JRB And what of Lady Macbeth's role in this scene?

PH It dramatizes her courage and the effort with which
she is able to control an incredibly difficult, torturing
situation. But I don't think the actress should exit
broken, ready for the sleep-walking scene. Much of the
energy and impetus of a Shakespearian play comes
from the fact that the protagonists come on in the
next scene in a way which you don't expect. I think
one should feel at the end of the banquet that here is
a woman who is now isolated from her husband, but
she can still cope; her strength is fantastic.

And then we see her sleep-walking . . . . I've tried
this scene (V.i) many different ways. It still eludes me.
I think it contains her whole life, her whole experience,
not just the fragments of the murder; it has the per-
ception of dreams. I honestly don't know what is the
progression of this scene. It is not purgation. It may be
that as Lady Macbeth leaves the stage, she has, for this
instant of time, purged enough of her torment to have
sleep. But I prefer to think that this is a segment of
the journey towards death. As she says, 'Give me your
hand', and 'To bed, to bed, to bed, to bed,' the sexual
bond, the life-giving bond, has been broken and there
is a great desire to reinstate it – which we know will
not happen. There are many new recognitions and great
imaginative reach. I could make a case for the sleep-
walking being a liberation of her imagination, so that
she is almost like the early Macbeth when he roams
imaginatively over the consequences of every action.
She always had sensibility, but she had deliberately
controlled it; now the blinkers are off. She is terribly

clear-sighted.

The scene is pointless if it is the incoherent fragments of dream. It all has specific meaning, and a specific progress and development. And that's what is heart-breaking, perhaps; because I think the final effect on the audience must be to break their hearts. The doctor and the waiting woman tell us how to look at the scene – that's what they're there for, like different shots in a film – and finally they're struck dumb.

JRB We have talked about particular moments, characters and scenes, but little of the shape and effect of the play as a whole.

PH It is the shortest of the great plays and there is a con-centrated feeling to it; it has a feverish rhythm. It's very, very quick, and its movement very economical. It also has a deliberate spread at the end of some scenes, when you settle down to a slow *andante* after the *presto* events earlier.

It does seem to me – and I'm speaking subjectively as someone who's been privileged to feel the play on my pulses by working on it twice – that architecturally it is consummate. I do not believe that the Folio text has been cut; I really don't. The extant texts of some of the other plays may not be performing texts; as most dramatists do even to this day, Shakespeare or his printers may have put back for publication what-ever they had cut from a performance. But if this play is cut, I swear it is in the sense that this is what he wanted it to be. This is what it is.

It is the most efficient piece of architecture, extra-ordinary in its rhythm. In modern performance you really can't put an interval anywhere without loss. You certainly can't have two intervals. The onrush of events, the consequence of actions, the development of the nightmare once Macbeth is king, is all gone if you have an interval. So last time I did it without any interval; and it seemed to be much better.

The play's demands on all the actors' emotional agility are vast and speedy. And I think it makes great demands on an audience. One is always reminded in this instance that Shakespeare worked with a dozen or so master actors who were all sharers of the company and who doubled everything; you have to have a company of consummate actors.

JRB And you have to have a stage which you can wipe clean of one image and superimpose another absolutely at once.

PH *Macbeth* with scenery that changes in any sense – even something going up and down – is impossible. The stage has to be a space which becomes what the characters say it is; and the intercut of scene to scene is crucial. Hecate should come down and the cauldron should come up: those are the only scene changes.

JRB And yet, with all these difficulties, *Macbeth* still holds you?

PH I would be very sad if I thought I wasn't going to do the play again in my life, because it's something you have to just go on tussling with. Unlike a conductor, a theatre director doesn't return to the great master-pieces often enough. The first time you do a play it may have an irreplaceable freshness; but knowledge comes only from doing it and redoing it, and doing and doing and doing. I'm still very fascinated with the journey from the little seed of evil in the individual's mind encouraged by the cranky old women who act out of malice and because they are outside society. The way that little seed grows into an act of murder, a *coup d'état*, the sickness of a whole country and the sickness of all the people within it; and the theatrical means by which that is done – the use of Hecate and the masque. There's a journey there I'd like to go again in order to try to get closer to the play.

But it's no accident, of course, that it's the unlucky play. Some people say that is because it was always done when a company was about to be disbanded and had to have good box-office. Once *Macbeth* was announced, all the actors knew times were bad. But there is something about living with evil that has a very debilitating effect on everybody who works on it. I've noticed that twice. None of us likes to think that humankind has quite that capacity for evil. To recognize this in a play and to recognize it in our-selves is a chastening and compelling experience. And that's why audiences want to go on seeing it. It re-mains, paradoxically, one of the most popular plays.

Afterword

John Russell Brown

'*Macbeth* is the shortest of Shakespeare's tragedies and the simplest in its statement: *Thou shalt not kill.*' So Alfred Harbage started his introduction to the Pelican edition of the play in 1956. No one is likely to write so confidently today. Rather we might stand his judgment on its head: *Macbeth* is the shortest of Shakespeare's tragedies but the most complex and subtle in its statement. We might even wonder whether 'Thou shalt kill' is not one of its statements, in the sense that it shows men and women drawn to violence by many motives: heroism, loyalty, sexual attraction, love, retaliation, expediency, inner necessity, isolation, fear, self-destruction, self-preservation. But if present-day understanding cannot be as simple as it was twenty-five years ago, the contributors to this book, each working to his own brief, do establish two important facts about the play which could be important guides to future inquiry.

First, it has become increasingly clear that the organizing principles in *The Tragedy of Macbeth* have to be sought at a level of consciousness in the characters below that which is expressed fully in the denotive meaning of the words they speak. One sign of this is the way in which the central characters can be played in opposing ways, especially if a few convenient deletions are made to the text. In particular the balance of power and initiative between Macbeth and Lady Macbeth is nowhere defined with any certainty. Their first scene together hinges on the weight, pitch, speed, intonation of a very few and simple words, and on the degree of intimacy, mutual agreement or desire for dominance that exists between the two characters:

>   – My dearest love,
> Duncan comes here tonight.
>   – And when goes hence?
> – To-morrow – as he purposes.
>   – O, never
> Shall sun that morrow see!   (I.v.55-8)

This is only the first of a series of encounters that involve central issues of the play but are open to a variety of impersonations. Moreover, Robin Grove has argued that words sometimes seem to express a consciousness of other scenes of which the speaker cannot be aware. For Macbeth, especially, as Michael Goldman has argued, the progress of consciousness in speech can seem like the product of an unwilled movement into deeper, irresistible involvement. Derek Russell Davis has suggested that many of the most crucial decisions taken in the play are involuntary, caused by an instinctive, unnamed self-hatred. Sometimes it seems as if 'nothing is but what is not' (I.iii.142).

Lady Macbeth's sleep-walking scene is easy to categorize as a guilty nightmare or a frenzied, half-crazed search for purgation, or even as possession by evil spirits, but as Peter Hall has said the progress of the scene is hard to discern, between the obvious moments of great emotional power, such as the inarticulate 'Oh, oh, oh!' which the Doctor identifies as a 'sigh' showing that the 'heart is sorely charg'd' (V.i.50-1). How many of her words express fear? How many guilt, or defiance, longing for peace and oblivion, sexual desire, tenderness? Why does she slip into childish rhyme? Why does she go through the motions of washing her hands? To what extent is she making conscious choices? This is a scene that can be given coherence and credibility only after the actress has studied her whole part with great care and experimented with many ways of making the disjointed lines live in performance. The inner complexity of this tragedy is here most obvious and its nature most hidden from our immediate understanding. Quoting the text does not help very much to define the power and purpose of this scene.

R.A. Foakes's opening contribution makes much the same point with regard to Macbeth himself. He does not understand himself when he says that 'ambition' is the only spur that causes him to murder Duncan: that text is no clear signpost to the heart of the play's action. Lady Macbeth might be nearer to his true state of mind when she asks:

> Art thou afeard
> To be the same in thine own act and valour
> As thou art in desire? (I.vii.39–41)

From the very start of the play, Professor Foakes argues, Macbeth is 'prisoner to his own imagination', his unspoken, unstillable, unspeakable thoughts.

The second striking agreement about the play, between the contributors to this book, silences an older notion that this is a tragedy about two people, the other characters being ciphers used only to fill out the tale and, after a long preparatory scene in Act IV, to represent an opposing reality just before the play closes. We are now encouraged to think that all the characters are carefully framed to serve a special and difficult purpose: to present a complicated series of contrasted personal and political relationships that, in turn, sets up a complicated system of dependency and power in which all have to try to function. In *King Lear*, Shakespeare used an ancient British setting to free the play from easily defined notions of belief; and so he was able to explore 'What man is', unaccommodated and without any of the inherited beliefs that customarily gave assurances. In *Macbeth*, written about the same time or a little later, the setting of ancient Scotland gives a comparable political and moral freedom to the drama, not by removing loyalties and certainties but by opposing the demands of different human bonds one against the other. Ideas about 'what becomes a man', a husband and wife, a family, a master, a king, a dependant, a commonwealth are repeatedly at issue. In these concerns the witches take their place, offering a female-dominated, destructive, half-crazed world that is an alternative to normality and gives to Macbeth a vision of absolute destruction:

> though the treasure
> Of nature's germens tumble all together,
> Even till destruction sicken. (IV.i.58–60)

In particular, Michael Hawkins has discerned four different political systems at work in the play and Peter Stallybrass has shown how the witches define yet a fifth. Brian Morris, by looking carefully at the religious references in the text and comparing them to Shakespeare's earlier invocations of Christian belief and practice, has argued that *Macbeth* is distinctive among plays drawn from Holinshed's *Chronicles* in that its hero does not acknowledge 'heavenly powers' or the possibility of repentance and grace. One point clearly emerges from the book as a whole: this is not a play that Shakespeare wrote for the gratification of his royal patron. An appendix in the notes to chapter 8 takes clear, and I believe conclusive, issue with H.N. Paul's *The Royal Play of 'Macbeth'* (New York, 1950), a study which has had a very wide and limiting influence on later criticism.

One further understanding may grow by reading this new collaborative book: *Macbeth* could well be the most danger-ous of Shakespeare's plays. For a start, its theme and structure are unusually hard to grasp, as we have just noted. Then, there are great difficulties involved in staging. Many short scenes have to establish themselves very quickly in contrast to powerful and sustained episodes immediately preceding. The Porter can fail to be either funny or credible. The 'Old Man' of II.iv has noble verse to support him, but his relation-ship to Ross and Ross's relationship to Macduff are hard to define during their brief exchanges. At the end, in Act IV, there are two problems: first, whether to stage Hecate and the witches in subservience to her – and it is notable how many of the contributors to this book give importance to this short scene despite an earlier consensus that it is spurious – and then, how to bring on Lennox with the anonymous 'Lord' so that the ironic and then more open talk registers credibly. Unlike the earlier Old Man, Lennox cannot bring a clear, contrary reference from outside the on-going drama, but has to present, suddenly, an active and astute political wariness. Scene vi of the last act is perhaps most difficult of all; it begins:

Drum and colours. Enter Malcolm, Siward, Macduff *and their* Army *with boughs.*

Malcolm Now near enough; your leavy screens throw down,
And show like those you are.

That is neatly said, but in performance represents a complicated manoeuvre that can easily look ridiculous or take up an inordinate amount of time. Frequently, modern directors delete the 'leavy' boughs.

These, of course, are marginal practical problems, and the true extent of the danger of this play can be better gauged by studying the notable actors and directors who have not matched up to its demands. The two leading roles present performers with crisis after crisis. For example, Lady Macbeth has to command attention on her first solo appearance as she is reading a letter and then move rapidly to extreme states of excitement and resolution. Macbeth has spoken only seventeen words before he has, as Banquo says, to 'start, and seem to fear / Things that do sound so fair' (I.iii.51–2). A few scenes later he has to *see* an imaginary airborne dagger and make the audience believe that, while he draws another, real dagger from its sheath. In the last act Lady Macbeth has the sleep-walking scene as the crown of her performance – an intense, isolated and almost uncharted appearance – and Macbeth veers between defiance and fear, confidence and suicidal despair. The last meeting with Macduff is charged with deep feeling, beginning with the ferocious, 'Turn, hellhound, turn' (V.viii.3) and encompassing both Macbeth's 'I will not fight with thee' and 'I will not yield', within five lines of each other. A desperate, physically demanding fight is the long conclusion to the play for Macbeth and for the greatly tired and tested actor who performs him.

This play demands of its players strength, vivid imagination, fine control, deep and subtle understanding, and a willingness to set free and present reactions that are normally below the surface of consciousness. All actors in the cast will be caught up in 'terrible imaginings', double senses and violent deeds; and they will need to keep very cool heads to maintain the torrents and eddies of the ongoing drama. A student of the play, it seems to me, requires his own measure of these resources if he is to make his own assessment of what lies hidden in the words of the text.

Index

255

Index

Index

257